How to Use Your
Business or Profession
As a Tax Shelter

How to Use Your Business or Profession As a Tax Shelter

JUDITH COWAN ZABALAOUI

Reston Publishing Company, Inc.
A Prentice-Hall Company
Reston, Virginia

The Entrepreneur Press

Library of Congress Cataloging in Publication Data

Zabalaoui, Judith.
  How to use your business or profession as a tax
shelter.

  Includes index.
    1. Tax shelters—Law and legislation—United States.
2. Small business—Taxation—Law and legislation—
United States. 3. Corporations—Taxation—Law and
legislation—United States. I. Title.
KF6297.5.Z3 1983   343.7305′23   83-2963
  ISBN 0-8359-2985-X   347.303523
  ISBN 0-8359-2988-4 (pbk.)

Copyright 1983 by
Reston Publishing Company, Inc.
A Prentice-Hall Company
Reston, Virginia 22090

10 9 8 7 6 5 4 3 2

Printed in the United States of America.

To my husband,
NASH,
for all the reasons he knows so well

Contents

Acknowledgments

The creation of a book is a curious thing. It is at once the most solitary of activities, and yet no one creates a book alone. And so it is with this book.

There are many people to whom I owe credit and appreciation. Such a list must begin with my parents. They began teaching me fundamental business concepts when I was about eight years old. Our first "classroom" was a grocery store which would fit quite comfortably in the living room of the home my parents now own. Later our classroom was a fast-food business.

My parents taught me the virtues of hard work, and good thinking, self-discipline, risk-taking, and, above all, the sheer joy of being a business owner. My mother added an extra by teaching me that women can be attractive and feminine without giving up the ability to think or strive for great goals.

My husband and children deserve a special thank you for going through it with me. The long months of "Don't make any plans—I'm working on the book this weekend" were tolerated with grace and humor. They have also been my greatest cheering section and providers of moral support.

I also want to thank my clients who encouraged me to undertake the book and who were considerate to a fault about my time during its writing.

Special accolades go to my associates at Resource Management, Inc. The number of times they literally did my job for me while I was writing can only be estimated. They kept the business thriving and pulled up my slack without complaint. They are among the finest financial planners in our industry, but equally important, they are extremely fine people.

Ellen Fort, our corporate CPA, checked my examples and helped make them more useful by her suggestions. The suggestions of Chuck Miller, our pension designer were invaluable in improving the chapter on retirement plans.

The entire book was improved considerably by the talents of Susan Barker, my editorial consultant.

Extra special thanks go to Sue Halsrud. She took typing home, working absurd hours to provide me with readable copy to edit and rewrite. She worked against deadlines with as much concern as if the book were hers. By her contribution she has stamped her ownership on the book. She had help from Mary Bruch, a lovely young woman on our staff who deserves special thanks for her efforts.

Lastly, my appreciation to Fred Easter at Reston Publishing who was kind and courteous through missed deadlines and changing tax law. Fred's encouragement was a great help in keeping my morale up during the birth of the book.

How To Use Your
Business or Profession
As a Tax Shelter

1

Choosing a Form of Business Organization

You're self-employed and you're good at what you do. When it comes to performing your professional service or running your business, you feel confident of the best way to do things. But with "financial planning and all that stuff," to use one of my client's descriptions, you're not so sure.

Being self-employed is quite special. When things go well, you can take the credit and feel great. But when things go badly, the worry, frustration, stress, and sense of failure are all yours, also. Being self-employed is a great deal more than just the way you earn your living. Because you put so much of yourself into your work, and take time and energy that would otherwise be yours and your family's, you want to enjoy more benefits than you could in a salaried job. This is where my advice can be of help.

I frequently compare my profession of Certified Financial Planner (CFP) to dentistry. People almost always agree that both are valuable services, and certainly one is better off for having seen the CFP or the dentist—but too frequently, people wait for the pain before seeking us out. You may visit your dentist in response to an errant cavity or a broken tooth; April 15 will, in many instances, be painful enough to prompt you to see me.

But what often prevents people from seeking out a tax advisor is resignation, the fact that they don't really believe much can be done. I hope to persuade you otherwise. There *are* ways to fight your tax bill, and, furthermore, tax saving impacts very heavily on your business activity.

In order to appreciate how important tax planning is to you as a business owner, let's think through the relationship between after-tax personal dollars and corporate sales. Let's assume that both you and your corporation are in the maximum tax brackets—50% for you; 46% for your corporation—and that you earn 10% of gross as a profit before taxes or sales.

When your corporation pays its 46% taxes, that 10% return shrinks to 5.4%. When you withdraw your 5.4% profit, you pay 50% personal tax, so your 5.4% profit now becomes 2.7%! In other words, to have *one* additional spendable dollar, you have to increase company sales by $37.00.

The flip side of the same point is, of course, *that any strategy that results in a $2.00 tax reduction for your firm is equivalent to increasing gross revenues by $37.00.*

If you are unincorporated, but in the 50% bracket personally, you will have to increase business gross revenues by $20.00 to end up with *one* additional after-tax dollar.

This example sums up what tax planning is all about: recognizing the opportunities available to reduce your taxes and installing the mechanisms to utilize these opportunities.

As a business owner or professional, you have unique opportunities. I want to take you through a number of options and look at how your choice of business organization affects each.

If you're like most self-employed individuals, you worry about protecting yourself, family members, and business associates in the event of your death, disability, or retirement. The financial-planning concerns of the self-employed seem to center in these major areas: what personal financial benefits can be gained from your business for yourself and your family; what tax benefits can be obtained; how money can be made without "Uncle Sam" taking the lion's share of the profits; and how family and business associates can be protected. The answers to these questions are governed almost exclusively by the form of business organization you choose.

The tax law recognizes three forms of business organization: sole proprietorship, partnership, and corporation. In addition, there is one important hybrid, the Subchapter S corporation. For each of these forms there is also a number of tax and nontax factors to be considered when planning for your business or professional practice.

Five important nontax factors to be considered for business organization are:

1. Period of existence
2. Liability exposure
3. Creation of subsidiaries
4. Relative costs of organization
5. Transfer of ownership interest

Seven important tax factors that also need to be considered are:

1. Treatment of income
2. Second taxation of distribution of income to owner(s)
3. Social Security
4. Fringe benefits deductible by the business but not taxable to the owner(s)
5. Deferral possibilities through fiscal year choice, deferred compensation, retirement plans
6. Income averaging possibilities
7. Dividend deduction in retained earnings

These factors will be discussed in detail for each possible form of business organization.

SOLE PROPRIETORSHIP

The sole proprietorship form of organization is frequently chosen because the owner is, in fact, the business. Although your accountant will treat your business as separate from you, legally you and the business are inseparable.

A sole proprietorship is, by far, the simplest form of business to set up and operate. This fact may account for its enormous popularity. In the United States, there are approximately nine million proprietorships. In total, they account for $220 billion in sales each year.

Nontax Factors

Period of Existence

The sole proprietorship realistically ceases to exist when the proprietor is no longer an active participant. Where this is quite literally true, the business will probably not continue after the death, disability, or retirement of the proprietor.

As a sole proprietor, your choices for you at retirement or for your heirs at your death are: liquidation, continuance of the business, a lifetime or death gift of the business, or an outright sale of the business. Liquidation is the worst of all the alternatives because it usually ends up as a forced sale of assets at bargain prices. Continuance of the business at your retirement may be possible if you have good successor management. What frequently happens in these instances is that the retired business owner is not really retired but just unpaid. Continuance of the business by your executor at your death is rarely a long-term solution unless there is a family member both capable and willing to take over the business and keep it going. In the absence of such a family member, the executor or executrix will probably begin liquidation and/or look for a buyer—running the business only as an interim measure. You could give your business interest away—either at retirement as a life gift, or at death. Which solution is best depends on the nature of the business and the individuals involved.

If you elect to sell your business, federal tax law takes the position that since a sole proprietorship is not recognized as a separate entity apart from the owner, the sale is not of a single interest but is a sale of all the individual assets of the business. Because businesses are usually buying and selling inventory and equipment on an ongoing basis, you will likely recognize some portion of your sale as ordinary income rather than long-term capital gain.

This differs from the sale of an incorporated business. That transaction is basically a sale of stock and, as such, is the sale of a single asset. Since businesses rarely sell in their first year, the sale of an incorporated business normally results in long-term capital gain.

Liability Exposure

Basically, a sole proprietorship is a one-owner business, and you and the business are legally inseparable. This is especially true in the area of liability exposure. As owner, you are liable personally for all the debts of your business.

Creation of Subsidiaries

If you foresee the need to divide your business activities through the creation of subsidiaries, you should use the corporate mode of organization. A sole proprietorship does not allow for the existence of subsidiaries.

Relative Cost of Organizing

The advantage of opting to organize as a sole proprietorship, of course, is that it is the least costly (in legal and accounting fees) to establish and maintain.

Transfer of Ownership Interest

This is not an option available to sole proprietors.

Tax Factors

Treatment of Income

The simplicity of organizing as a sole proprietorship also extends to your tax treatment. Although your accounting system treats you as a separate unit, you will be taxed personally on the profits of your business. There is no direct tax on a proprietorship.

As owner, you compute your business profits on Schedule C of form 1040 by listing the income of the business and deducting business expenses. This net figure is then added to your personal income.

Second Taxation on Distribution of Income to Owner(s)

This is not a consideration in the case of sole proprietorships.

Social Security

You will pay self-employment tax (social security for the self-employed). These rates are lower than the combined rates you pay once incorporated.

Fringe Benefits

The sole proprietorship lends itself to fewer fringe benefits than a corporation. Refer to Table 1–2 on fringe benefits for more information on what may be available to your business.

Deferral Possibilities, Income Averaging, and Dividend Deduction

These are not available with a proprietorship, because it is not a taxable entity.

PARTNERSHIP

Partnerships are rather complex business organizations and are the least used of all the business forms available. There are about one million partnerships in the United States, producing about $83 billion in annual sales.

Nontax Factors

Period of Existence

Basically the federal tax law says that a partnership is terminated only if no further business is carried on by any of the partners or there is a sale or exchange of 50% or more of the total interest in partnership capital and profits within 12 months.

When a member of the partnership dies or resigns, there may be a technical termination under the laws of many states, but the partnership can continue as an entity for tax purposes under the provisions of federal law.

According to federal tax law, a partnership interest is a capital asset; therefore, the sale of a partnership interest should result in capital gain. However, there are many assets that are exempted from capital-gains treatment. If you sell your interest in a partnership, you could end up with all capital gains, all ordinary income, or some combination of the two, depending on what assets your partnership was holding at the time of sale.

If the partnership is liquidated and you receive property distributions, you recognize no gain or loss until you dispose of the property.

Liability Exposure

As a partner in a general partnership, you have personal joint and several liability for partnership obligations. What this means in practical terms is that any of your personal assets (such as house, car, jewelry, and investments) may be claimed by business creditors for unpaid debts of the business.

Creation of Subsidiaries

The partnership does not allow for the existence of subsidiaries. If you foresee this need for your business, you should opt for incorporation.

Relative Costs of Organization

A partnership is a separate entity from its shareholders. If you elect this mode, the costs you may incur will include:

1. Legal fees
2. State filing fees
3. Annual franchise fees
4. Cost of setting up and maintaining books
5. Cost of preparing income tax returns

Deductibility of Organizational Costs

If you elect to become a partnership, no deduction is allowed for accounts paid or incurred to organize your partnership or to promote the sale of an interest in your partnership. Such expenses include commissions, professional fees, and printing costs for issuing and marketing partnership interests.

However, other organizational expenses may be deducted ratably over a period of not less than 60 months. The expenses eligible for this 60-month amortization must be incident to the partnership creation and chargeable to the capital account.

If a partnership is liquidated before the end of the 60-month period, any expenses not yet deducted may then be deducted as a loss.

Transfer of Ownership Interest

To transfer interest in a partnership requires consent of all partners (unless the partnership agreement allows otherwise). The addition of a new partner in some cases creates a new partnership, which can become a problem.

Tax Factors

Treatment of Income

Although your accounting system treats your partnership as a unit separate from you and your partner(s), a partnership is not a taxable entity. It does file a tax return, Form 1065, but this is strictly an information return. A partnership is frequently referred to as a conduit. Income simply flows through, and you pick up your share of partnership profits as gross personal taxable income.

Second Taxation

This is not an option available to partnerships.

Social Security

As a partner, you must pay self-employment tax, with rates lower than the combined rates of a corporation.

Fringe Benefits

Corporations provide more opportunities for fringe benefits than partnerships. Refer to Table 1–2 for specific information.

Deferral Possibilities, Income Averaging, and Dividend Deduction

Partnerships are not taxable entities, so there are no mechanisms for these tax factors.

CORPORATIONS

Corporations are legal, taxable entities that are separate from their stockholders.

The corporate mode predominates in economic importance. There are almost 1.5 million corporations in the United States, and their combined sales are about $1.5 *trillion* for average sales of $1 million per year. (Contrast this to average sales of $25,000 per year for sole proprietorships and $83,000 per year for partnerships.) These facts will lead you to the conclusion that the more business you do, the more advisable incorporating will become. There are many reasons why this is an accurate conclusion: we will be considering them throughout the book.

Nontax Factors

Period of Existence

The period of existence of a corporation is assumed to be indefinite, as changes in ownership have no effect on the ability of the business to continue.

Liability Exposure

As a stockholder in a corporation, your liability is limited to your capital contribution except for a few, quite extraordinary circumstances. It should be especially noted that the corporate structure cannot shield you from professional liability, only from normal business liabilities.

Creation of Subsidiaries

If you foresee the need to divide the activities of your business through the creation of subsidiaries, you have no choice but to be a regular corporation.

Relative Cost of Organizing

One question tax advisors are frequently asked is how much it costs to incorporate.

The costs vary enormously, according to the size of your firm and the complexity of your accounting needs. As a rule of thumb, however, you should be able to justify $2,000—$3,000 in tax savings to consider incorporating.

There have been a number of books on the subject of incorporating yourself. Frankly, I subscribe to the old adage that anybody who acts as his own financial planning team has a fool for a client. There are several critical decisions to be made early on in this process, and I believe that the cost of a good corporate attorney, a certified public accountant (CPA) and a certified financial planner is money well spent.

I will try to alert you to the necessary decisions you will have to make, as well as factors to consider when making these decisions, so that you will know what you need and be in a position to assess the professionals with whom you talk. Reading one book, however, cannot possibly make you an expert able to handle the myriad of details in establishing a corporation.

A corporation is a separate entity from its shareholders, but the costs you might incur include:

1. Legal fees
2. State filing fees
3. Franchise fees
4. Costs of setting up and maintaining books
5. Costs of preparing income tax returns
6. Additional costs of Social Security

Deductibility of Organizational Expenses

As with a partnership, deductible expenses must be incident to the creation of the corporation and chargeable to the capital account. Allowable expenses include fees paid for legal expenses in drafting the corporate charter, bylaws, minutes of organizational meetings, and terms of original stock certificates. In addition, fees paid for accounting services and fees paid to the state of incorporation also qualify for deduction. If you incur expenses for temporary directors or in relation to organizational meetings of your directors or stockholders, these, too, may be deducted.

If you are raising money for your corporation by selling shares of stock or other securities, expenses incurred in this regard are not deductible. Examples of such nondeductible expenses are commissions, professional fees, and printing costs.

Organizational costs relative to the corporate mode are ordinarily deductible in the year of dissolution. If you meet certain conditions, however, you can elect to amortize them ratably over a period of 60 months or more. Your amortization starts with the month your corporation begins business and must be elected by the time of filing the return for the tax year your corporation begins business.

Transfer of Ownership Interest

Transfer of ownership is accomplished by transfer of a certificate of ownership shares. Because of the ease with which this transaction can be made, you will probably want to consider the corporate mode if you are considering transferring ownership interests to either family members or as a partial sale to raise capital.

Tax Factors

Treatment of Income

Treatment of income is one of the most significant factors to be considered in the corporate mode. When you incorporate your business, technically you are no longer self-employed, but are an employee of your corporation. This puts you in a peculiar situation of being both employee and employer.

The corporation is a taxable entity. How income you receive personally is treated for personal tax purposes depends on the way in which you take income from your corporation. Your choices are:

1. Compensation for work you do as an employee. This can take the form of salary, bonus, and/or various fringe benefits,
2. Dividends as a shareholder, and/or
3. Cash or property given to you to redeem your stock.

Salary, bonus, and dividends are taxed to you personally as ordinary income. Cash or property given to you to redeem your stock will be return of principal, ordinary income, or capital gains, depending on the circumstances of the redemption.

Second Taxation

Only the corporate mode produces dividends that are not deductible to your corporation but are fully taxable to you. The term "double taxation" has real meaning in this context. Let's contrast the tax difference between dividends and compensation through salary and bonus.

Gross Revenues	$500,000	$500,000
Expenses	350,000	350,000
Salary	75,000	150,000
Corporate Net	75,000	–0–
Corporate Tax	15,750	–0–
Personal Tax on $75,000 Salary and $58,750 Dividends	50,877	59,002
Combined Tax	66,627	59,002
Difference Due to "Double Taxation"	7,625	

As you can see from the example, there is an additional $7,625 in taxation created by taking dividends rather than salary. Please don't conclude at this point that (a) you would rather not be incorporated or (b) that if you do incorporate, you'll pull all your profits out as salary.

I'm always distressed to hear of people who have rejected the corporate mode because they are convinced that there is no cure for the problem of double taxation. Being incorporated has real advantages, and there are ways other than either salary or dividends to take money from your corporation. (See Chapter 5.)

Social Security

As a stockholder/manager of a corporation, you are an employee of the corporation—not self-employed—for purposes of the Social Security tax. Table 1–1, on comparisons, will make this difference very clear.

TABLE 1–1
Self-Employed Vs Corporate-Employed Social Security Tax Comparisons

Year	Wage Base	Corporate/Sub S (employee)		Sole Prop/Partnership (self-employed)	
		Tax Rate†	Maximum Tax*	Tax Rate†	Maximum Tax
1978	$17,700	6.05%	$1,070.85	8.10%	$1,433.70
1979	22,900	6.13	1,403.77	8.10	1,854.90
1980	25,900	6.13	1,587.67	8.10	2,097.90
1981	29,700	6.65	1,975.05	9.30	2,762.10
1982	31,800	6.70	2,130.60	9.35	2,973.30
1983	33,900	6.70	2,271.30	9.35	3,169.65
1984	36,000	6.70	2,412.00	9.35	3,366.00
1985	38,100	7.05	2,686.05	9.90	3,771.90
1986	40,200	7.15	2,874.30	10.0	4,020.00
1987	42,600	7.15	3,045.90	10.0	4,260.00

*Remember that both the employee and employer pay this rate. In effect you pay twice: once as an employee of your corporation and again as the employer.
†The Social Security Commission, which is still deliberating at this writing, may change the tax rates for 1984–1987.

Here is an *example* to illustrate this point in another way.

Let's assume you are self employed and earn more than $33,900 in 1983. Your self-employment tax will be $3,169.65. However, if you had become incorporated, you would have paid $2,271.30 as an employee, and your corporation would have paid another $2,271.30 on your behalf for a combined tax of $4,542.60—an extra $1,372.95. Before you conclude, however, that you don't want to incorporate, remember that the employer's contributions for Social Security are deductible as business expenses.

Your share as an employee is not deductible, but then neither is the self-employment tax.

Fringe Benefits

Table 1–2 provides summation of the differences between proprietorships, partnerships, and corporations with regard to fringe benefits deductible by the business but not taxable to owners. As the table demonstrates, the regular corporate mode is the most generous in terms of fringe benefits.

TABLE 1–2
Deductibility of Fringe Benefits by Mode of Organization

	Proprietorship	Partnership	Corporation	Subchapter S
Company car	Yes	Yes	Yes	Yes
Business travel and entertainment	Yes	Yes	Yes	Yes
Educational costs	Yes	Yes	Yes	Yes
Life insurance	No	No	Yes	No
Disability insurance	No	No	Yes	No
Medical insurance	No	No	Yes	No
Medical reimbursement	No	No	Yes	No
Deferral opportunities	No	No	Yes	No
Keogh	Yes	Yes	No	No
IRA	Yes	Yes	Yes	Yes
Pension and profit-sharing plan	No	No	Yes	Yes

Fringe benefits are an extremely good way to take corporate income in the most advantageous way (deductible to the corporation but not taxable to you). For a full treatment of these benefits see Chapter 4. Insofar as you can take compensation in these forms, you literally take tax-free income.

Dividends

Dividends are probably the worst possible form in which to take corporate income, since both you and your corporation must pay income tax on these monies. A newcomer to the corporate mode will frequently decide that the best solution is to take all the corporate income as compensation.

The Internal Revenue Service (IRS) frequently challenges this technique on the grounds of unreasonable compensation. The basic IRS guideline is whether your compensation compares with that of a person performing similar services for a corporation he does not control.

Prior to the Economic Recovery Act of 1981 (ERTA), unearned income (rents, dividends, interest, and so forth) could be taxed at brackets as high as 70%, whereas earned income (salary, commissions, bonuses and so forth) could be taxed only at brackets up to 50%. While ERTA placed a 50% ceiling on all income, regardless of its nature, it did not altogether eliminate the problem of unreasonable compensation. Remember that compensation is fully deductible by the corporation in arriving at its taxable income, whereas dividends are not. Dividends are paid from after-tax corporate dollars. Therefore, being able to pay a corporate owner compensation rather than dividends results in a reduction of the corporation's taxable income.

In short, thanks to the Economic Recovery Act of 1981, dividends and compensation are taxable to you in the same bracket, but dividends are taxed twice—once to the corporation and once to you personally.

Wealth Building

One of the most significant advantages of being incorporated is that you can control your taxable income by limiting your salary. Corporate earnings in excess of your salary needs can be used to provide various fringe benefits or can be accumulated in the corporation. If accumulated earnings are invested in stocks of other companies, 85% of dividend-income received can be excluded from taxation (see Chapter 7).

Because of the complexity of the tax treatment of corporations, there are many misconceptions about the best ways of withdrawing income from the corporation. Indeed, many people reject the corporate mode based on these misconceptions.

Let's assume for a moment that you are a business owner (or a professional); that gross receipts from your business are $500,000; that your business expenses are $350,000; that you want to fund a retirement plan to the maximum allowable limits and minimize income taxes. Your taxes with and without being incorporated are as follows for 1983.

	Sole Proprietorship/ Partnership	Corporation
Business gross	$500,000	$500,000
Expenses	350,000	350,000
Salary	N/A	100,000
Retirement plan contribution	15,000*	25,000**
		$ 25,000
Corporate taxable income	N/A	25,000
Personal taxable income	135,000	100,000
Personal income tax	51,502	34,190
Corporate income tax	–0–	3,750

Combined taxes	51,502	37,940
Retained earnings	–0–	21,250***

*Keogh plan—1983 Limits—15% to maximum of $15,000.

**Combination pension and profit-sharing plan set at 25% of compensation.

***Corporate net after corporate taxes have been paid.

(To see how these taxes were calculated, see Appendix B.)

This short example, I believe, reveals several points:

1. A corporate owner can more easily control the flow of personal taxable income.
2. Because your corporation is a taxable entity, business profits are "averaged" between two taxable entities rather than flowing completely to you personally.
3. While you are paying two taxes, you are not paying "double taxation" since the combined taxes are less than the personal taxes alone.

And that's only on the income side. Let's look at the example now with an eye to wealth building.

	Proprietorship/ Partnership	*Corporate Owner*
Investment in a retirement plan	$ 15,000	$ 25,000
	$150,000	$100,000
	– 15,000 Keogh	–34,190 Tax
	– 51,502 Tax	
Available cash	83,498	65,810
Retained earnings	–0–	21,250
Total	98,498	112,060
	(13,562)	

It is true that the corporate owner has less actual spendable cash, but his/her wealth building is $13,562 greater than that of the proprietor/partner. This leads me to the first of many rules of thumb regarding incorporation. Since incorporation is an extremely effective device for wealth building, you should consider the corporate mode as soon as your business produces more income than you need to live on.

Deferral Possibilities

Because the proprietorship, partnership, and Subchapter S corporation are income conduits, the only business mode that allows for deferral opportunities is the corporation. The corporate mode permits deferral through deferred compensation, fiscal year choices, and retirement plans.

Deferral Through Deferred Compensation

In tax planning, the advantages of deferral are taken as a truism. However, clients frequently say to me, "If we're only postponing the inevitable, why bother? If I'm going to pay these taxes anyhow, what's the point of deferral?" And, indeed, that may sum up your feeling about deferring income to defer taxes. Nonetheless, I hope that by exploring the advantages, you will be convinced to consider deferral mechanics.

Let's make some assumptions now and look at how the numbers work out. Let's assume that your corporation grosses $750,000 a year; your expenses are $500,000; and you have been cleaning the corporation out every year. Now you're considering deferring half your income.

	Without Deferral		*With Deferral*
Corporate gross	$750,000		$750,000
Expenses	500,000		500,000
Salary	250,000		125,000
Taxable corporate net	–0–		$125,000*
Personal tax**	$109,002	($62,500)	$ 46,502
Corporate tax**	–0–		37,250
Combined tax	$109,002		$ 83,752
Tax savings		($25,250)	

*Deferred compensation is deductible to the corporation when *withdrawn* by the executive.

**At 1983 rates.

During the deferral period, your corporation has an increased tax liability because deferred compensation is not deductible until withdrawn. The deferred compensation is carried on the books as a promissory note, and an account may or may not be established to invest these funds. You may or may not be entitled to interest, depending on your deferred compensation agreement with your corporation.

Let's assume you defer income for ten years, at which time you retire and take deferred compensation rather than salary. If the tax structure remained the same, the combined personal and corporate taxes would also remain the same since your corporation gets a $125,000 a year deduction for deferred compensation and you take taxable compensation of $125,000. Now let's see what that $25,250 a year in tax savings has done.

First, check Appendix G. Assume that your money has been invested at 12%. Go to the column labeled 12% and run your finger down to ten years. You'll see the factor 3.1058; multiplied times $25,250 it results in $78,421, the amount your $25,250 will grow to in ten years at 12%. Remember, this was earned on money you kept rather than sending it off to Washington. There's no mystique about it—it's simply the result of the time value of money. (The table does not consider the tax aspects of the investment.)

The tool that creates this kind of deferral is a deferred-compensation plan. In simple terms, this is a nonqualified plan whereby a company provides you with a periodic right to defer a portion of your compensation.

The chief advantage to you is, of course, that it lowers your current income-tax bill by postponing the recognition of income to later years. The chief disadvantage to you is that you have, in place of current income, an unsecured promise that your company will pay the promised benefits. The right to the benefit may be subordinated to corporate creditors if your business gets in trouble.

The advantage to your business is that the company is not obligated to segregate any assets to fund its obligation to you. Additional cash will thereby be available and yet you will retain your future right to the income.

One very important disadvantage to your corporation is postponement of the tax deduction for your compensation until distribution.

Although there is no necessity to fund a deferred compensation plan, the corporation may accumulate the needed cash in mutual funds, annuities, or other investments. It is critical that title to those assets remains in the company.

In order to take advantage of this provision, you should have a deferred-compensation agreement drawn up by an attorney. Items to be included are: the amount of percentage of salary to be deferred, the number of years the plan is to be in effect (both the number of years funds will be deferred and the number of years compensation will be deferred) and the conditions under which the deferral compensation will be paid. The agreement may include provisions for bonuses, if desired. Chapter 5 deals with deferred compensation in some depth.

Deferral Through Fiscal-Year Choices

Many factors will determine your choice of fiscal year. Most of these are considered in Chapter 2. If, however, a fiscal year other than the calendar year is chosen, you will find deferral opportunities available to you.

Let's assume you choose as your company fiscal year June 30 and you are a calendar-year tax payer. From January-December 19X1, you take a salary of $100,000. In March or April your accountant begins getting ready for your corporate year-end. As s/he tells you that corporate profits (after your salary) are going to be about $100,000, you decide to take a $50,000 bonus to reduce corporate profits to $50,000. We'll see in a moment that this is a very desirable level.

The personal result of having a fiscal year different from your personal year is this: You earned the $50,000 in 19X1 and took taxable receipt in 19X2. The corporate results are that your business took the deduction in fiscal 19X2 and no advantage was lost by deferring this payment to you. In addition, the business kept its cash until late in the fiscal period, and had an opportunity to assess the profit picture before declaring a bonus.

Deferral Through Retirement Plans

Occasionally when I suggest to a business owner that this is one of the best business tools available, I get a response like, "Judith, I'm only 35 years old. I plan to work 30–35 more years. I don't want my money tied up that long. Why should I think about a retirement plan now?"

The remark misses the boat on two scores. One, it fails to acknowledge the tremendous time value of money, as we have just seen, and two, it fails to recognize the tremendous tax advantage of retirement plans. Depending on how young the investor is, a relatively small commitment may be all that's necessary. With my young clients, I stress the time value of money because young people can achieve really dramatic retirement goals without a backbreaking sacrifice now.

Frankly, as a certified financial planner, I wish I could put every 20-year-old in the country in a retirement plan. It would give them independence from fears of old age and would allow the government some leeway in solving the problems of Social Security. I pray none of my clients (or my family) ever live through the fear many senior citizens have lived through as talk of Social Security cutbacks is in the nightly news.

The next objection I hear is, "I don't want my money tied up." This objection fails to recognize the tax advantages of retirement plans. I remind my clients that "Uncle Sam" picks up about half the tab for their retirement plan.

The point to remember is this: You don't really have a choice between putting the money in the bank or putting the money in your retirement plan—the choice is between sending half of it to Washington as taxes; putting half in the bank (where you will pay about half the earnings as taxes); or putting *all* of it in your retirement plan and sheltering the earnings as well as deducting the contribution.

Don't get confused about whose money it is!

Let's get down to the specifics of retirement plans now. Please remember that this is simply an overview. I'm going to hit the high points here but Chapter 8 will discuss retirement plans in depth.

A retirement plan is basically a qualified pension, profit-sharing, stock bonus, annuity, or bond purchase plan. Although there are admittedly some aggravations in qualifying your retirement plan and in meeting ongoing requirements, you will be encouraged to do so by the very favorable tax treatment these plans receive.

For openers, your company gets a current tax deduction whether or not employees' interests are forfeitable. Neither you (as owner/employee) nor any of your participating employees are taxed on contributions going into the plan. The contributions go into a trust established for this purpose, and the trust is not taxed on its earnings. (Unrelated business income is an exception to this general rule.) Distributions from the retirement plan receive extremely favorable tax treatment.

Retirement plans are also exempt from gift taxes when you irrevocably designate a beneficiary to receive the death benefits. If your beneficiary does not take a lump-sum distribution at your death, employer-paid death benefits are excluded from your estate.

There is a variety of retirement plans, but they basically fall into two broad categories: defined contribution or defined benefit.

Defined Contribution Plans   With defined contribution plans, you "define" your contribution in terms of your compensation. Your contribution is a set percentage of your compensation up to the lesser of 25% or $30,000.

Defined Benefit Plans   With defined benefit plans, you "define" your benefit (what you will take out as opposed to what you will put in). Your contribution is then determined on what you need to contribute annually to accumulate a capital base on which the earnings will generate the benefit defined.

The benefit maximum is the lesser of $90,000 or 100% of your average compensation for the three consecutive years during which you receive your highest pay. There is no maximum annual contribution since you must contribute annually whatever is necessary to fund the capital base needed to pay the defined benefit.

With these somewhat brief descriptions in mind, let's take a look at an example of the tax and cost results of various contributions to a retirement plan. Assume that the business grosses $750,000; that business expenses before paying the owner's salary are $600,000; and that the owner wants to come close to "zeroing out" the corporation.

	Contributions to the Retirement Plan			
	10%	15%	25%	40%*
Gross revenues	750,000	750,000	750,000	750,000
Expenses	600,000	600,000	600,000	600,000
Salary	135,000	130,000	120,000	107,000
Retirement plan	13,500	19,500	30,000	42,800
Corporate net	1,500	500	–0–**	200
Corporate income tax	225	75	–0–	30
Personal income tax	51,502	49,002	44,002	37,550
Cash available after tax—personal	83,498	80,998	75,998	69,450
Cash available after tax—corporate	1,275	425	–0–	170

*This will be available to business owners in certain circumstances. Chapter 8 will expand on this possibility.

**Frequently referred to as "zeroing out."

Now let's draw a few conclusions. Since we came very close to zeroing out the corporation, corporate taxes are not a factor in our thinking. Results on the personal side, however, are quite satisfactory.

Let's contrast the difference between a 10% contribution and a 40% contribution.

Personal income taxes down	$13,952
Cash available after taxes down	14,048
Increase in contribution to the retirement plan	29,300

In other words, by putting an additional $29,300 in your retirement plan, you lower your personal income tax by $13,952. The reality is that Uncle Sam is paying 47% of your contribution. You can see why retirement plans are considered the finest tax shelters available.

Remember one of our earliest observations: when your business produces more income than you need to live on, consider incorporation and use the deferral mechanisms available. There really is no magic number determining at what point incorporation is "right"—it's a matter of profit in excess of your personal need.

Income Averaging Possibilities

In order to fully appreciate the income averaging possibilities of a corporation, you should study the personal and corporate tax rate schedules (Table

1–3 and 1–4). The income-tax rates for individuals filing joint returns reach comparable corporate levels at the taxable income levels shown in Table 1–4.

TABLE 1–3
Corporate Tax Rates

Taxable Income	Prior to 1982	1982	1983 & After
0 to $25,000	17	16	15
Over $25,000 but Under $50,000	20	19	18
Over $50,000 but Under $75,000	30	30	30
Over $75,000 but Under $100,000	40	40	40
Over $100,000	46	46	46

TABLE 1–4
Personal Tax Rates

Taxable Income	Prior to 1982	1982	1983
$ 7,600–$11,900	18	16	15
11,900– 16,000	21	19	17
24,600– 29,900	32	29	26
35,200– 45,800	43	39	35
45,800– 60,000	49	44	40

As you can see from the tables, corporate tax rates are considerably lower than personal tax rates. It takes $75,000 of corporate taxable income to reach the 40% tax bracket, but it only takes about $33,000 of personal taxable income to reach that bracket. The solution to this problem is clear: Split the income between yourself and your corporation up to the point that your respective brackets are almost equal.

Let's look at some more examples:

Gross receipts	$750,000	$750,000	$750,000	$750,000
Expenses	500,000	500,000	500,000	500,000
Salary	100,000	150,000	200,000	250,000
Corporate net	150,000	100,000	50,000	–0–
Corporate income tax	48,750	25,750	8,250	–0–
Personal income tax	34,190	59,002	84,002	109,002
Combined taxes	82,940	84,752	92,252	109,002
Retained earnings	101,250	74,250	41,750	–0–

If you look back at Tables 1–3 and 1–4, you'll see that you reach the 48% tax bracket at $85,600 of personal taxable income and the 46% tax bracket at $100,000 of corporate taxable income. It's only logical to split income up to this point.

When you split income or average-out income between yourself and your corporation, you end up with retained earnings. (Profits remaining after corporate taxes have been paid.) This leads us to the fifth and last tax factor to consider in your choice of business form.

Dividend Deductions on Retained Earnings

I said earlier that it distresses me to hear new clients say they want to zero out the corporation. There are at least two good reasons not to do so. The first, the advantage of income averaging, we've just seen. The second is that by zeroing out you will have no retained earnings.

Retained earnings (accumulated earnings) are primarily the way in which a business grows. From a tax angle, it's better to let your business grow and take the growth later as a long-term capital gain than to withdraw the earnings as currently taxable personal income. But there is a far more significant argument for retained earnings. Dividends received from domestic corporations are subject to an 85% dividends-received tax deduction. To appreciate what a potent tool for wealth building this can be, look at the following example:

	Personal Investment 50% Tax Bracket	*Corporate Investment 46% Tax Bracket*
Investment of $250,000 at 10% dividend rate equals	$25,000	$25,000
Less exclusions:		
85% corporate exclusion		21,250
Married filing joint exclusion	200	
Taxable income	24,800	3,750
Tax rate	50%	46%
Personal income tax	12,400	1,725
Amount of taxes saved		10,675
Percentage saved		86%

The assumption of the example is that after-tax funds are invested. For the corporation, of course, after-tax funds are retained earnings. The example also assumes that you and your corporation are in the maximum tax bracket—46% for the corporation; 50% for you. Only dividends are eligible for the exclusion. The investment is therefore assumed to be in dividend-paying stocks.

Reflect for just a moment now on the advantages of not zeroing out. You can average out your income, thus lowering the combined taxes, then invest the corporate retained earnings and exclude 85% of the dividends earned from taxation.

Let's now *recap* some of the advantages of being incorporated:

1. Indefinite life
2. Limitation of personal liability for business risks
3. Opportunity to create subsidiaries
4. Ease of transferability of ownership interest
5. Opportunities to defer income and income taxation
6. Opportunities for fringe benefits that are deductible by the corporation but not taxable to you personally
7. Income averaging possibilities
8. Dividend deduction on retained earnings.

Although there are no hard and fast rules about when you should incorporate, there are *two rules of thumb to use as guidelines:*

1. Tax savings from incorporation should be at least $2,000 to $3,000 to justify its additional costs. These tax savings will probably only be possible if the second rule of thumb is true.
2. Your business profits should exceed your personal income needs. Since most tax-saving techniques require the use of corporate income and/or foregoing of personal income, incorporation will not produce much tax saving if you are unable to forego some current personal income.

Assuming you meet one or both of these rules, you're ready to look at your tax savings opportunities in depth in the coming chapters.

SUBCHAPTER S CORPORATION

So far we've looked at the proprietorship, the partnership, and the corporation as forms of business organization. The last form we want to consider is the Subchapter S corporation.

Subchapter S corporations were statutorily allowed in 1958. The idea behind their creation was to minimize the effect of federal income taxes as a factor when choosing a mode of business organization by allowing tax treatment similar to partnerships and nontax treatment similar to corporations. What happened in practical terms, however, was the creation of a type of business organization that differed from a corporation or a partnership.

On October 19, 1982, the President signed the Subchapter S Revision Act of 1982, which will be effective for taxable years beginning after 1982 and which has as its major purpose to redirect Subchapter S toward its original goal. The fundamental effect of the act is to allow qualifying businesses elect the corporate form for nontax purposes (for example, limited liability) and to enjoy the advantages of the partnership mode for income tax purposes.

In order to be a Subchapter S corporation, all shareholders must consent to the election. However, a person who becomes a shareholder after the corporation is a Subchapter S corporation does not have to consent and cannot terminate the election by refusing to consent. The election can be made on or before the 15th day of the 3rd month of the current tax year or any time during the preceding year. Unless terminated, the election is effective for all later years.

Nontax Factors

A Subchapter S corporation is essentially a hybrid of partnerships and corporations. In essence, a Subchapter S is a true corporation that elects to be treated like a partnership for federal income tax purposes. This special tax treatment is available only to certain qualified corporations whose shareholders elect it.

To qualify for Subchapter S election, your corporation must meet all of the following conditions:

1. It must be a domestic corporation.
2. It cannot be a member of an affiliated group.
3. It cannot have more than 35 shareholders.
4. It cannot have a foreign trust as a shareholder.
5. It must have only one class of stock, but voting differences are permitted and straight debt is excluded.
6. It must not have a resident alien as a shareholder.

Period of Existence

While termination of the tax treatment election may be voluntary or involuntary, the corporation continues until dissolution. Its life as a legal entity is not affected by disaffection of shareholders.

The election can be voluntarily revoked by shareholders' consent. The election may be involuntarily terminated, however, by any one of the following four events. First, a new shareholder who owns more than one-half of the voting stock can terminate the election by exercising his/her right of revocation. Second, the corporation can cease to qualify as a Subchapter S. For example, your corporation accepts another corporation as a shareholder or you issue a second class of stock. An event causing failure to meet any of the eligibility requirements terminates the election as of the date of the event. Third, pre-1983 law dictated an involuntary termination if gross receipts from sources outside of the United States equalled more than 80% of total corporate gross receipts. The Subchapter S Revision Act of 1982 eliminates this rule. Fourth, pre-1983 law dictated that if passive investment income (income from interest, dividends, rents, royalties, annuities, and/or gains from sales of stock or securities) equalled more than 20% of total corporation gross receipts, the Subchapter S election would be involuntarily terminated. Under the Subchapter S Revision Act of 1982, passive investment income will not generally result in termination, but it may result in involuntary termination if the electing corporation has accumulated earnings and profits from regular corporate years and has 25% or more of passive income in each of three consecutive years. Income in excess of the 25% limit in any year is taxed to the corporation at a 46% rate.

The IRS may waive an involuntary termination. The Senate Finance Committee Report states that the IRS is expected to be reasonable in granting waivers. Waivers may be granted in situations where the corporation had acted in good faith and a requirement was inadvertently breached but no tax avoidance resulted.

Liability Exposure

Generally, stockholder liability is limited to capital contributions. Limited liability does not extend to professional liability.

Creation of Subsidiaries

A corporation owning a subsidiary is not eligible for Subchapter S status.

Relative Cost of Organization

Cost may include: legal fees, state filing fees, cost of setting up and maintaining books, and fees for tax return preparation. See Chapter 2 for details.

Transfer of Ownership Interests

This is essentially the same as for corporations, provided the total number of shareholders is 35 or fewer after the transfer. Involuntary revocation of the Subchapter S corporation occurs if there are more than 35 shareholders.

Tax Factors

Treatment of Income

Subchapter S is a true corporation, but it is treated like a partnership for federal income tax purposes. The statutory term for a Subchapter S corporation is "small business corporation," which is a misnomer since there are no restrictions on the amount of capital or assets.

In general, a Subchapter S corporation is not subject to federal income tax. A Subchapter S corporation must compute its taxable income, however. The computation is very similar to that of an individual with the exceptions described in the following paragraphs.

Generally, net capital gains in excess of $25,000 and 50% of taxable income (if the later is in excess of $25,000) is taxable to the corporation. This taxation, however, is not applicable if the corporation has had Subchapter S status for each of the preceding three years or Subchapter S status each year of its existence if it is less than three years old.

The corporation is liable for any increase in tax that can be attributed to early disposition of property which was subject to the investment tax credit if the property was acquired when the corporation was not a Subchapter S corporation. Disposition of the property triggers the recapture, not the Subchapter S election.

As mentioned earlier, a corporation with earnings and profits that were accumulated before the corporation elected Subchapter S status is taxable on excessive passive investment income.

Items of income, loss, deductions, or credit must be separately stated.

Deductions that would not be available to a partnership are not allowable to a Subchapter S corporation. Such deductions include personal exemptions, foreign or possessions taxes, charitable contributions, net operating losses, and certain added itemized deductions allowed to individuals.

A Subchapter S corporation may make the same elections regarding amortization of their organizational expenditures as a regular corporation.

The dividend received deduction of 85% is not available to a Subchapter S corporation.

As a shareholder in a Subchapter S corporation, you will have income and losses passed through the corporation to you and allocated to you on a per-share, per-day basis. This tax treatment was only true of losses prior to the 1983 law. Capital gains and losses resulting from sales or exchanges of capital assets are passed through to you as capital gains or losses.

Second Taxation

Since a Subchapter S corporation is not a taxable entity, this does not apply.

Social Security

Social Security functions exactly the same here as it does in a regular corporation.

Fringe Benefits

The Subchapter S Revision Act of 1982 changed one advantage that Subchapter S corporations had enjoyed over partnerships. Under prior law, owner/ managers of a Subchapter S corporation were considered to be employees of the corporation. Conversely, a partner was not his own employee. The result of prior regulations was that shareholder employees of Subchapter S corporations could enjoy tax-favored fringe benefits for which partners in a partnership were not eligible. The new law changes that treatment of fringe benefits for any person who owns more than 2% of the outstanding stock of the Subchapter S corporation. As a result of the new law, treatment of fringe benefits for any person owning more than 2% of the stock in a Subchapter S corporation is the same as that for a partner in a partnership.

The practical results of this change in the law are that amounts for medical care of an owner/employee owning more than 2% of a corporation stock are not deductible by the corporation. Such amounts are deductible by the owner/employee personally but are subject to the 5% floor that is applicable under the provisions of the Tax Equity and Fiscal Responsibility Act of 1982. Corporations that were Subchapter S corporations as of September 28, 1982, may retain existing fringe benefits for tax years through 1987. The retention of these existing fringe benefits is allowed provided the corporations do not fail the old passive income test—that is, that gross receipts from passive income do not equal more than 20% of total corporate gross receipts, and a majority of the stock is not transferred.

Deferral Possibilities

Deferral possibilities of the Subchapter S corporation are limited to those that do not depend upon having income taxes at the corporate level or holding income in the corporation. (See Table 1–2.)

Income Averaging Possibilities and Dividend Deduction on Retained Earnings

These options are not available to the Subchapter S corporation.

For persons who know where they stand in relation to some of the tax and nontax factors we've discussed but are still unsure which form of business organization is most advantageous, Table 1–5 may be useful.

TABLE 1–5

Differences Between Proprietorships, Partnerships, Subchapter S and Corporations by Factors

Factor to Be Considered	Proprietorship	Partnership	Subchapter S	Corporation
Period of Existence	Ceases to exist when the sole proprietor is no longer active	Terminated by agreement or upon sale or exchange of 50% or more of total interest within 12 months	Continue until dissolved—not affected by the disaffiliation of shareholders The Subchapter S election may be revoked or terminated involuntarily if qualifications are not met	
Liability Exposure	Unlimited personal liability for debts of the business	General partners have joint and several liability for partnership obligation. Limited partners have liability only to the extent of capital contributions	Generally, stockholder liability is limited to capital contributions. Limited liability does not extend to professional liability	
Creation of Subsidiaries	no	no	no	yes
Relative Costs	Least costly—very few costs associated	Costs to be incurred may include: legal fees, state filing fees, fees to set up and maintain books, fees for tax return preparation. A thorough, protective partnership agreement is essential and expensive		
Deductibility of Organization Costs	N/A	No deduction for costs incurred to promote the sale of interests. Other organization expenses may be deducted ratably over a period of not less than 60 months	Organizational expenses normally deductible in the year of dissolution. Under certain conditions, an election to amortize ratably over a period of 60 months is possible. Election must be made by the income-tax filing date for the tax year corporation begins business	
Social Security Comparisons	Pay self-employment tax—not deductible. Rate less than combined rate of corporation and employee		As an employee of the corporation, pay social security tax. Your corporation matches the tax. Combined tax is greater than self-employment tax. Corporate contribution deductible. Personal contribution not deductible.	

TABLE 1–5 (continued)

Differences Between Proprietorships, Partnerships, Subchapter S and Corporations by Factors

Factor to Be Considered	Proprietorship	Partnership	Subchapter S	Corporation
Transfer of Ownership Interest	By sale or gift of the business	Requires consent of all partners (unless partnership agreement allows otherwise)	Accomplished by transfer of certificate of ownership shares. Transfer must meet requirements of Subchapter S election—35 or fewer shareholders who are individuals or estates and not nonresident aliens	
Treatment of Income	Not a taxable entity—Income flows through to the proprietor. Net income of business becomes proprietor's personal gross	Income determined at partnership level and flows through to each partner. Partners are personally taxed whether or not a distribution has been made. Ordinary income at the partnership level is ordinary income to each partner—capital gains and/or losses at the partnership remain as such to each partner. Operating losses are passed through to partners to the extent of partners' basis	Income determined at corporate level and flows through to each shareholder. Shareholders pay personal tax on their portion of corporate income. Operating losses flow through to shareholders and may be used to offset other income	Corporation is a taxable entity. Income to shareholders is taxed at the personal level according to the nature of income, for example, salary, fringe benefit, and dividend. Operating losses cannot be passed through to shareholders
Federal Income Tax Returns Required	Schedule C of Personal 1040	Information Return Form 1065. Partnership is not a taxable entity	Corporate return Form 1120-S. Subchapter S is not a taxable entity	Corporate return Form 1120. Corporation is a taxable entity
Capital Gains	N/A	Capital gains retain their character when passed through to partners. This is true even if the partnership has an operating loss	Capital gains from sales or exchanges of capital assets pass directly through to shareholders	Corporate capital gains are taxed at the corporate level

TABLE 1–5 (continued)

Differences Between Proprietorships, Partnerships, Subchapter S and Corporations by Factors

Factor to Be Considered	Proprietorship	Partnership	Subchapter S	Corporation
Capital Losses	N/A	Carried through to individual partners. Partners may use these losses to offset individual capital gains and ordinary income to a maximum of $3,000 may be carried forward	Capital losses pass directly through to shareholders. If losses exceed gains, they can be used to offset the shareholders' personal capital gains and/or, within the usual limit, deducted from their other income	Capital losses are deducted to the extent of capital gains. Capital losses not currently used may be carried back three years or carried forward five years
Undistributed Earnings	N/A	Partners are taxed individually on all income whether or not the income has been distributed	All income is passed through the corporation and becomes taxable income to the shareholders	Because a corporation is a taxable entity and not simply an income conduity as are the other forms of business, a corporation is allowed to accumulate income for reasonable business needs. The limit to be accumulated without question (or penalty) is $150,000 for personal sevice corporations and $250,000 for all other corporations. Accumulation in excess of this amount must either be justified as reasonable business needs or will be subject to a penalty tax.
Dividends Received Exclusion	None to the business since they are not taxable entities. Individually the partners or shareholders may take $100 ($200 if married filing jointly) as available on the individual 1040.			Corporations may exclude from income 85% of dividends received
Fringe Benefits: Company Car	Only the portion attributable to business use is deductible. Personal use is not deductible			
Business Travel and Entertainment	Must be adequately substantiated and must be of a legitimate business nature.			

29

TABLE 1–5 (continued)

Differences Between Proprietorships, Partnerships, Subchapter S and Corporations by Factors

Factor to Be Considered	Proprietorship	Partnership	Subchapter S	Corporation
Educational Costs	In the absence of a qualified program, only deductions for educational costs which "improve or maintain skills" or are "job-related" are allowed. With an Employer Educational Assistance Program these expenses are excluded from an employee's gross income and are deductible by the employer.			
Life Insurance	No deduction allowed			Employer-paid group term insurance, up to $50,000 per employee is allowed. The premium on this policy is not taxable to the employee but is deductible to the corporation. For benefits in excess of $50,000, the taxable cost is determined by the Uniform Premium table which is in the IRS regulations.*
Disability Insurance	No deduction allowed for premiums paid			Deduction is allowed for premiums paid.
Medical Insurance	No business deduction allowed. Personal deduction of medical expenses is limited to 5% of adjusted gross income.			Premiums deductible by corporation—not taxable to the employee. Benefits received are normally tax free.
Medical Reimbursement	— Not available —			Under a medical reimbursement plan a corporation may deduct medical expenses reimbursed to an employee. These expenses are deductible to the corporation but tax-free to the employee.
Opportunities to Defer Taxation by Deferring Income	— Not available —			Deferred compensation various retirement plan option; accumulated earnings.

TABLE 1–5 (continued)

Differences Between Proprietorships, Partnerships, Subchapter S and Corporations by Factors

Factor to Be Considered	Proprietorship	Partnership	Subchapter S	Corporation
Keogh Plans	Yes	Yes	No	No
IRA	The Economic Recovery Tax Act allows every working person, whether or not they participate in a qualified retirement plan, to make a tax deductible contribution of 100% of earned income to a maximum of $2,000 to an IRA.			
Pension & Profit Sharing Plans	Limited to IRA and/or Keogh		With defined contribution—up to a total of 25% of compensation not to exceed $30,000. With defined benefit—as needed to fund predetermined benefit. Benefit cannot exceed $90,000 or $100% of average compensation for three highest consecutive years.	
Interest Free Loans		— Not of benefit —		If properly structured, an interest-free loan from a corporation to an employee should not result in taxable income

*Five-year bracket	Cost per $1,000 of protection for one-month period
under 30	$.08
30–34	.10
35–39	.14
40–44	.23
45–49	.40
50–54	.68
55–59	1.10
60–64	1.63

The costs are arbitrary and bear no relationship to the actual premiums paid for the coverage.

The Mechanics of
Becoming Incorporated

A careful reading of Chapter 1 has probably convinced you that you fall into one of these three categories:

1. Purely from a tax perspective, you cannot benefit by incorporation; or
2. Your tax situation can be improved so marginally that the cost of incorporating and the additional work of being incorporated are the deciding factors; or
3. You should definitely be considering incorporation.

This chapter will help you answer questions about the costs and extra work generated by the incorporation process and maintenance of the corporate mode.

The decision to incorporate triggers dozens of other decisions, called here "things to decide" and "things to do."

Things to decide include:

1. Name of the corporation
2. State of incorporation
3. Capital structure

4. The Subchapter S election

5. Directors and officers

6. Stockholder/employee salaries and form of payment

7. Fringe benefits, life insurance, retirement

8. Working on the ongoing professional relationships

9. Fiscal year

10. Accounting method

Things to be done include:

1. Review of agreements formed prior to incorporation

2. Articles of incorporation, filing, payment of fees

3. By-laws

4. Organizational meeting

5. Initial board of directors meeting

6. Licenses

7. Applications for workmen's compensation and unemployment compensation under corporate name

This is a formidable list, but don't get discouraged. It's not that bad. Let's go through it now, item by item.

THINGS TO DECIDE

Name of the Corporation

If you are incorporating an existing business, you may decide not to change the name. The Model Business Corporation Act (MBCA), however, requires that the corporate name contain the word "corporation," "company," "incorporated," or "limited," or an abbreviation. Jurisdictions differ as to whether "company" or "co." is adequate to indicate incorporation, so if you prefer not to use "corporation" or "incorporated" be sure to check local laws before you spend any money on such items as signs, letterhead, or business cards.

Be very careful that your corporate name does not mislead the public about your corporate purpose, as this is in violation of the MBCA. Local law may prohibit the use of certain words such as "bank," "trust," "insurance," or any wording that would lead the public to believe you're a nonprofit organization, or an official organization of the government, labor, or a profession.

The MBCA also prohibits selecting a name that another firm has registered or a name that is deceptively similar to a registered name.

Although the secretary of state in your state will have to approve your name, the approval is no protection from another company's filing a claim that your corporate name is unreasonably similar to theirs.

Some other regulations are:

1. Not using the name of a living person without express consent.
2. Using English letters or characters in most states. Foreign names are usually acceptable.

Aside from the legal considerations, you will presumably want to choose a name that describes your business, that "sounds good"; and that is short enough for signs, letterhead, business cards, and the like.

Choosing the State of Incorporation

If you expect to do all, or most, of your business in your home state, you will probably prefer to incorporate in that state. Some states allow you to incorporate out of state and still do business in your home state. Others do not. If you are in a state with a rather onerous corporate tax rate, you may consider incorporating out of your state. Check your state regulations to see if this would be possible.

Some areas in which state laws differ are:

1. Some states require shareholders' meetings to be held in the state of incorporation. (If this is important one way or the other to you, check your state's laws.)
2. State liability laws are not universal. Under some state laws, shareholders may be liable for certain corporate liabilities (especially for monies due employees).
3. State corporate laws vary regarding the percentage of vote required for certain corporate acts.
4. State laws on directors' liability vary.
5. State laws may differ regarding the right to own real estate for both business purposes and as investment.
6. State laws can vary on the amounts and the sources from which dividends may be paid.
7. State laws regarding the number and kind of incorporations are not universal. Some states require as few as one; others as many as three. Identity of the investors may or may not have to be revealed.

State Tax Factors To Be Considered

The kinds of taxes that individual states may charge are:

1. *Property tax.* This is normally assessed by the state in which the property is located, as opposed to the state of incorporation. If you anticipate that your business will own real estate, check this one out.

2. *Tax on intangible property.* May be levied on the value of securities, bank balances, accounts receivable, and so forth.

3. *Tax on the going value of the firm, called a capital-stock tax.* Those states that levy such a tax provide a formula by which the value is calculated.

4. *State income tax.* Look particularly at: deductions for interest, depletion, contributions, depreciation, and federal income tax paid. Determine the state's treatment of capital gains (may differ from federal) and the treatment of loss carry-forward and carry-back (the use of losses in previous and subsequent years). This is especially important if your business is somewhat volatile with high profits in one year and losses another.

5. *Franchise taxes.*

6. *Incorporating fees.*

The state-by-state listing at the end of this chapter breaks down all taxes for each state.

Capital Structure

The term "capital structure" refers to the type of corporate securities and debt which are to be used and their ratio to each other. Those most commonly used with closely held corporations are: common stock (sometimes with 2 or more classes); preferred stock; and promissory notes.

These securities and/or debt instruments are issued in exchange for assets transferred into your corporation.

Factors To Be Considered

In determining the capital structure of your corporation, you should consider several factors.

1. The probability of the business' profit and loss and how much of your personal wealth you are willing to commit.

2. Your future income tax consequences, if the business is very successful, as corporate earnings and/or capital are distributed.

3. The avoidance of a capital structure that would restrict your electing Subchapter S if you wish to (for example, a Subchapter S corporation can only have one class of stock).

4. The comparative advantages of a tax-free or taxable transfer.
5. The potential income tax consequences if you wish to transfer depreciable property into the corporation and obtain a stepped-up income-tax basis.

The point of all these considerations is to determine:

1. Which assets do you want to transfer into your corporation?
2. At what total value do you want your corporation capitalized?
3. Do you want to take stock or debt as evidence of the assets transferred?

If You Take Debt

If, however, you loan assets to the corporation (taking a debt instrument) your corporation can deduct the interest it pays you on the debt. Equally important, the corporation can repay its debt as a return of principal with no personal tax consequences to you. An example illustrates these differences.

Stock-Income Tax

Business Gross	$50,000
Expenses	–0–
Taxable Corporate Income	$50,000
Corporate Tax	8,250
Available for Distribution as Dividend	$41,750
Personal Taxes @ 50%	20,875
Total Distribution	41,750
Combined Taxes	29,125

Debt-Income Tax

Business Gross	$50,000
Interest on Debt	41,750
Taxable Corporate Income	8,250
Corporate Tax	1,237
Available for Distribution as Dividend	7,013
Personal Taxes @ 50%	24,381
Total Distribution	48,763
Combined Taxes	25,618

Repayment of Debt

In this instance you take a large distribution from your company as repayment of your loan to that company. The distribution will be tax free as a return of principal.

It's easy to understand why, purely from a tax point of view, you are better off maximizing debt and minimizing equity in your capital structure. But if you go to extremes, your corporation will be categorized as "thinly capitalized," and the Internal Revenue Service may challenge you. Usually, what they do then is to restructure and "redefine" some interest payments as dividends which results in additional corporate taxes.

Code section 385, effective in early 1983, allows the Treasury Department to prescribe regulations to determine whether an interest in a corporation is treated as stock or debt.

You will want to explore the provisions of code section 385 with your tax advisor when setting up the debt structure of your business, but basically, the section provides a general presumption that an instrument issued by a corporation with a debt-to-equity ratio of 10:1 or more will be treated as equity. An exception is made for instruments whose terms and conditions, together with the corporation's financial structure, would be satisfactory to banks or other lending institutions making ordinary commercial loans.

For straight debt instruments, an additional "safe harbor" rule is provided if:

1. The corporation's debt-to-equity ratio determined in the ordinary way does not exceed 10:1, and
2. The corporation's inside debt-to-equity ratio does not exceed 3:1. Liabilities to independent creditors are not considered when determining the inside ratio.

Debt will be considered stock for tax purposes unless your corporation passes the tests described above or unless the loan is made on terms under which a commercial lender would have made the loan.

The Commissioner and the courts will determine the nature of "debt" issued prior to passage of code section 385. They will look for debt with characteristics of stock such as a variable yield which is a function of corporate profits, no fixed maturity date, and subordination to other creditors. Debt with characteristics of stock combined with a high debt-to-equity ratio may result in redefinition and a loss of the interest deduction.

One more advantage that will encourage you to consider debt over equity is that debts are an acceptable reason to accumulate retained earnings. You should, of course, follow IRS guidelines for documenting your debt very carefully.

If You Take Stock

If you accepted mostly stock as evidence of the assets transferred, then part of what your corporation pays you as earnings may be dividends. This is the worst possible way to take money from your corporation because: (1) the corporation is not allowed to deduct dividend payments when computing corporate tax and (2) a large distribution to you will have to be treated as a dividend for which you must pay personal income tax.

Common Stock

Common stock has several characteristics:

1. A corporation is normally under no legal obligation to pay any return (dividend) to the owners of common stock.
2. A corporation normally has no obligation to repay funds used for the purchase of common stock (not to be confused with buy-back arrangements).
3. Common stock is normally voting stock and therefore provides holders a voice in management.
4. A corporation's growth usually accrues to common stock, so that common stockholders are usually the most generously rewarded.

You will want to issue common stock first. How many shares you issue depends upon two things: (1) your needs (for example, will you be making gifts of stock for estate-planning purposes or to employees for management purposes), and (2) state filing costs. These are frequently a function of the number of shares authorized.

Preferred Stock

The second kind of stock you may issue is preferred stock. Remember, though, that if you're making a Subchapter S election you can only have one class of stock.

Preferred stock is a sort of hybrid of common stock and bonds. Like stock, it is considered equity capital and therefore carries neither interest obligation to the corporation nor predetermined payback. The dividend payout, however, is recorded in the articles of incorporation at a fixed rate that the corporation is obligated to pay. This is similar to the interest obligation on a bond. Preferred shareholders are given priority over common stockholders in their respective claims to dividends, just as they are in the event of dissolution or liquidation.

Preferred shares are frequently redeemable at the option of the corporation, and rarely, if ever, grant their holders any voice in the management of the corporation. A frequent use of preferred stock is to give one group of shareholders priority in earnings. Other uses for preferred stock are:

1. To give key employees a work incentive without relinquishing control.

2. To reduce your taxes by making it a gift to your children. The dividends are then taxed in their brackets (which may be significantly lower than yours), and you have not given up any control.

3. To put a large portion of the value of the business in preferred stock for yourself; and then gift nonvoting common stock to your heirs. This has the effect of freezing the value of the business through the preferred stock and letting future corporate growth accrue to the common stock—a very good estate-planning device.

4. To keep it for its investment income when you sell your business. By holding some shares, you may also keep the purchase price more manageable for the buyer.

If possible, it is recommended that you make such decisions about your preferred stock at incorporation. Preferred stock that is issued tax free in a reorganization or as a dividend on common stock may become federal tax code section 306 stock. Preferred stock will become Section 306 stock if your corporation had earnings and profits at the time the preferred stock was issued. Conversely, preferred stock issued at incorporation is not Section 306 stock.

Section 306 Stock

The Internal Revenue Code Section 306 creates a form of stock which is referred to simply as Section 306 stock. Code section 306 stock is any stock, except common stock, that a shareholder receives in a reorganization in which gain or loss to any extent is not recognized but only to the extent that the effect of the transaction is substantially the same as the receipt of a stock dividend.

It is important to avoid Section 306 stock, if possible, because proceeds from the sale of Section 306 stock are considered *ordinary income*, even though the stock would be considered a capital asset otherwise.

Let's look at an illustration. Suppose you had stock with an original value of $50,000. You held the stock more than one year and sold it for $100,000. A comparison of the tax implications follows:

	As a Capital Asset	As Section 306 Stock
Sale price	$100,000	$100,000
Cost basis	50,000	50,000
	$ 50,000	$ 50,000
Less long-term capital gains deduction (60%)	$ 30,000	N/A
Taxable @ 50%	20,000	$ 50,000
Taxes due	$ 10,000	$ 25,000
	$15,000	

Section 1244 Stock

You should definitely include a provision for federal tax code section 1244 stock, which is basically common stock issued by small business corporations. This stock, commonly called 1244 stock, allows an advantageous alternative without corresponding negative compromises.

If you sell Section 1244 stock at a loss, or if it becomes worthless, you can take up to $50,000 in *ordinary* loss per year ($100,000 on a joint return) regardless of how long you held the stock.

The following example will demonstrate the advantage.

	Long-term Capital Loss	Section 1244 Stock
Purchase price	$50,000	$50,000
Sale price	25,000	25,000
Loss	($25,000)	($25,000)
Deductible portion of loss	$12,500	$25,000

The long-term capital loss represents a loss on the sale of stock you held more than one year. Allowable losses are the lesser of:

1. The taxable income for the taxable year reduced (but not below zero) by the zero bracket amount. (See Appendix B.)
2. The applicable amount, or
3. The sum of:
   a. The excess of the net short-term capital loss over the net long-term capital gain, and
   b. One-half of the excess of the net long-term capital loss over the net short-term capital gain.

You may deduct $3,000 per year of the loss and carry it forward until completely used.

The requirements for a 1244-stock deduction are:

1. The stock must be common stock of a domestic corporation. It can be either voting or nonvoting common.
2. The stock must be issued in exchange for money or other property. Stock issued for service does not qualify as 1244 stock.
3. Only the first $1,000,000 of stock qualifies.
4. The stock will not qualify as Section 1244 stock if, during the five-year period prior to the shareholder's loss or during the period of corporate existence, if less than five years, the corporation earned

more than 50% of its gross receipts from royalties, rent, dividends, interest, annuities, and sales or exchanges of stock or securities.

Ordinary losses on 1244 stock are limited to the basis[1] originally acquired. You cannot use subsequent capital contributions to lift your basis on 1244 stock.

If you are considering a business about which you have some real concern, a Subchapter S election combined with 1244 stock will maximize your deductions in the event the business operates for a while at a loss and then goes under.

Two important points remain about 1244 stock:

1. The ordinary-loss deduction is available only to the person to whom the stock was issued *originally*. Avoid making gifts of 1244 stock.
2. You can sell your 1244 stock for less than your basis and realize an ordinary loss. The stock does not have to become worthless.

There's also an interesting use for 1244 stock. If you're considering a new business, IRS takes the position that any expenses incurred to investigate the feasibility of the business are not deductible *unless you enter into the business*. However, if you incorporate before you do your investigating, and later determine that the business is not feasible, you can liquidate the corporation· and take the loss freely through 1244 stock (within the maximums). Your articles of incorporation should specifically provide for code section 1244 stock.

Par Value Stock

I often get questions about the benefits of par value stock. At one time, nearly all stock issued was par value stock. This stock has a fixed value stated on the stock certificate, so as the value of the business changes the par value becomes increasingly inaccurate. Unless your state requires par value stock, you will probably not prefer this option.

Stock Redemption

If you take a large distribution from your company, intending it as a partial redemption of your stock, you are in essence saying, "buy back some of my stock." In most cases the distribution will be treated as a dividend. The result is illustrated in the example on page 37.

---

[1]Basis generally is the number you subtract from the amount you receive from a sale to determine your gain or loss. It will normally be what you invested in the property being sold. Basis is often adjusted for specific situations and/or property.

Taxable or Tax-Free Incorporation

The first thing to realize about a taxable or tax-free incorporation is that this has nothing to do with the Subchapter S election. I've said to many clients: "let's incorporate you as a tax-free incorporation" and heard them respond, "Judith, I thought we had decided against the Subchapter S election." This is a reasonable and perfectly logical mistake.

The terms "taxable incorporation" or "tax-free incorporation" refer to recognition or nonrecognition of gain or loss on assets transferred into a new corporation.[2] The Subchapter S election refers to the taxation of corporate profits earned by the ongoing business operation.

The inclination of most of us, I suspect, is to see the terms, "taxable" and "tax free" and conclude that there is nothing to decide. A tax-free incorporation has to be better. What possible virtue could there be in recognizing gain if you don't have to? Well, there are some circumstances in which you may come out ahead by recognizing gain at the point of incorporation. This section will explore those circumstances.

The decision to be taxable or tax free is governed by Internal Revenue Code Section 351 as a nonelective provision. When certain conditions are met, you're a tax-free incorporation, but under other conditions, you're a taxable incorporation. So, if you are convinced that being a taxable corporation is to your advantage, you must take certain steps to meet the code requirements.

The fact that it's more difficult to meet the requirements for a taxable corporation has always seemed to me reason enough to explore it with clients. Tax regulation frequently seems to dictate that the easiest way for us to do things is the most profitable to the federal government!

Tax-Free Incorporation

Since the requirements for tax-free incorporation are the easiest, let's explore them first. The term "tax-free" is actually a misnomer—it should be called "tax deferred." When you dispose of the stock you take in exchange for the assets transferred into the corporation, you recognize the gain.

Code section 351 provides that *no gain or loss* will be recognized when assets are transferred to a corporation if:

1. The person or persons who transfer assets to the corporation own at least 80% of the voting power of all voting stock and at least 80% of all other classes of stock after the incorporation.

---

[2]The word "recognize" as used in connection with taxation has a very specific meaning. Gains, losses and/or income are taxable when "recognized."

2. The person or persons who transfer assets to the corporation receive *only* stock and securities of the corporation.

3. The corporation cannot assume a liability from the transferors or assume a liability on any assets transferred if (a) there is not a bona fide business purpose, (b) the major motivation is to avoid taxes, or (c) the sum of the liabilities assumed, combined with existing liabilities on the assets, is greater than the adjusted basis of all property transferred.

Notice that this tax-free transfer is a double-edged sword. It gives you the right to defer taxes by making a tax-free transfer, but it also prohibits the recognition (and therefore the deductibility) of losses.

Assets That May Be Transferred To The Corporation

Property, both real or personal; cash; or stock or securities of other corporations may be transferred.

There are three situations in which you may have taxable gain even in a tax-free incorporation. Those situations are:

1. Issuance of stock for services
2. Issuance of stock and "boot" in exchange for assets
3. Assumption of liabilities

Issuance of Stock for Services

If you transfer "services" to your corporation as opposed to assets, you do not necessarily nullify federal code section 351. However, the transferor receiving stock for services is not counted for purposes of satisfying the 80% control provision. The control provision is still satisfied if the remaining stockholders have the control required. One critical consideration is that you are immediately taxable on the fair market value of the stock or securities that you accept in exchange for your services. In other words, the effect is to have received income.

Issuance of Stock and Boot in Exchange for Assets

Code section 351(a) dictates that you must receive only stock or securities in exchange for assets transferred into the new corporation. True to form, however, code section 351(b) modifies this by allowing you to receive money or other property *in addition* to stock and securities. The emphasis is important, because if no stock or securities are received, the transaction is not a transfer but a sale, and, of course, immediately taxable. Anything received other than the stock and securities of the new corporation is considered "boot."

If you receive boot as part of a tax-free incorporation as governed by code section 351, you must recognize gain on the transaction but only to the extent of the boot you receive. Let's take an example. You transfer into your corporation a building in which you intend to conduct your business or profession. Your basis in the building is $100,000; fair market value of the building is $200,000. In return you take $150,000 of stock and $15,000 in cash. Although there is $100,000 of gain on the building, you recognize only $15,000—the boot you receive.

Since Uncle Sam makes up his own rules, it may not surprise you to learn that losses don't work the same way. You cannot trigger the recognition of loss by accepting boot. If the fair market value of the building in our example was $50,000 (or indeed, anything less than $100,000), you would not be permitted to take the loss.

We will see later that two keystones of tax planning are to defer taxes and to convert ordinary income to capital gains whenever possible. With a tax-free incorporation, however, you have to be careful or you may convert capital gain to ordinary income. (If you're not sure why the distinction is so important, you may want to read Appendix B.)

Normally, if boot does trigger gain, it is treated as ordinary income if you have owned the asset being transferred at a gain for less than one year. If you have owned the asset for more than one year, the gain is normally treated as long-term capital gain.

This happens normally—but not always. The exceptions are:

1. Depreciable assets: If you transfer a depreciable asset and take some boot with your tax-free corporation, the recognized gain is treated as ordinary income, regardless of your holding period,[3] if you, your spouse, minor child(ren) and grandchild(ren) combined own 80% of the new corporation (federal code section 1239).

2. Personal property transfer: If your transfer is personal property on which you have taken depreciation, those prior depreciation deductions are subject to recapture[4] as ordinary income (again, regardless of your holding period) to the extent of recognized gain (code section 1245).

3. Real property transfer: If your transfer is real property, prior excess

---

[3]The length of time you own an asset. Normally, selling an asset that you have owned more than one year results in long-term capital gains.

[4]The term recapture is very descriptive, since what is "recaptured" is income-tax liability. This is the result of being required to claim as ordinary income items that had been taken in past years as ordinary deductions. The most frequent example is depreciation.

depreciation deductions are recaptured as ordinary income to the extent of recognized gain. Excess depreciation results from taking accelerated depreciation (federal code section 1250).

The last of the special situations is a tax-free transfer in which there is an assumption of liability.

Assumption of Liabilities

We have just seen that if you accept cash or other property in addition to stock in your new corporation, you are required to recognize gain to the extent of such boot.

Under certain circumstances, the assumption of a liability by your corporation may be treated as boot. Let's look at those situations.

Let's assume, that, like most taxpayers, you want to make maximum use of tax advantages. In thinking about what you will transfer to your new corporation, you decide to transfer your house, with its rather large mortgage, and pay off your home with pre-tax corporate dollars.

The result of the transfer is boot in the amount of the liability. Why? Because federal code section 357(b) says that if your principal purpose in having your corporation assume your liability or acquire your property subject to a liability is to avoid tax, you have received boot in the amount of the liability. This also holds for any transfer that is not for a bona fide purpose.

You are also deemed to have received boot if the liabilities assumed by your new corporation are greater than the basis of the assets transferred to it. Don't load up an asset with debt and then transfer it in. In addition to triggering taxable gain by the receipt of boot, the basis in your stock will be zero. Why? Because federal code section 358 says your basis in the stock is determined by starting with the basis in the assets, *subtracting the total liabilities transferred to the corporation,* and adding the gain you recognized on the transaction.

Liabilities are not treated as boot if they are deductible and/or they are a payment to a retiring partner or a deceased partner's successors for his/her share of the business.

Taxable Incorporation

If you fail to meet the requirements of code section 351, as a tax-free incorporation, then the transfer of assets to your corporation is governed by Internal Revenue Code Section 1001, a taxable incorporation. The basic effect of this transaction is the same as having made a sale of assets to your corporation.

Let's take a look at two assets that might typically be transferred into a new corporation:

	Cost	Depreciation Taken Prior To Transfer	Fair Market Value
Asset 1 Land	$ 10,000	N/A	$ 35,000
Asset 2 Building	$100,000	$25,000	$200,000

Tables 2–1 and 2–2 present the results obtained using these figures for both tax-free and taxable incorporation.

TABLE 2–1
Results of a Tax-Free Incorporation

	Transferors		Taxable Gain Deferred	Corporation		
	Basis	Fair Market Value		Basis	Fair Market Value	Depreciation Base*
Before Transfer Land	10,000	35,000	25,000			
After Transfer Land				10,000	35,000	N/A
Stock in New Corp.	10,000	35,000	25,000			
Before Transfer Building	75,000 Cost 100,000 Minus Depr. 25,000 75,000	200,000	125,000			
After Transfer Building				75,000	200,000	75,000
Stock in New Corp.	75,000	200,000	125,000			

*For personal, nonbusiness assets, the depreciation basis is the lower of fair market value or basis in the hands of the transferor(s) prior to transfer.

Let's figure out what Tables 2–1 and 2–2 are trying to tell us. Assume the building was being depreciated straight-line[5] with a useful life of 20 years; 5 have already been taken.

$$(\$100,000 \div 20 \text{ years} = 5,000 \times 5 \text{ years} - \$25,000)$$

If you opt for tax-free incorporation, the newly formed corporation will

[5]Depreciation deducted in even increments over the life of the asset.

TABLE 2–2
Results of a Taxable Transfer

	Transferors		Taxable Gain Recognized	Corporation		
	Basis	Fair Market Value		Basis	Fair Market Value	Depreciation Base
Before Transfer Land	10,000	35,000	25,000			
After Transfer Land				35,000	35,000	N/A
Stock in New Corp.	35,000	35,000				
Before Transfer Building	75,000	200,000	125,000			
After Transfer Building				200,000	200,000	200,000
Stock in New Corp.	200,000	200,000				

probably use 15-year, straight-line depreciation, as allowed by the Economic Recovery Tax Act of 1981.

$$(\$75,000 \div 15 \text{ years} = \$5,000/\text{year for } 15 \text{ years})$$

The transferors save on personal income taxes as follows:

$125,000	taxable gain (deferred)
× 40%	taxable portion
$ 50,000	
× 50%	tax rate
$ 25,000	taxes deferred by taking tax-free incorporation

But your savings are really being financed by your new corporation through "lost" depreciation deductions.

If your corporation started with a depreciation basis of $200,000—straight-line for 15 years—the depreciation write-off would be $13,333/year for 15 years. Assuming your corporation was in the maximum corporate bracket of 46%, the loss would be:

Depreciation with $200,000 basis	$13,333
Depreciation with $ 75,000 basis	5,000
Depreciation deduction lost	8,333
at 46%	$ 3,833

In 6½ years your corporation would have earned a tax saving and still have 8½ years of depreciation left. This analysis largely ignores the time value of money, however, and $25,000 expanded today, when money earns 10%–11% in a money market fund, has a significant time value.

Assuming for the moment that the assets you want to transfer into your corporation are such that a step-up in depreciation basis is very meaningful to you, what should you be particularly careful about?

Depreciation Recapture

The first thing to watch out for is depreciation recapture. If you transfer realty to your corporation, the difference between accelerated depreciation[6] and straight-line depreciation is treated as ordinary income.

If you transfer personal property to your corporation, *all* depreciation previously deducted is treated as a recapture of ordinary income. With transfers of personal property, it doesn't matter what method of depreciation you use—it's all recaptured.

Converting Capital Gains to Ordinary Income

The next thing to watch out for, and this is particularly applicable to a closely held business, is inadvertently converting capital gains to ordinary income. The provisions of federal tax code section 1239 are such that if you sell depreciable property to a corporation in which you own directly or indirectly 80% or more of the value of the stock, any gain realized is *taxed as ordinary income*.

Let's look at Tables 2–1 and 2–2 again in light of this provision and assume that you will own 80% or more of the corporation you are establishing. The taxes saved by deferring look like this:

$125,000	taxable gain
× 50%	tax rate
$ 62,500	taxes deferred by taking a tax-free incorporation

Under these conditions, your corporation would require 16½ years to recoup through depreciation (remember that 15 years was the schedule). If we plug the time value of money into equation, the figures on taxable incorporation really get left at the gate.

Let's look now at some conditions that not only get an increased depreciation basis for your corporation, but may also encourage you to consider a taxable incorporation.

---

[6]Depreciation deducted faster than on a pro-rata basis. Schedules for accelerated depreciation are specifically spelled out in the federal tax code.

If You Own An Appreciated Asset

A taxable corporation should be considered if you own an appreciated asset (nondepreciable) that your corporation will use as a business asset.

Let's look at the land in our example. Suppose your corporation improved the land in some way and sold it for $70,000. You would have a long-term capital gain immediately recognizable at transfer of $25,000—a tax bill of $5,000.

$$(\$25,000 \times 40\% = \$10,000 \times 50\% = \$5,000)$$

Your corporation would have a taxable gain of $35,000 ($70,000 sale price minus $35,000 basis), at 28% corporate rate, resulting in a tax bill of $9,800.

If you were a tax-free incorporation, you would have had no tax at transfer, but your corporation would have had a taxable gain of $60,000 ($70,000 sale price minus $10,000 basis), a 28% corporate rate and a tax bill of $16,800. The combined tax savings is $2,000.

Loss Deduction

Another situation for considering a taxable corporation is if you have losses on the assets you are transferring in and if you will own 50% or less of the outstanding stock of the newly formed corporation. If you meet these conditions, you can take a loss deduction.

If you plan to elect a Subchapter S treatment, do consider a taxable incorporation. This is particularly the case if the assets to be transferred in have a low basis relative to their fair market value. The loss that can be passed through a Subchapter S is limited to your basis in your stock. A taxable incorporation gives you basis of fair market value of the assets transferred in and permits greater loss pass-through deductions[7] later.

Income Splitting

To a very real degree, a taxable incorporation represents an opportunity for income splitting of the type we discussed with the land. Think carefully about the assets you own that might become business assets. Are there any opportunities for paying some of the taxes now as capital gains and the balance later through the corporation?

Another way of splitting income is to remember that a taxable incorporation results in a greater basis in your stock. Consequently, when you dispose of your stock in the new corporation, you will be taxed only on the

---

[7]These are discussed in Chapter 1 in the section on Subchapter S shareholders' income tax treatment.

appreciation of the business since incorporation. In other words, you will be "splitting" the gain on the assets and the gain on the business in different tax years, and perhaps at lower rates.

The Question Of Need

To determine how much total value to transfer to your corporation, you will need to do some projections. If you're incorporating an ongoing business this is not too difficult to do with some degree of accuracy. If you're starting a new business, it may be little more than sophisticated crystal ball gazing. In any event, you need to answer the question of need as carefully as possible. Consider:

1. Will you have heavy growth needs? If so, can your growth be financed from current income, or will you need to transfer assets to the new corporation to accommodate the growth?
2. How much will you need in fixed assets: buildings, equipment, and fixtures? Will you transfer in cash or transfer in these assets if you already own them? Have you considered owning them personally and leasing them to your corporation? (More about this in Chapter 5.)
3. How much gross income will be required to end up with a spendable dollar? Look at operating ratios in your business to try to find an answer. (Study industry norms if you're starting a new business.)
4. How fast will inventory turn over? What will it cost to carry your inventory needs?
5. What will you do about a short-term cash crunch? Do a cash-flow projection. Project on a month-by-month basis what cash will be coming in and what cash will be going out. Even profitable businesses have cash-flow problems!
6. Will you borrow or sell equity in the new business, if you can't finance the business with existing personal assets?
7. What can go wrong and how will these problems affect any financing? Suppose your growth projections are off either way? Growing too fast or too slow are both problems with which financial arrangements are concerned. Suppose your customers don't pay on time? Suppose your equipment breaks down and you have to lease from outside sources or replace ahead of your projected schedule of equipment replacement?

You know the areas that are liable to mean trouble for your business. Think them through carefully and arrange your financial structure accordingly.

The Subchapter S Election

Now that you've decided on your capital structure, you can decide whether or not to make the Subchapter S election. When considering this question, it may be useful to review the characteristics of a Subchapter S corporation.

Basically, a Subchapter S is a hybrid with characteristics of a partnership and a regular corporation. The Subchapter S election allows the business to avoid corporate tax. Earnings simply flow through the Subchapter S to shareholders and are taxed to the shareholders at their respective brackets.

Losses behave the same way, and may be used by shareholders to offset income from sources other than the business.

Let's take a look at two situations and/or objectives that might indicate the use of Subchapter S election:

1. Suppose this new corporation is not your sole source of income; you either have a job and/or investment income. With a Subchapter S election, corporate operating losses can be used to offset your other income. Since new businesses frequently lose money the first year or two, the election is frequently taken for new operations.
2. If you expect your income to be so high that you're concerned about "unreasonable compensation," a Subchapter S election could be considered.

In my opinion, the two major motivations for Subchapter S are for pass through of losses to offset other personal income and to address the unreasonable compensation problem.

Subchapter S frequently involves a complex set of decisions. I would encourage you to seek good tax advice before deciding on this election.

Officers and Directors

You need to decide who are to be your officers and directors. State requirements differ somewhat in this area, so check these out before drawing up your bylaws.

The system generally works as follows: Your bylaws will either spell out the number of directors or establish the procedure for determining the number of directors. The majority of states call for three—most make an exception of the professional corporation and some make an exception to allow fewer than three directors, if fewer than three own all the stock. Some states require that your directors be residents of the state of incorporation. Some states require that your directors be stockholders. The board of directors meets and selects the officers. Some states require that the shareholders be directors, others leave qualifications to the bylaws.

Generally accepted corporate titles for officers include: chairman of the board, president, vice president (frequently of something specific such as advertising, marketing, or finance), secretary, recording secretary, treasurer, controller, and corporate counsel. As a rule, the only offices that must be filled are president, secretary, and treasurer. One officer holding two positions is disallowed in many states.

Some states permit the shareholders rather than the board of directors to select officers. If you have a preference for this method, check your state's requirement.

Large companies almost always pay their directors a salary. Relatively small businesses frequently pay their directors, especially those who do not own stock. If your firm has good growth potential you may want to consider including on your board some business people you admire and/or your corporate CPA, attorney, or CFP. For a relatively small fee, you may get some excellent guidance on the management of your business!

Your bylaws should spell out procedures for removing both officers and directors.

Stockholder/Employee Salaries and Form of Payment

If your business generates more income than you need as personal income, you will have to decide how much to take as salary and what fringe benefits the business is to provide for you.

I frequently suggest to my clients that we "back into" the salary. I like to start with the personal budget, how much you need, after taxes, to live on. The idea is to figure your needs accurately and take this as salary. In addition to your salary, you will need money for income-tax payments and/or tax-shelter investments to minimize personal income taxes. Now go down the list of items in your personal budget and determine if any of them can be paid with corporate dollars. (See Chapter 4.)

Plan to accumulate your full allowable retained earnings. It is $150,000 for professional corporations and $250,000 for regular corporations. This is what you can accumulate without penalty even if you have no "business need." If you have legitimate business needs you can accumulate whatever you need to satisfy them.

Be careful not to pay yourself "too much," or the IRS may claim some portion was a dividend. The budget I've included in Appendix J is one that I encourage my clients to work through for the previous 12 calendar months. It provides a good handle on how much you spend for personal-living needs and is your point of departure in determining your salary requirements from the business. Determine this point of departure, and if there are business profits beyond this need, move on to fringe benefits, then to retained earnings.

Fringe Benefits, Insurance, Retirement Funds

During the incorporation process, think about what you would like to do for yourself, your business associates, and your employees regarding fringe benefits. A good beginning is to prepare the employee census (financial inventory worksheets, Appendix J). Think carefully about the future of these people with your firm. In what ways can you encourage their greater interest in the business?

This is also a good time to reflect on your role in the business. If you left the business through death, disability, or retirement, what would happen? Could someone now in the business continue to operate it? If so, why not arrange for this person to buy out your family at your death or if you become disabled? A buy/sell agreement funded with life insurance or disability insurance is a good way to arrange these transactions.

I get very distressed when I go to a new business client and discover that all the key people are between 50 and 60 years old and that younger executives are not being brought into key positions. Give some serious thought to your business' continuity: How will it be provided for? By whom? Under what condition? How will you use your fringe benefit and retirement program to help with younger employees? How can you use business insurance to facilitate these decisions?

You will probably not be able to decide any of these questions at this point, but you should be thinking about them as you go through the book.

Working with Your Existing Professional Relationships

One of the hardest decisions a business owner has to make involves his existing professional relationships. Frequently, the scenario is something like this. You start a business, and the most natural thing in the world is to put your business bank accounts in the bank where your personal accounts are. Your friend (cousin, ex-college roommate, or brother-in-law) has been doing your personal tax return for years and is a competent bookkeeper, so naturally he looks after your business account as well. The attorney who drew up your will seems pretty competent and so is retained as your business attorney.

Everything seems okay for a while, maybe even years, but somewhere along the way your business outgrows the bank (or banker), the CPA, and the attorney. You've gotten bigger and have more sophisticated problems than your initial team of professionals can handle. Sound familiar?

It's a problem every owner of a growing business faces at some point in the business growth cycle. Sometimes you get lucky and enjoy professional relationships that mature with your business but, unfortunately, this is not always the case.

In my role as financial planner, I have sometimes had to recommend

that a client change banks, attorneys, or CPA. This is frequently very painful for my client, for two reasons. One is the very human problem of terminating what has often been a long-term relationship. The second is purely financial. "Trading up" financial advisors is costly in terms of fees. You spend more on financial advice and guidance when you bring in a CFP to design and coordinate a financial plan with your CPA, attorney, and banker. It may be hard for you to accept how valuable spending this extra money can be.

If you are faced with this problem, here are some ideas to keep in mind:

1. Good financial advice should result in profits, not costs. In my firm, for example, we do not take on new clients who cannot expect to make profits at the end of 12 months. We expect our fee to be paid with reduced taxes and increases on investments. Ask yourself what inadequate financial guidance is costing you.

2. On the human side, are you sure your present advisors want to retain your account? They may be very uncomfortable, knowing your business requires specialization beyond their skills. They may be spending more time on your account than the fee justifies but are reluctant to raise the fee because they are not sure how much more time they require to do the job than a specialist would. I have heard clients express amazement that their advisors were actually relieved to be taken off the account.

3. A good CFP can help you assess other members of the financial planning team (and vice versa). A good CFP can work as an "idea person" with your CPA or attorney who may be an excellent technician. You may find that bringing in a CFP to design and coordinate your finances with your existing team of advisors will eliminate the need to disturb these relationships.

Choosing a Fiscal Year

We talked earlier about the advantages of having a corporate fiscal year that differs from your personal tax year. The initial choice of fiscal year is largely in your control and does not require permission from the commission of the IRS. If you make a bad choice, however, and wish to change your accounting year you will need the commissioner's permission, which is rarely granted if your motivation is tax-saving. In order to get permission to change your taxable year, you must present a good case for having valid business reasons for the change. Your initial choice, however, may be based entirely on tax-saving motives. Obviously, then, you should give the choice of your taxable year some serious consideration.

According to the federal tax law, your taxable income is calculated on the basis of your taxable year. Your choices, outlined in federal code section 441, are as follows:

1. Calendar year. The calendar year is a 12-month period that ends on December 31.

2. Fiscal year. A fiscal year is any 12-month period that ends on the last day of any month except December.

3. 52–53-week year: A 52–53-week year is a fiscal year that always ends on the same day of the week that either (a) occurs for the last time in a calendar month or (b) falls nearest the end of a calendar month. A 52–53-week year will vary, as the name implies, from 52 to 53 weeks.

4. Short period: A short period is allowed under certain conditions only. This is a period of less than 12 months that may be used for your initial return, your final return, or if you're making a change in your accounting period.

Let's look now at some of the factors that will influence your choice of tax year.

You will most likely choose to end your year when your normal business activity is at its lowest point. For example, many retail businesses use a January 31 fiscal year to allow for closing the year in January, typically their slowest month. If you don't have much control over the contracts in your business (personnel, shipping, leases, and so forth), then this may motivate you to set your fiscal year so that you are not harried with closing your year, taking inventory, and getting financial statements prepared at the same time you are trying to negotiate contracts.

You will get better professional help if the end of your fiscal year corresponds with the slack period of your legal and accounting professionals.

You will want to choose a 12-month period that reflects a complete business cycle for you, particularly if you're in a highly seasonal business. Not only will this more accurately reflect your profit picture for tax purposes, it will make your financial statements a more meaningful management tool for you.

Purely from a tax point of view, you may wish to defer personal income through using your corporate fiscal year. If you are a principal in more than one corporation, consider using a different fiscal year for each to give you maximum deferral opportunities. You cannot, by the way, split up one business into two corporations with two fiscal years. Unless each corporation is a separate taxable entity, you cannot use different tax years.

A Subchapter S corporation must use a calendar year or must establish a business purpose for a different taxable year to the satisfaction of the IRS.

Choosing an Accounting Method

One of the most critical decisions you have to make for your corporation is what accounting method to use. The accounting year or tax year governs only the opening and closing dates of your year. The accounting method

you choose governs when and under what conditions your income is reportable and when and under what conditions your expenses are deductible.

There are seven recognized methods of accounting. Each one has its own characteristics and, accordingly, may be right or wrong for you. The methods are:

1. Cash method
2. Accrual method
3. "Hybrid" method
4. Percentage-of-completion method
5. Completed contract method
6. Installment method
7. Deferred-payment sales method

Let's look at each individually with a special eye to the treatment of income and deductions. Then we will determine if you are legally permitted to use the method that seems to serve your needs.

Cash Method

The cash method is frequently referred to by tax professionals as "checkbook accounting." This nickname gives you a fairly good idea of how it works. Under the cash method, you realize income when you actually or "constructively" receive it during your tax year. How much you actually earn is immaterial—income on the books is not realized until received.

Deductions work the same way. Expenses are deductible when paid, not when incurred.

There are some items of income, however, that don't show up in the checkbook but are taxable. There are income items that have been "constructively received." "Constructive receipt" is an IRS concept that says: If you can have it simply by asking for it, it's taxable, even if you have elected not to ask for it. The most common example of this is interest on a bank savings account or a certificate of deposit that has been left for compounding. The interest is taxable when credited to your account because it is really yours. The fact that you elect not to withdraw it is immaterial; the same is true for bond coupons that you neglect to clip until the next tax year.

You may use the cash method if you do not use inventories to determine income or if you don't keep books of account. The major advantage is that you aren't taxed on receivables. You don't realize income until you actually collect it. It is also a far simpler bookkeeping system since there is no need for accruals, and you govern profits somewhat by governing income and outgo to some extent.

The major disadvantage is that the cash method does not reflect your business profits accurately.

I frequently suggest to clients in service-oriented businesses to use the cash method for taxation but to run a parallel accrual system for internal business management. Yes, Virginia, it's legal to keep two sets of books, as long as they are both accurate and are kept for different reasons.

Accrual Method

You *must* use the accrual method if you have to keep inventories. You *may* use the accrual method if you have adequate books and records, whether or not you keep inventories.

Under this method, income is taxable when you have the right to receive it. Expenses are deductible when you have incurred them. The actual receipt and disbursement of cash is immaterial to this method.

The IRS seems to be particularly vigilant regarding transactions between principals of a closely held corporation and the corporation and regarding transactions among family members, where the taxpaying entities use different accounting methods. If you are accruing expenses in either category, be very careful. You could lose your deduction.

Here's a good example. The corporation owes you money that it has accrued and taken as a deduction in the current tax year. Unless that expense is paid within 75 days of the close of the taxable year, the deduction will be lost. Year-end bonuses are the most frequent victims of this rule.

Although the accrual method has a little less flexibility in regard to controlling income and outgo for tax purposes, it more accurately matches income and expenses and over a several year period tends to even out taxable income.

"Hybrid" Method

The hybrid method mixes other recognized methods. The most common mixture is cash and accrual. Basically, the accrual method is used for purchases and sales of the goods and services the business provides for its customers. All other income and expense items are accounted for with the cash method.

The advantage is that relatively small amounts of income and expense (interest and dividends in particular) don't have to be accrued, since this is often more trouble than it's worth.

Any taxpayer may select this method if it doesn't distort the profit picture and if it is used consistently.

Percentage-of-Completion Method

You may use this method only if you have contracts that typically take more than one year to complete. Not surprisingly, it's most commonly used in the construction industry.

Under this method you will recognize a portion of the total contract price each year. That portion is determined according to the percentage of contracts completed in that year. These completions must be certified by architects or engineers. Expenses are deductible as they can be allocated to the portion of finished work.

This method tends to reflect income more accurately than any other method but frequently distorts the profit picture during interim work.

Completed Contract Method

Like the percentage-of-completion method, this method is more common in the construction industry than in other industries and can only be used if you have contracts that typically require more than one year to complete.

The name is very descriptive. The entire contract is reported in the year of its completion and all income is recognized from the contract and all expenses allocable to the contract are deducted.

This method is extremely accurate since all the figures are in when the profits are calculated. It eliminates interim estimates, which are frequently inaccurate. However, if you have several large contracts completed in the same tax year, your taxes may be higher than if you had evened out the income over more than one year.

Installment Method

You may elect the installment method for your business only if you deal in personal property and normally sell to your customers on the installment plan. The installment method is also available to you if you are a casual seller of either real or personal property. In order to qualify for this method as a casual seller, you must receive at least one payment in a taxable year following the year the sale takes place.

Income is recognized in each year that an "installment" is received. The amount of income recognized is a percentage of gross profit on the entire sale. This is best described with an example.

Let's assume you own a building that you sell for $200,000. Your adjusted basis is $100,000. The buyer agrees to pay you the $200,000 over 10 years at $20,000 a year. If you charge your buyer interest of 9% or more, the interest is not considered part of the selling price.

Here's how you figure your percentage of payment, which you will recognize as gain:

Selling Price	$200,000
Adjusted Basis	($100,000)
Gross Profit	$100,000
Selling Price	$200,000

Gross Profit Percentage is $100,000 ÷ $200,000 = 50\%$

As you receive each $20,000 payment, 50% is capital gain, and 50% is considered your return of basis.

If you are a dealer who sells primarily on the installment plan and you wish to select this method, be certain to isolate and record separately all of your cash transactions.

Deferred Payment Sales Method

Anyone is entitled to use the deferred payment sales method. Transactions that qualify for this treatment are basically installment sales in which the seller receives payment in the year(s) after the sale. To qualify for deferred payment method, you must file a timely election with the IRS.

THINGS TO DO

Review Agreements Formed Prior to Incorporation

Among the first things to do is to review any agreements that you formed prior to incorporation. Those agreements that should be given careful attention to ward off any potential problems with incorporation are:

1. *Labor contracts and/or employment contracts:* Does being incorporated break or affect these agreements?
2. *Leases:* Can these be put in the corporate name? Must the principal(s) sign on as well, or must they be left exactly as they were before incorporation? If so, will this be a problem?
3. *Contracts to provide services:* Are your customers or clients willing to stay with your new corporation, or will they insist that their contract is with you personally? The legal ramifications are important, but don't lose sight of the public relations aspects of this item. I always encourage my clients to send a letter to their clientele explaining that growth is the primary reason for the need to incorporate and to thank the clientele warmly for making the growth happen. Explain the advantages of continuity, more people available to handle their needs, and whatever other advantages incorporation may have *for the clientele*.

Draw Up the Articles of Incorporation

The articles of incorporation represent the very basis of your corporation's existence. Normally your attorney prepares the articles of incorporation and files them with the state. A designated state official will approve the articles and grant a charter, under which the corporation operates. Some states have prescribed forms; others allow more flexibility.

The articles of incorporation should describe or list the following items:

1. Corporate name

2. Business purpose: Describes the type of activities the corporation is permitted to perform. For a closely held corporation you will probably prefer a rather broad description.

3. Address of the corporate officer: This is normally the address to which your secretary of state will send all official papers. In some states this address is called the registered office.

4. Capitalization of the corporation: This section should describe how many shares of each type the corporation will be permitted to issue. Details regarding limitations, voting, rights to income, and any other rights or restrictions placed on the capitalization are spelled out here.

5. Names and addresses of incorporators

6. Names and addresses of initial directors if different from the incorporators

In some states, details regarding meetings of the board of directors and/or committees may be included. Other points that may be included are details on amending or repealing the bylaws and some details regarding the powers conferred on the directors and the classification of directors.

Bylaws

The bylaws contain the rules and procedures under which the corporation will operate. They should describe or list the following items:

1. Corporate offices: This may either be the principal office of the corporation or the address of the corporation's attorney. The bylaws should spell out the procedure for changing this address. The address is used for two important reasons: This is where shareholders are entitled to look at the books and records of the corporation and secondly, this is the address to which all official papers and notices are mailed.

2. Details regarding the directors: The bylaws should either state the number of directors or provide some formula for determining the correct number. Other details relative to the directors are: their qualifications; terms of office; how directors are removed and how vacancies are filled; when, where, and how often the directors will meet; how notices to directors are handled; quorum requirements for corporate action by directors; and compensation of directors.

3. Details of shareholders meetings: Procedures to determine time and place, voting details, procedures for giving notice to shareholders, rules regarding proxy voting, record dates, quorum requirements, and provisions for special meetings.

4. Details regarding officers: The selection of officers, their titles, duties, compensations, qualifications, and removal.

5. Accounting information such as the fiscal year, accounting method, and selection of accountants.

6. Details regarding the financial statements provided to the shareholders.

7. Limitation on rights to inspect books and records. Rights cannot be denied to a shareholder for a legitimate corporate purpose.

8. Details of capitalization and terms of stock transfer.

Organizational Meeting of Incorporators

Once your attorney has filed your articles of incorporation and has drafted your bylaws, you should hold an incorporators' meeting where several rather important items of business should take place. (We frequently suggest our clients hold this initial meeting in our offices with their attorney and CPA.) Your attorney will probably bring to this meeting your corporate seal, stock register, and minute book, unless those have already been given to you.

First, one of the participants should report on the filing of the articles of incorporation, payment of any organizational and/or filing fees due in your state, and any publications or recordings your state may require. The attorney almost always reports on the filing.

The next item of business is discussion and adoption of the bylaws. Again, the attorney normally reviews this document with the incorporators, who then elect the board of directors and authorize it to issue stock.

At this point, a motion should be made to enter the certificate of incorporation (sent from the state certifying the incorporation) and any other records presented at this meeting in the corporation's minute book.

If the incorporators and the board of directors are the same group of people, the meeting can continue with the incorporators wearing a board of directors hat, although for the purposes of the minutes it becomes a different meeting. If the board of directors and incorporators are different, then a board of directors meeting should take place as quickly as possible.

The first thing the board of directors should do is to designate a secretary charged with keeping minutes of the meeting. The board should then elect the officers of the corporation and determine their compensation. If employment contracts have been issued, these should be reviewed and adopted.

The board should review and adopt the bylaws of the articles of incorporation if your state requires it. It should review and adopt any outstanding contracts of the new corporation, especially those that have been transferred in; and then approve the corporate seal and review and adopt the form on which corporate stocks will be issued.

The board must also authorize reimbursement for expenses relative to the incorporation process. This allows deductibility of these expenses. (Refer to Chapter 1 for ways to make these expenses deductible.)

If your bank requires signature on any special forms or resolutions by the board of directors, it should be done at this meeting.

In addition, a resolution should be adopted to issue 1244 stock. (Refer to the section on capital structure in Chapter 2.) If the board of directors did not receive a formal notice of this meeting, put a waiver of the notice in the minutes. Be sure minutes of this meeting are drawn up and put in the minute book.

Licenses

During the period when you are deciding on the major points of your incorporation process and your attorney is drafting the articles of incorporation and the bylaws, you should be alert to any licenses your business may require. Be sure to make application as quickly as possible since issuance of some licenses takes quite a while.

Workmen's Compensation/Unemployment Compensation

You will also need to apply for workmen's compensation and unemployment compensation in your corporate name. Your CPA can help with this chore.

Federal Employer Identification Number

Be sure to get your federal employer identification number. This number is like a Social Security number for your corporation. Just call the IRS office in your area, and they will send you an application form. The form is quite simple, so you can handle this task yourself if you wish. If not, have the CPA apply.

That's it! If you have followed through step by step, by now you're a corporation or well on your way. All those delicious tax savings will soon be yours.

Now let me share a few pointers about this new "person" we've created. Yes, person. In the eyes of the tax law, we have literally created a living thing. It's important to remember that because some of the things you did prior to incorporation are off limits now. Income, for example, is not yours in the cash drawer. It belongs to the corporation—it's not yours until the corporation gives it to you in the form of a salary or bonus. I've had business owners take money from the cash register and tell me they had declared themselves a "bonus." That's skating on very thin ice.

Put yourself in the place of IRS for a moment. There's a pretty good precedent in tax rulings that you can incorporate *for no other reason than tax savings*. However, the service will certainly look to see that you are behaving as a corporation. You cannot enjoy the tax advantages of being incorporated *and* the flexibility and freedom of being unincorporated. You have to choose one alternative and conform to its structure.

The Importance of Minutes

Sometimes the principals in a closely held corporation take the minutes and, indeed, formal meetings of the board of directors rather lightly—*don't*. In a corporate audit, one of the first things the IRS agent (auditor) asks for are your corporate minutes. He or she wants to see proper corporate behavior conducted and recorded.

Federal corporate tax law, in my opinion, is a veritable mine field. Good minutes will help you avoid stepping on one of the mines. In the minutes you document your intentions relative to various transactions. It simply doesn't work after the fact to tell the service what you had intended. I can't stress enough how important the minute book is.

Some Areas To Which Your Minutes Should Pay Particular Attention

Compensation of Officers and Directors

Remember that compensation is deductible only if it is reasonable. If the IRS can make its case for unreasonable compensation, the payment is classified as a dividend. Minutes should reflect the responsibility borne by the executive, the special skills and/or training that individual brings to the job, how similar jobs are compensated in the industry, and how this compensation compares to the other executives' compensation.

Retained Earnings

You must have legitimate business needs for retained earnings in excess of the limitation. The minutes document these needs. Internal financing of planned expansion; upcoming acquisitions; deferred compensation; expected loss of a large contract resulting in decreased revenues; and liabilities in products or services are all reasonable. Avoid discussion of the tax advantages the corporation is enjoying on retained earnings.

Corporate Payouts

Be sure that the minutes record the payout as a deductible expense. Gifts, for example, must be corporate charitable contributions or gifts to employees of $25 or less to be deductible.

Acquisitions, Subsidiaries, Reorganization, etc.

The more taxable entities you can create, the lower your combined tax bill becomes. The service understands this concept better than you do and so will disallow these activities unless you can demonstrate genuine business need. Minutes are a way of doing so.

Fringe Benefits or Corporate "Perks"

Your minutes should always reflect the adoption or resolution to adopt plans to provide such benefits.

Transactions Involving Property or Corporate Stock

There is a rather large and complex body of regulations addressing these two areas. I would encourage you always to work with your tax advisor in any transaction involving real property or your corporation's stock. Your consultant can guide you as to the least tax-burdensome methods and will help you document the transaction in your minutes.

STATE INCORPORATION REGULATIONS

Following is state-by-state information on incorporation regulations. All of this material was current when this book was published.

ALABAMA

Where to File: Judge of Probate
County in which incorporated

Initial Costs:

Charter Fee: $45 (for use of the State of Alabama $20 and for use of judge of probate $25). Payment made once only to probate judge of county in which corporation is incorporated.

No-par value stock is taken at actual value if value is shown, otherwise at $100 per share.

Annual Corporate Taxes and Fees: Applies to domestic corporations only.

Franchise Tax: $3 on each $1,000 of capital stock paid in and subject to call. Minimum $25. No-par stock is valued at $100 unless book value shown to be otherwise.

Registration Fee:

Authorized Capital Stock	Fee
$25,000 or less	$10
$25,000–$50,000	$20
$50,000–$100,000	$30
$100,000–$150,000	$50
Over $150,000	$100

Stock Tax: All property not otherwise classified—20%

Share Tax: Stock is assessed at proportion of value and taxed at the rate in effect in the county in which the principal office of the corporation is located.

Income Tax: 5% on the net income. Deduction allowed for federal income tax paid or accrued.

ALASKA

Where to File: Commissioner of Commerce
Juneau, Alaska 99801

Initial Costs:

Organization Fee: Based on authorized capital stock.

Authorized Capital Stock	Fee
$100,000 or less	$35
Over $100,000 but not over $1,000,000	$35 plus 25¢ for each $1,000 or fraction over $100,000
Over $1,000,000	$260 plus $18 for each million or fraction over $1,000,000

If no-par, stock valued at $10 per share.

Minimum: $135

Bi-Annual Filing Fee: $100

Annual Corporate Taxes and Fees:

Corporation License Tax: $50

New industrial developments are tax exempt within certain limitations.

Annual Report Fee: $45.00. All corporate reports have a filing deadline of May 1 of each calendar year. However, a corporation is required to file a report only each biennium (once in two years), according to the date of their incorporation or qualification in Colorado.

CONNECTICUT

Where to File: Secretary of State
State of Connecticut
30 Trinity Street
Hartford, Connecticut 06115

Initial Costs:

Filing Articles of Incorporation:
Stock corporation $30
Nonstock corporation $6
Credit union $10

Annual Corporate Taxes and Fees:

Income Tax: Compute these three ways and take the highest of the three:

1. 10% of net income
2. 3.1 mills on certain items of capitalization
3. profit or loss + compensation to officers divided in half then add 5% tax to the balance

Franchise Tax: Non-stock . . Minimum $30
Stock . . . . . Minimum $50
1¢ per share up to and including first 10,000 shares
½¢ per share for each share in excess of 10,000 and up to and including 100,000 shares
¼¢ per share for each share in excess of 100,000 up to and including one million shares
⅕¢ per share for each share in excess of one million

Filing Annual Report: Stock $35
Biennial nonstock . . . . $ 7.50

DELAWARE

Where to File: Secretary of State
Division of Corporations
Dover, Delaware 19901

Initial Costs:

Organization Tax: Based on authorized capital stock as follows:

(a) Par Value Shares   Tax

Up to $2,000,000 . . . . 1¢ per $100
$2,000,001 to $20,000,000 . . . . $200 plus ½¢ for
                                             each $100 over $2,000,000
Over $20,000,000 . . . . $1,100 plus ⅕¢ for
                                             each $100 over $20,000,000

(b) No-Par Value Shares   Tax

Up to 20,000 shares . . . . ½¢ per share
20,001 shares to 2,000,000 shares . . . . $100 plus ¼¢ for
                                             each share over 20,000
Over 2,000,000 shares . . . . $5,050 plus ⅕¢ for
                                             each share over 2,000,000

Minimum tax is $10

Other Fees   about $35.00

*Special Filing Requirements: Certified copy must be recorded with the county recorder of the county in which the principal office is located.

Annual Franchise Taxes and Fees:

Franchise Tax: lesser of (1) or (2)

1. Based on authorized shares: 1,000 shares or less—$20; over 1,000 shares to 3,000 shares—$24.20; over 3,000 shares to 5,000 shares—$30.25; over 5,000 shares to 10,000 shares—$60.50; over 10,000 shares—$60.50 plus $30.25 for each additional 10,000 shares or fraction thereof in excess of 10,000 shares.
2. Based on assumed par value capital authorized shares: $121 for each $1,000,000 or fraction thereof; whenever assumed par value capital is less than $1,000,000, tax is an amount that bears same relation to $121 as assumed par value capital bears to $1,000,000. Minimum: $20. Maximum: $110,000.

Annual Report Filing Fee: $10.00

Income Tax: 8.7% of taxable income from business or property located in Delaware.
              Not handled by Secretary of State
              Handled by: Department of Finance
                          Division of Revenue
                          Wilmington, Delaware

DISTRICT OF COLUMBIA

Where to File: Office of Supt. of Corporations
                  Washington, D.C. 20000

Initial Costs:

Organization Fee:

Authorized Shares

Up to 10,000 shares .... 2¢ per share
The next 40,000 shares .... 1¢ per share
All shares over 50,000 .... ½¢ per share

License Fee: Minimum $20—varies according to amount of stock involved in corporation.

Indexing Fee: $2

Filing articles of incorporation: $20

Annual Corporate Taxes and Fees:

Income Tax: 9.9% of that portion of net income attributable to business in the District of Columbia plus income derived from District of Columbia sources.

Minimum: $25

Annual Report: $15

FLORIDA

Where to File: Secretary of State
Tallahassee, Florida 32301

Initial Costs:

Organization Fee:

(a) Par Value Shares	Fee
Up to $125,000	$4 per $1,000
125,001 to $1,000,000	$500 plus $1 per $1,000 over $125,000
$1,000,001 to $2,000,000	$1,375 plus 50¢ per $1,000 over $1,000,000
Over $2,000,000	$1,875 plus 25¢ per $1,000 over $2,000,000

(b) No-Par Value Shares	Fee
Up to 1,250 shares	50¢ per share
1,251 to 10,000 shares	$625 plus 10¢ per share over 1,250
10,001 to 20,000 shares	$1,500 plus ¹⁄₂₀¢ per share over 10,000
Over 20,000 shares	$1,505 plus ¹⁄₄₀¢ per share over 20,000

Minimum filing tax is $30

The fee for filing certificate of designation of address of office for service of process and of resident agent is $3.

Note: Florida has a stamp tax for original issues.

Annual Corporate Taxes and Fees:

Annual Report Fee: $10

Income Tax: 5% of net taxable income. Based on adjusted federal income, with modifications, allocable to Florida.

Intangible Personal Property Tax: One dollar per $1,000 of the just value as of December 31

GEORGIA*

Where to File: Secretary of State
Corporations Division
Plaza Level—West
200 Piedmont Avenue, SE
Atlanta, Georgia 30334

Initial Costs:

Reservation Fee: $3

Filing Fee: $15 for certificate of incorporation

County Filing Fee: $18

Publication Fee: $60

*Special Filing Requirements: Charter granted by the Secretary of State in accordance with Title 22, Georgia Code Annotated, and a copy filed with the clerk of Superior Court. All documents are received and disbursed by the Secretary of State's office, to include all fees that are required.

Annual Corporate Taxes and Fees:

License Tax: Based on net worth including capital stock, paid in surplus and earned surplus:

Net worth over	But not over	Tax
0	$10,000	$10
$10,000	25,000	20
25,000	40,000	40
40,000	60,000	60
60,000	80,000	75
80,000	100,000	100

100,000	. . . .	150,000	 125
150,000	. . . .	200,000	 150
200,000	. . . .	300,000	 200
300,000	. . . .	500,000	 250
500,000	. . . .	750,000	 300
750,000	. . . .	1,000,000	 500
1,000,000	. . . .	2,000,000	 750
2,000,000	. . . .	4,000,000	 1,000
4,000,000	. . . .	6,000,000	 1,250
6,000,000	. . . .	8,000,000	 1,500
8,000,000	. . . .	10,000,000	 1,750
10,000,000	. . . .	12,000,000	 2,000
12,000,000	. . . .	14,000,000	 2,500
14,000,000	. . . .	16,000,000	 3,000
16,000,000	. . . .	18,000,000	 3,500
18,000,000	. . . .	20,000,000	 4,000
20,000,000	. . . .	22,000,000	 4,500
22,000,000	 5,000		

Income Tax: 6% of net income from property owned or business done in Georgia

Stock Tax: $1 per $1,000 value of bonds and debentures

HAWAII

Where to File: Director of Regulation Agencies
Honolulu, Hawaii 96810

Initial Costs:

Incorporation Fee: 20 cents per $1,000 on total amount of authorized capital. Minimum of $50. Maximum of $1,000.

Fee for No-Par Stock: Computed on the basis of $10 per share

Annual Corporate Taxes and Fees:

Annual Exhibit Fee: $10

Income Tax: 5.85% on first $25,000 net taxable income; 6.435% on excess of net taxable income over $25,000

Excise Tax: Rates range from .0015% to 4%

IDAHO

Where to File: Secretary of State
Boise, Idaho 87300

Initial Costs:

Filing Fee: $60 + $20 for initial franchise tax

Annual Corporate Taxes and Fees:

Franchise Tax: Prorated according to corporate income for the year
                 Minimum: $20

Income Tax: 6.5% of Idaho income

ILLINOIS*

Where to File: Secretary of State
                 Springfield, Illinois 62700

Initial Costs:

License Fee: Computed at the rate of $\frac{1}{20}$th of 1% (50¢ per $1,000) in the
               amount of stated capital and paid-in surplus represented in
               Illinois, with minimum of 50¢.

Filing Fee: $75.00

Initial Franchise Tax: Assessed at the rate of $\frac{1}{10}$th of 1% ($1.00 per $1,000)
                         on the stated capital and paid-in surplus represented
                         in this state with a minimum of $25 and a maximum
                         of $1,000,000.

*Special Filing Requirements: Certificate of incorporation issued by the
Secretary of State is recorded with recorder of deeds of the county in which
the registered office is located.

Annual Corporate Taxes and Fees:

Annual Report Fee: $15

Annual Franchise Tax: Computed at the rate of $\frac{1}{20}$ of 1% for the 12-
                        months' period commencing on July 1 of the year
                        in which such tax is payable. Minimum: $25
                        Maximum: $1,000,000 for combined annual
                        franchise tax and the supplemental annual fran-
                        chise tax.

Minimum Annual Franchise Tax:

$25   if the sum of its stated capital and paid-in surplus is $500,000 or less

$50   if the sum of its stated capital and paid-in exceeds $500,000 but
      does not exceed $1,000,000

$200   if the sum of its stated capital and paid-in surplus exceeds $1,000,000
       but does not exceed $10,000,000

$500 if the sum of stated capital and paid-in surplus exceeds $10,000,000

Capital Stock Tax: Based upon value of all corporate assets over valuation of real estate and tangible personalty.

Income Tax: 4% based upon the corporation's federal taxable income allocated and apportioned to Illinois—$1,000 standard exemption allowed for 1 full year.

Replacement Tax: 2½% based upon the corporation's federal taxable income

INDIANA

Where to File: Secretary of State
Indianapolis, Indiana 46200

Initial Costs:

Organization Fee: Par or no par

Filing Articles of Incorporation (domestic corporations for profit)
Minimum fee for first 1000 shares or less, plus certificate fee . . . $36.00
1001 through 200,000 shares . . . . 2¢ per share
200,001 through 1,000,000 shares . . . . 1¢ per share
Additional shares over 1,000,000 shares . . . . 0.2¢ per share

Annual Corporate Taxes and Fees:

Income Tax: Any corporation doing business in Indiana is required to compute its Indiana income tax under both the Gross Income Tax Act and the Adjusted Gross Income Tax Act. The corporation will pay the greater of the two taxes, applying payments made under either act against the ultimate amount due. In addition, corporations with Indiana adjusted gross income will generally be subject to the supplemental net income tax. (The calculations and terms of the two are too lengthy and complicated for this report; we recommend that you check with the Department of Revenue.)

Annual Report: $15

IOWA*

Where to File: Secretary of State
2nd Fl. Hoover Bldg.
Corporation Department
Des Moines, Iowa 50319

Initial Costs:

Organization Fee: For filing articles of incorporation and issuance of the certificate of incorporation—$50

County Recorders' Fee: $3 per page

*Special Filing Requirements: Secretary of state forwards copy to county recorder of county in which the registered office is located. This applies to domestic corporations only.

Annual Corporate Taxes and Fees:

Annual License Fee: $5 for stated capital up to $20,000; $10 over $20,000 to $40,000; $15 over $40,000 to $60,000; $20 over $60,000 to $80,000; $25 over $80,000 to $100,000; $30 over $100,000 to $150,000; $35 over $150,000 to $200,000; $40 over $200,000 to $250,000; $45 over $250,000 to $300,000; $50 over $300,000 to $350,000; $55 over $350,000 to $400,000; $60 over $400,000 to $500,000; $70 over $500,000 to $600,000; $80 over $600,000 to $700,000; $90 over $700,000 to $800,000; $100 over $800,000 to $900,000; $110 over $900,000 to $1,000,000; $175 over $1,000,000 to $2,500,000; $250 over $2,500,000 to $5,000,000; $350 over $5,000,000 to $10,000,000; $800 over $10,000,000 to $50,000,000; $1,200 over $50,000,000 to $100,000,000; $1,600 over $100,000,000 to $200,000,000; $2,000 over $200,000,000 to $300,000,000; $2,500 over $300,000,000 to $500,000,000; $3,000 over $500,000,000.

Income Tax: Based upon income attributable to Iowa at the rate of 6% on first $25,000 of taxable income, 8% on next $75,000, 10% on the next $150,000 and 12% on amounts over $250,000.

KANSAS*

Where to File: Secretary of State
Topeka, Kansas 66600

Initial Costs:

Application and Recording Fee: $50—Domestic; $70—Foreign

Incidental Fees: Approximately $30

*Special Filing Requirements: Certified copy must be recorded in office of registrar of deeds in county in which the registered office is located.

Annual Corporate Taxes and Fees:

Annual Franchise Tax: 1% per $1,000 of shareholders' equity attributable
                         to Kansas. Minimum: $10. Maximum: $2,500.

Income Tax: Based upon Kansas income at rate of 4½%. A surtax of 2¼%
               is added on income over $25,000.

KENTUCKY*

Where to File: Secretary of State
                  Frankfort, Kentucky 40601

Initial Costs:

Organization Fee:

(a) Par Value Shares   Fee

1–20,000 shares . . . . 1¢ per share
Next 180,000 shares . . . . ½¢ per share
Balance over 200,000 shares . . . . ⅕¢ per share

(b) No-Par Value Shares   Fee

1–20,000 shares . . . . ½¢ per share
Next 180,000 shares . . . . ¼¢ per share
Balance over 200,000 shares . . . . ⅕¢ per share

Minimum . . . . $10 + $15 for filing fee

Filing Fees: $20

*Special Filing Requirements: Endorsed copy filed with county clerk of the
county of the corporate registered office.

Annual Corporate Taxes and Fees:

License Tax: 70¢ on each $1,000 based on capital employed in the state.
                Minimum: $10

Income Tax: First $25,000 attributable to the state—3%; the next $25,000—
               4%; the next 50,000—5%; over $100,000—6%

LOUISIANA*

Where to File: Secretary of State
                  Baton Rouge, La. 70800

Initial Costs:

Organization Fee:

(a) Par Value Shares   Fee

Par value under $25,000 . . . . $10
Par value over $25,000 . . . . $50

(b) No-Par Value Shares   Fee

Under 10,000 shares $10
Over 10,000 . . . . $50

Filing Fee: $35

*Special Filing Requirements: Recorded in the office of recorder of mortgages of the parish in which registered office is situated.

Annual Corporate Taxes and Fees:

Franchise Tax: Basis for computation is determined by taking arithmetical average of: (1) ratio that net sales in Louisiana and other revenue attributable to Louisiana bears to total net sales in regular course of business and other revenue, and (2) ratio of value of property in Louisiana to value of all property. All shares taken at book value. Rate: $1.50 per $1,000. Minimum: $10

Income Tax: First $25,000—4%
Next $25,000—5%
Next $50,000—6%
Next $100,000—7%
Anything over $200,000—8%

MAINE

Where to File: Secretary of State
Augusta, Maine 04333

Initial Costs:

Organization Fee:

(a) Par Value Shares   Fee

$2,000,000 or less . . . . $10 for each $100,000
$2,000,001 to $20,000,000 . . . . $200 plus $50 for each
$1,000,000 over $2,000,000
Over $20,000,000 . . . . $1,100 plus $20 for each
$1,000,000 over $20,000,000

(b) No-Par Value Shares   Fee

20,000 shares or less . . . . ½¢ per share, but not less
                                                 than $10

Over 20,000 to 2,000,000 shares   . . . $100 plus ¼¢ per share over
                                                 20,000 shares

Over 2,000,000 shares   . . . . $5,050 plus ⅕¢ per share
                                                 over 2,000,000 shares

Minimum is $10 ($20 if both par and no-par shares are used)

<u>Filing Fees</u>: $65 and $50 for articles of incorporation

Annual Corporate Taxes and Fees:

<u>Annual Filing Fee</u>: $30

<u>Income Tax</u>:   4.95% of Maine net income up to $25,000 plus 6.93% over
                   $25,000

MARYLAND

<u>Where to File</u>:   State Dept. of Assessments, and Taxation
                     Baltimore, Maryland 21201

Initial Costs:

Organization Fee:

Authorized Capital Stock	Fee
Up to and including $100,000	$20
Over $100,000 up to and including $1,000,000	$20 plus $1 for each $5,000 or fraction in excess of $100,000
Over $1,000,000 up to and including $2,000,000	$200 plus $10 for each $100,000 or fraction in excess of $1,000,000
Over $2,000,000 up to and including $5,000,000	$300 plus $15 for each $500,000 or fraction in excess of $2,000,000
Over $5,000,000	$390 plus $20 for each $1,000,000 or fraction in excess of $5,000,000

No-par value stock valued at $20 for tax purposes.

Minimum tax is $20.

Recording Fee: $20 plus $2 for each page over five.

Annual Corporate Taxes and Fees:

Annual Filing Fee: $40

Income Tax: 7% of net income allocable to Maryland

MASSACHUSETTS*

Where to File: Secretary of State
Corporation Division
One Ashburton Place
Room 1717
Boston, Massachusetts 02108

Initial Costs:

Organization Fee: $\frac{1}{20}$ of 1% of total amount of authorized capital stock
with par value (use $1 if par value less than $1) and 1¢
per share for all no-par shares

Minimum Fee: $150 on original amount authorized

*Special Filing Requirements: Must be filed with the Corporate Commis-
sioner and the Secretary of State.

Annual Corporate Taxes and Fees:

Excise Tax: $2.60 per $1,000 on allocated tangible property or net worth
plus 9.5% of net income attributable to Massachusetts.
Minimum: $228

Annual Report Fee: $70

MICHIGAN

Where to File: Department of Commerce
Corporation Division
P.O. Box 30054
Lansing, Michigan 48909

Initial Costs:

Organization Fee: Minimum fee is $35. Maximum fee for domestic
regulated investment companies is $40.

Filing Fee: $35

Annual Corporate Taxes and Fees:

Annual Report Fee: $15

Single Business Tax: 2.35% of "adjusted tax base" (sum of federal taxable income and adjustments as apportioned to Michigan)

MINNESOTA

Where to File: Secretary of State
St. Paul, Minnesota 55100

Initial Costs:

Treasurer's Fee: $70 for the first $25,000 or 2,500 shares of no-par value stock. Add $1.25 for each $1,000 or fraction thereof over $25,000 or 100 shares no-par stock.

Filing Fee: $15

Annual Corporate Taxes and Fees:

Income Tax: Based on net income earned in or allocable to activities in Minnesota less allowable deductions.   Rate: 12%

1. Any year beginning after 12/31/81 and before 1/1/83
   First $25,000 of income 9%
   Excess over $25,000 . . . . 12%
2. Calendar year 1983 and any year beginning after 12/31/82
   First $25,000 of income 6%
   Excess over $25,000 . . . . 12%

MISSISSIPPI*

Where to File: Secretary of State
Jackson, Mississippi 39200

Initial Costs:

Organization Fee:

Up to and including $5,000 in authorized
capital stock $25
Over $5,000 capital stock . . . . $25 plus $2 each
$1,000 over $5,000

Minimum is $25.   Maximum is $500.

For no-par stock, the sale price of the stock issued if it is fixed by the charter of the corporation or an amendment thereto will be deemed par value. Otherwise the maximum fee of $500 must be deposited and, within 30 days after the approval of the charter, a proper certificate filed with the state disclosing the sale price per share as fixed by the directors or shareholders.

*Special Filing Requirements: Must be filed with the chancery clerk of the county where the corporation's principal office is located. Notice of incorporation must be published within 30 days in a newspaper in the county of the principal place of business.

Annual Corporate Taxes and Fees:

> Annual Filing Fee: $10
>
> Income Tax: Based upon income attributable to Mississippi at the rate of 3% for the initial $5,000 and 4% for amount thereover.
>
> Franchise Tax: $2.50 per $1,000 of taxable income capital employed in Mississippi. Minimum: $25

MISSOURI

Where to File: Secretary of State
Corporation Division
P.O. Box 778
Jefferson City, Missouri 65102

Initial Costs:

> Incorporation Fees: Based on authorized capital.

$30,000 or less	$53.00	$110,000	$ 93.00
35,000	$58.00	120,000	$ 98.00
40,000	$58.00	125,000	$103.00
45,000	$63.00	130,000	$103.00
50,000	$63.00	140,000	$108.00
55,000	$68.00	150,000	$113.00
60,000	$68.00	160,000	$118.00
65,000	$73.00	170,000	$123.00
70,000	$73.00	180,000	$128.00
75,000	$78.00	190,000	$133.00
80,000	$78.00	200,000	$138.00
85,000	$83.00	250,000	$163.00
90,000	$83.00	300,000	$188.00
95,000	$88.00	500,000	$288.00
100,000	$88.00	1,000,000	$538.00

Annual Corporate Taxes and Fees:

Franchise Tax: ¹⁄₂₀ of 1% of par value of outstanding stock and surplus or portion thereof employed in Missouri or the assets of the corporation, whichever is greater.

Income Tax: 5% of net income allocable to Missouri after federal income tax deduction.

Registration Fee: If registration filed in July—$10; August—$15; September—$25; October—$30; November—$25; December—$40.

MONTANA

Where to File: Secretary of State
Helena, Montana 59601

Initial Costs:

Filing Articles: $15

License Fee: Based on number of taxable shares.

(a) Par Value Shares: Each $100 unit = 1 taxable share.
(b) No-Par Shares: Each authorized share is considered having $1 par value (every 100 shares = 1 taxable share).

Taxable Shares	Fee
1 through 1,000 shares	10¢ for each share
1,001 through 2,500 shares	8¢ for each additional share through 2,500 shares
2,501 through 5,000 shares	6¢ for each additional share through 5,000 shares
5,001 through 10,000 shares	4¢ for each additional share through 10,000 shares
All shares in excess of 10,000	2¢ for each additional share over 10,000 shares

Annual Corporate Taxes and Fees:

License Tax: 6¾% based on total net income received from all sources within or allocable to Montana. Minimum: $50.

NEBRASKA

Where to File: Secretary of State
Lincoln, Nebraska 68500

Initial Costs:

Organization Fee:

Authorized Capital Stock:

$10,000 or less $40
Over $10,001 to $25,000 . . . . $70
Over $25,001 to $50,000 . . . . $100
Over $50,001 to $75,000 . . . . $150
Over $75,001 to $100,000 . . . . $200
Over $100,000 . . . . $200 + $2 to each
                                            additional $1,000

Filing Fee: $3 per page, $15 for certificate with seal.

City Clerk's Fee: $4 for first 200 words and 6¢ for each 10 words thereafter
                      for articles filed in his office.

Reservation of Corp Name: $15

Annual Corporate Taxes and Fees:

Occupational Tax: Based on the amount of paid-up capital stock accord-
                      ing to the following table:

When paid up capital stock exceeds	But does not exceed	Such annual tax shall be
$ 0	$ 10,000	$ 10
10,000	20,000	15
20,000	30,000	22.50
30,000	40,000	30
40,000	50,000	37.50
50,000	60,000	45
60,000	70,000	52.50
70,000	80,000	60
80,000	90,000	67.50
90,000	100,000	75
100,000	125,000	90
125,000	150,000	105
150,000	175,000	120
175,000	200,000	135
200,000	225,000	150
225,000	250,000	165
250,000	275,000	180
275,000	300,000	195
300,000	325,000	210
325,000	350,000	225
350,000	400,000	250
400,000	450,000	275
450,000	500,000	300
500,000	600,000	340

600,000	700,000	380
700,000	800,000	420
800,000	900,000	460
900,000	1,000,000	500
1,000,000	10,000,000	500 plus $300 for each million or fraction thereof over and above one million dollars.
10,000,000	15,000,000 4,500
15,000,000	20,000,000 5,500
20,000,000	25,000,000 6,500
25,000,000	50,000,000 7,500
50,000,000	100,000,000 8,000
100,000,000 8,250

Minimum: $10.

Income Tax: Income or franchise tax applies to taxable income of corporation derived from sources within state. Tax is flat percent of adjusted federal income tax liability of corporation with respect to tax income for taxable year.

Rate of tax for corporations whose income consists exclusively of foreign or interstate commerce is 25% of rate for individuals on first $25,000 of taxable income and 27½% of such rate in excess of $25,000.

NEVADA

Where to File: Secretary of State
Capital Complex
Carson City, Nevada 89710

Initial Costs:

Organization Fee:

Authorized Capital Stock	Fee
$25,000 or less	$50
$25,000.01–75,000	$75
$75,000.01–200,000	$115
$200,000.01–500,000	$175
$500,000.01–1,000,000	$250
Over $1,000,000	$250 for first $1,000,000 and $125 for each $500,000 or fraction thereof.

No-par is considered to be $10 per share (for computing filing fees on new corporations and qualifications only).

Minimum fee is $25. $50 plus $5 for new corporations.

Certification Fee: $5 per copy

Annual Corporate Taxes and Fees:

Annual Fee: $20 plus $5 penalty if not filed on time. This is for filing the annual list of officers, directors, and agent.

NEW HAMPSHIRE

Where to File: Secretary of State
Concord, New Hampshire 03300

Initial Costs:

License Fee:

Authorized Capital Stock	Fee
$15,000 or less	$ 60
Over $15,000 up to $50,000	100
Over $50,000 up o $150,000	300
Over $150,000 up to $250,000	400
Over $250,000 up to $500,000	800
Over $500,000 up to $1,000,000	1500
Each additional $100,000 above $1,000,000	100

No-par value stock is valued at $50 per share for first 20,000 shares and $1 per share thereafter.

Filing Fee: $25

Annual Corporate Taxes and Fees:

Income Tax: Imposed on taxable business profits at a rate of 8% plus the surtax of 13.5% (effective rate of tax 9.08%).
Minimum: $250

Franchise Fees: A franchise fee equal to the license fee paid upon filing its original articles of incorporation plus an amount equal to any additional license fees for increases in its authorized capital stock, if any.   Minimum: $60
Maximum: $2,000

Report Filing Fee: $60

NEW JERSEY*

Where to File: Secretary of State
Trenton, New Jersey 08600

Initial Costs:

Organization Fee: Based upon number of shares of authorized capital stock. Rate is 1¢ per share up to 10,000 shares and ¹/₁₀¢ per share in excess of 10,000 shares. Minimum is $25. Maximum is $1,000.

Filing Fee: $35

Recording Fee: $35 varies for over 2,500 shares

*Special Filing Requirements: Certified, conformed copy must be recorded with the county clerk of the county where the principal office is located.

Annual Corporate Taxes and Fees:

Report Filing Fee: $15.

Business Income–Net Worth Tax: 9% + .002 of adjusted net worth.

Sales Tax: 5% on taxable sales

Business Personal Property: 5% of original cost × .013

NEW MEXICO*

Where to File: State Corporation Commission
Sante Fe, New Mexico 87501

Initial Costs:

Organization Fee: $1 on each $1,000 of authorized capital stock. No-par value stock is valued at $1 per share. Minimum is $50.

*Special Filing Requirements: Must be filed with county clerk of county where the principal office is located. Certificate of incorporation must be published once within 30 days. Proof of publication must be filed with the state corporation commissioner.

Annual Corporate Taxes and Fees:

Franchise Tax: Based on book value of the portion of corporation's capital stock represented by property and business in New Mexico. Rate: 55¢ per $1,000 of taxable capital stock. Minimum: $10.

Net Income Tax: 5% of the corporation's entire net income or portion thereof taxable in New Mexico.

Annual Report Fee: $10

NEW YORK*

Where to File: Secretary of State
                 Albany, New York 12200

Initial Costs:

  License Fee:

    Based on authorized capital stock . . . . 50¢ per 1,000 for par
                                                              value stock; 5¢ per share
                                                              for no-par stock.

  Minimum Fee: $10

  Filing Fee: $50

*Special Filing Requirements: The Secretary of State certifies and transmits a copy to the county clerk of the county where the principal office is located.

Annual Corporate Taxes and Fees:

  Franchise Tax: The larger of (1) 10% of entire net income allocated to New York; (2) 10% of allocated part of 30% of entire net income, salaries to officers and/or stockholders controlling in excess of 5% of issued capital stock, less $15,000 and any net loss for the year; (3) 1.78 mills on each dollar of allocated business and investment capital; or (4) a minimum tax of $250. In addition there is a tax of 9/10 of a mill on each dollar of allocated subsidiary capital.

NORTH CAROLINA*

Where to File: Secretary of State
                 Raleigh, North Carolina 27600

Initial Costs:

  Charter Tax: 40¢ per $1,000 of the authorized capital stock   Minimum: $40.   Maximum: $1,000.   No-par value shares are valued at $100 per share

  Filing Fee: $5

*Special Filing Requirements: Must be recorded with the registrar of deeds in the county where the registered office is located.

Annual Corporate Taxes and Fees:

Income Tax: 6% of net income allocable to North Carolina

Franchise Tax: $1.50 per $1,000 of the largest of three alternate bases.

1. The amount of the capital stock, surplus, and undivided profits apportionable to the state; or
2. 55% of appraised value of property in the state subject to local taxation plus the assessed value of intangible property subject to taxation; or
3. The book value of real and tangible personal property in the state less any debt outstanding which was created to acquire or improve real property in the state.

Intangible Taxes: May be applicable

NORTH DAKOTA

Where to File: Secretary of State
Bismarck, North Dakota 58501

Initial Costs:

Organization Fee:

Authorized Capital Stock	Fee
$30,000 or less	$30
Over $30,000	$30 plus $10 for each $10,000 over $30,000

No-par value stock is deemed to have a value of $100 per share.

Filing Articles: $20; affixing certificate and seal—$12

Annual Corporate Taxes and Fees:

Income Tax: Based on net income attributable to sources within the state at the following rates: First $3,000—3%; over $3,000 up to $8,000—4%; over $8,000 up to $15,000—5%; over $15,000—6%.

Annual Report Fee: $10

OHIO

Where to File: Secretary of State
Columbus, Ohio 43200

Initial Costs:

Organization Fee:

Authorized Capital Stock
Base and Rates for Filing Fees:

The fee for filing and recording of articles of incorporation is based on the number of authorized shares as follows:

The first 1,000 shares	10¢ per share
Next 9,000 shares	5¢ per share
Next 40,000 shares	2¢ per share
Next 50,000 shares	1¢ per share
Next 400,000 shares	½¢ per share
Shares in excess of 500,000	¼¢ per share

The minimum fee (regardless of this computation) is $75.

Registration of Shares Fee: $25 minimum

Annual Corporate Taxes and Fees:

The corporate franchise tax liability is the greater of:

1. 0055 mills on the net worth of the corporation; or
2. .046 on the first $25,000 of net income plus .087% on net income in excess of $25,000; or
3. $150 + surtax

A credit against a corporation's franchise tax liability is allowed for a portion of the tangible property taxes paid on manufacturing machinery and equipment acquired after January 1, 1978.

OKLAHOMA

Where to File: Secretary of State
                   Oklahoma City, Oklahoma 73100

Initial Costs:

Organization Fee: For filing articles and issuing certificate of incorporation, ¹⁄₁₀ of 1% of authorized capital stock. Minimum $50—foreign corporations; Minimum $25—domestic corporations.

No-par stock is deemed to be valued at $50 per share.

Annual Corporate Taxes and Fees:

Franchise Tax: $1.25 for each $1,000 or fraction thereof of the corporate capital used, invested, or employed in Oklahoma. Minimum fee: $10.   Maximum fee: $20,000.

Income Tax: 4% based on income derived from property owned and business transacted in the state, less applicable credits.

OREGON

Where to File: Corporation Commissioner
Salem, Oregon 97301

Initial Costs:

Organization Fee:

When authorized capital stock exceeds	But does not exceed	The fee is
. . . .	$5,000	$10
$5,000	$10,000	$15
$10,000	$25,000	$20
$25,000	$50,000	$30
$50,000	$100,000	$50
$100,000	$250,000	$75
$250,000	$500,000	$100
$500,000	$1,000,000	$125
Over $1,000,000		$200

No-par value shares are deemed to have a par value of $10 each.

Minimum fee is $10.

Filing Fees are also imposed.

Annual Corporate Taxes and Fees:

License Fee: Based on authorized capital stock. If the capital stock does not exceed $5,000, the fee is $10; exceeding $5,000 but not $10,000—$15; exceeding $10,000 but not $25,000—$20; exceeding $25,000 but not $50,000—$30; exceeding $50,000 but not $100,000—$50; exceeding $100,000 but not $250,000—$75; exceeding $250,000 but not $500,000—$100; exceeding $500,000 but not $1,000,000—$125; exceeding $1,000,000—$200. No-par shares valued at $10 each.

Income Tax: Based on Oregon proportion of total net income at the rate of 7½%.

Excise Tax: 7½% on net income. Minimum: $10

PENNSYLVANIA

Where to File: Department of State
Harrisburg, Pennsylvania 17101

Initial Costs:

Filing Fee: $75

Annual Corporate Taxes and Fees:

Capital Stock Tax: 10 mills per dollar of taxable portion of the actual value of the whole capital stock.

Income Tax: 10.5% of net income allocated to Pennsylvania

Corporate Loans Tax: Tax is imposed at the rate of 4 mills on the nominal value of indebtedness on which interest is paid. Nominal value is determined by dividing the rate of interest into the amount of interest actually paid.

RHODE ISLAND

Where to File: Secretary of State
                 Providence, Rhode Island 02900

Initial Costs:

Filing Articles of Incorporation: $110

Certificate of Incorporation Fee: $30

Annual Corporate Taxes and Fees:

Income Tax: Corporations are subject to one of two taxes: business corporation tax or corporate franchise tax, whichever yields the higher amount. The minimum tax under each calculation is $100.

Corporate Net Income Tax: 8%

Franchise Tax: This tax is levied at $2.50 per $10,000 of authorized capital stock. Nonstated par value stock is valued at $100

SOUTH CAROLINA

Where to File: Secretary of State
                 Columbia, South Carolina 29200

Initial Costs:

Incorporation Tax: 40¢ for each $1,000 of aggregated value of shares authorized plus $5 filing fees. No-par value stock is deemed to be valued at $10. Minimum is $40. Maximum is $1,000.

Miscellaneous Fee: $5

Annual Corporate Taxes and Fees:

License Tax: One mill on each dollar paid to the corporation on account
of capital stock and paid-in surplus.   Minimum fee: $10

Annual Report Filing Fee: $5

Income Tax: 6% of net income attributable to in-state business.

SOUTH DAKOTA

Where to File: Secretary of State
Pierre, South Dakota 57501

Initial Costs:

Organization Fee:

Authorized Capital Stock

$25,000 or less	$40
Over $25,000 and not exceeding $100,000	$60
Over $100,000 and not exceeding $500,000	$80
Over $500,000 and not exceeding $1,000,000	$100
Over $1,000,000 and not exceeding $1,500,000	$150
Over $1,500,000 and not exceeding $2,000,000	$200
Over $2,000,000 and not exceeding $2,500,000	$250
Over $2,500,000 and not exceeding $3,000,000	$300
Over $3,000,000 and not exceeding $3,500,000	$350
Over $3,500,000 and not exceeding $4,000,000	$400
Over $4,000,000 and not exceeding $4,500,000	$450
Over $4,500,000 and not exceeding $5,000,000	$500
Over $5,000,000	$500 plus $40 for each additional $500,000 over $5,000,000**

**Effective July 1, 1982, the maximum amount charged under this sub-division may not exceed $16,000.

No-par value stock is valued at $100 per share.

Annual Corporate Taxes and Fees:

Annual Report Filing Fee: $10

TENNESSEE*

<u>Where to File</u>:   Secretary of State
                       Nashville, Tennessee 37200

<u>Initial Costs</u>:

   <u>Charter Fee</u>:   Based on authorized shares.

      (a) <u>Par Value Shares</u>   <u>Fee</u>
         Up to 20,000 shares . . . . .1¢ per share
         Next 180,000 shares . . . . .½¢ per share
         Balance over 200,000 shares . . . . . . .⅕¢ per share

      (b) <u>No-Par Value Shares</u>   <u>Fee</u>
         Up to 20,000 shares . . . . .½¢ per share
         Next 1,980,000 . . . . .¼¢ per share
         Balance over 2,000,000 shares . . . . . . .⅕¢ per share

   Minimum: $10

*<u>Special Filing Requirements</u>:   Certificate of incorporation with the secretary of state's certificate must be recorded in the office of the registrar in the county in which the principal office of the corporation is located.

<u>Annual Corporate Taxes and Fees</u>:

   <u>Gross Receipts Tax</u>:   The tax is computed on one of two methods at the option of the taxpayer.

     1. ½ of 1% of the gross amount of receipts from intrastate business.
       Minimum: $25

     2. On the amount of issued and outstanding capital stock at the following
       rates: Capital stock up to and including $25,000 . . . . $5
              Over $25,000 and up to and including $50,000 . . . . . . $10
              Over $50,000 up to and including $100,000 . . . . $20
              Over $100,000 up to and including $250,000 . . . . $30
              Over $250,000 up to $500,000 . . . . $50
              Over $500,000 and less than $1,000,000 . . . .$100
              Over $1,000,000 . . . .$150

   Minimum: $5.   Maximum: $150
   Banks and banking corporations are exempt.

   <u>Excise Tax</u>:   Based on net earnings arising from business done in the state for the fiscal year preceding the return date at the rate of 6%.

   <u>Franchise Tax</u>:   Based on the larger of: (1) total capital stock plus surplus and undivided profit or (2) value of real tangible personal property. 15¢ per $100.   Minimum: $10

TEXAS

Where to File: Secretary of State
                 Austin, Texas 78700

Initial Costs:

Organization Fee: $100

Annual Corporate Taxes and Fees:

Franchise Tax: $4.25 per $1000 of the corporation's stated capital, surplus and undivided profits allocated to Texas on a gross receipts basis; or the regular minimum tax of $55, whichever is greater. A corporation with less than $1 million total assets may pay based on assets shown on its federal income tax return. The tax on this "short form" may be as low as $35.

UTAH

Where to File: Lt. Governor
                 Salt Lake City, Utah 84114

Initial Costs:

Organization Fee: 1/20% of authorized shares par value. No-par shares are valued at $1 each. Minimum is $50. Maximum is $525.

Filing Fee $25

Annual Corporate Taxes and Fees:

Franchise Tax: 4% based on income attributable to the state.
                 Minimum: $25.

Income Tax: 4% of net income derived from Utah sources. If you qualify and pay franchise tax, then you don't have to pay income tax.

Annual Report Fee: $5

VERMONT

Where to File: Secretary of State
                 Montpelier, Vermont 05601

Initial Costs:

Organization Fee:

If authorized capital stock exceeds	But does not exceed	The fee is
$	$5,000	$20
$5,000	$10,000	$40
$10,000	$50,000	$80
$50,000	$200,000	$160
$200,000	$500,000	$320
$500,000	$1,000,000	$475
$1,000,000	$2,000,000	$800
$2,000,000		$800 plus $150 for each $1,000,000 or fraction thereof over $2,000,000

No-par value stock is deemed to have a value of $100.

Minimum tax is $20.

Annual Corporate Taxes and Fees:

Annual Report Fee: $2 for Vermont corporations
$35 for foreign corporations

Income Tax: 5% on Vermont net income of $10,000 or less; $500 plus 6% over $10,000 for $10,001—$25,000; $1,400 plus 7% over $25,000 for $25,001—$250,000; $17,150 plus 7½% over $250,000 for $250,001 and over.   Minimum: $50

VIRGINIA

Where to File: State Corporation Commission
Richmond, Virginia 23200

Initial Costs:

Charter Fee:

Capital Stock	Fee
Not over $50,000	$20
Over $50,000 and less than $3,000,000 .	40¢ for each $1,000 or fraction thereof
$3,000,000 and over	$1,200

No-par stock valued at $100.

Filing Fee: $10

Recording Fee: $10 (over 4 pages add $2 per page)

Annual Corporate Taxes and Fees:

Income Tax: 6% based on net income attributable to business within the state.

Franchise Tax: Based upon maximum authorized capital stock. If the value of the maximum authorized capital stock is up to $25,000 the tax is $20; $25,000.01–$50,000—$40; $50,000.01–$100,000—$80; $100,000.01–$300,000—$120; $300,000.01–$500,000—$200; $500,000.01–$1 million—$400; $1 million–$50 million—$400 + $20 per $100,000 or fraction over $1 million; $50–$100 million—$10,200 + $150 each million or fraction over $50 million; over $100 million—$20,000

Registration Fee: Based upon maximum authorized capital stock as of January 1. If the authorized capital stock has a value of up to $15,000, the fee is $10; over $15,000 but not over $25,000—$20; over $25,000 but not over $50,000—$25; over $50,000 but not over $100,000—$30; over $100,000 but not over $300,000—$40; over $300,000—$50. No-par value stock is to be valued at $100 per share.

Filing by local clerk of court: Circuit court of city or county where registered office is located—$12

WASHINGTON

Where to File: Secretary of State
Legislative Building
Olympia, Washington 98504

Initial Costs:

Filing Fee:

Authorized Capital Stock	Fee + 25% surtax
$50,000	$50
Over $50,000 up to and including $1,000,000	$50 plus $1 for each $1,000 over $50,000
Over $1,000,000 up to and including $4,000,000	$1,000 plus 40¢ for each $1,000 over $1,000,000
Over $4,000,000	$2,200 plus 20¢ for each $1,000 over $4,000,000

No-par shares have value of amount to be allocated to stated capital from consideration for issuance.

Minimum is $100. Maximum is $5,000

Surtax of 25% on all filing fees.

Annual Corporate Taxes and Fees:

Annual Report Filing Fee: $5

Business and Occupation Tax: Gross receipts tax imposed for act or privi-
lege of engaging in business activities in
state, unless business specifically exempted.
Rates depend on nature of business activity.

WEST VIRGINIA*

Where to File: Secretary of State
Charleston, West Virginia 25300

Initial Costs:

Filing Fee: For certificate of incorporation, $10. (No incorporation tax, but
charter license tax; see annual fees.)

*Special Filing Requirements: The Secretary of State issues a certificate of
incorporation to be recorded in the county clerk's office in the county where
the principal office is located or in the office of the clerk of the county court
of the county in which the corporation does its principal business.

Annual Corporate Taxes and Fees:

License Tax: Based on authorized capital stock. If the authorized capital
stock is $5,000 or less—$20; over $5,000 to $10,000—$30;
over $10,000 to $25,000—$40; over $25,000 to $50,000—$50;
over $50,000 to $75,000—$80; over $75,000 to $100,000—$100;
over $100,000 to $125,000—$110; over $125,000 to $150,000—
$120; over $150,000 to $175,000—$140; over $175,000 to
$200,000— $150; over $200,000 to $1,000,000—$180 plus 20¢
on each $1,000 or fraction thereof over $200,000; over
$1,000,000 to $15,000,000—$340 plus 15¢ on each $1,000 or
fraction thereof over $1,000,000; over $15,000,000—$2,500.
No-par value stock is to be valued at $25 per share unless
originally issued for a higher consideration.
Minimum: $250

Income Tax: 6%, applicable to a corporation's taxable income as defined
by federal law with modifications.

WISCONSIN*

Where to File: Secretary of State
Madison, Wisconsin 53700

Initial Costs:

Filing Fee:

(a) Par Value Stock . . . . $1.25 per $1,000 or fraction
                                             thereof authorized par value

(b) No-Par Value Stock . . . . 2½¢ per share

Minimum is $70.00

*Special Filing Requirements: Certified copy recorded within 30 days with
the registrar of deeds of the county where the corporation's registered office
is located.

Annual Corporate Taxes and Fees:

Franchise/Income Tax: Based on net income derived from business trans-
                                      acted and property located in the state—7.9%

Annual Report Fee: $10.00

WYOMING

Where to File: Secretary of State
                        Cheyenne, Wyoming 82001

Initial Costs:

Organization Fee:

Articles of incorporation or articles of continuance and issuing a certificate
of incorporation, fee is based on the par value of the authorized shares.
(No-par shares shall be assessed a value of $1 for computation purposes.)

Not exceeding $50,000 . . . . $ 50.00
$50,001 to $100,000 . . . . 100.00
Over $100,000 . . . . 100.00 for the first $100,000 plus $.50
                                         for each additional $1,000

Annual Corporate Taxes and Fees:

Annual Corporate Report License Tax: (both domestic and foreign)
If assets located and employed in Wyoming are valued at:

$50,000 or less . . . . $ 10.00
Over $50,000 including $100,000 . . . .   20.00
Over $100,000 including $500,000 . . . .   50.00
Over $500,000 including $1,000,000 . . . . 100.00
Each additional $1,000,000 or fraction thereof 10.00

Corporations with assets wishing to keep the
charter in good standing 10.00

Putting Together
Your Financial Planning Team

Over the years, many people have remarked to me how difficult it is to assemble a financial planning team. Some questions that concern most people are:

1. What kind of professionals should be on my team?
2. What should they do?
3. How can I assess their capabilities?
4. Who directs and coordinates their activities?

Following is a list of those professionals who may be members of your financial planning team, and a brief description of what you should expect them to do for you.

LAWYERS

The theory that lawyers are all-knowing—competent in everything from wills to predicting the profit potential on a "hot tip"—is one of the most destructive theories around. Good attorneys, interestingly, never make exaggerated claims of what they can do and are quick to tell clients when their questions go beyond the scope of their expertise.

Unfortunately, there are many attorneys who won't admit that there is something they don't know and so either charge the client while learning new skills or give advice that is beyond their expertise. Lawyers are particularly quick to give investment advice and yet are frequently not competent in this area.

What Should Your Attorney Do?

Your attorney should draw up all legal documents, take the time to understand exactly how they fit into your overall financial plans, and share possible ways to make them fulfill your financial objectives. Once these conversations have been concluded, your attorney should see that the documents are completed on a timely basis and that they incorporate the decisions you and s/he have made together.

Your attorney will also advise you on the legal aspects of investments, but he or she is probably not trained to assess the profit potential. If your attorney has some expertise, it should be evidenced by some credential or registration, such as Chartered Financial Analyst, Certified Financial Planner, or Registered Investment Advisor. Your attorney should be willing to share thinking and to be receptive to the ideas of your other advisors on a periodic basis.

Find out what other relationships your attorney may have. For example, one of my client's attorney has an ongoing relationship with a tax shelter syndicator. The syndicator refers clients to the attorney for legal work and the attorney, in turn, refers potential investors to the tax-shelter syndicator. The arrangement is neither illegal nor unethical, but, as his client, you are entitled to know about it.

At Resource Management, Inc. we consider the attorneys extremely important team members, *but* we ask that they perform only those functions appropriate to their profession.

CERTIFIED PUBLIC ACCOUNTANTS

The CPA is another extremely valuable team member. He or she should function solely as an accountant, answering tax questions relative to your investments and determining the tax impact of alternative investment strategies in your tax-planning program.

Expect to pay a good CPA fairly well. My experience has been that a good one saves you more than he or she costs.

We bring the accountant in early in the tax-planning process. For any given calendar year, we begin planning the taxes in January to February of that year, roughly 15 months early.

BANKERS

A client's banker is rarely a regular member of the financial team. Unless your assets are heavily mortgaged or you "tie up" assets quite heavily for a line of credit, it is rare to include your banker as a regular participant in your planning.

INSURANCE AGENTS

Your insurance agent should meet the following criteria:

1. He or she should have the freedom to shop the insurance market for you and should not be tied to only one insurance company.
2. He or she should not have an absolute bias for "cash value" insurance policies but should be open to considering term insurance if that seems better for you.
3. Your insurance agent should not suggest insurance to you as a solution for every financial planning concern but should recognize that only a small percentage of financial planning problems can be solved with insurance.
4. Your insurance agent should be willing to be a team member and should not attempt to isolate you from other financial planning team members.

FINANCIAL PLANNERS

Two analogies have been used to describe financial planners. One describes us as the quarterback on the financial planning team. Another describes us as the conductor of an "orchestra" composed of the other team members.

Both descriptions are accurate. The job of the financial planner is to do thorough data gathering; to make an in-depth assessment of your current financial situation and your financial objectives; to design a financial plan that maximizes the use of your financial resources (income and/or assets) for the achievement of your financial objectives; and to coordinate the activities necessary to implement your financial plan. Your financial planner must be a highly competent professional.

If I were choosing a financial planner I would insist on several things. The first would be certification from the College for Financial Planning in Denver.[1] This designation is granted after passing a five-course curriculum,

---

[1] 9725 East Hampden Ave., Suite 200, Denver, Colorado 80231.

consisting of: introduction to financial planning, risk management, investments, tax planning and management, and retirement and estate planning.

Certification qualifies a financial planner for membership in the Institute of Certified Financial Planners. Your financial planner should be a member of this organization.[2]

Because of its strong educative commitment financial planners should be active members of the International Association for Financial Planning (IAFP).[3] The IAFP is also strongly committed to a high level of ethical standards in the industry, and a financial planner must agree to abide by its code of ethics to remain a member.

There are also other things to look for in choosing your financial planner. He or she should do very thorough data gathering. In addition to "hard" information—your assets, liabilities, spending patterns, income tax liability, and so forth—your financial planner should learn about you. He or she should know, for example, what your financial objectives are, how you feel about risk taking, how your family relationships are, and whether you will have to take care of aging family members.

You should feel comfortable with your planner when answering these questions. After all, a financial planner's job is not to pass judgment on your objectives but to help you recognize which ones are realistic and then help you to achieve them.

I would be even more careful in assessing a financial planner who represents only one life insurance company or who works for a brokerage firm. I hasten to add that I know good financial planners in both settings, but I still feel that an extra measure of caution should be brought to the relationship because these financial planners have less freedom to select from the open market.

I would also ask for referrals from the financial planner's clients. Some financial planners feel that it is unfair to ask this of their clients, and I understand and respect this position. Most financial planners, however, have a few clients who have graciously agreed to perform this task on their behalf. If the planner you're considering is reluctant to provide client referrals, ask for a referral to other professionals with whom they have worked—a client's CPA or attorney, for example.

Types of Financial Planners

There are two types of financial planners: fee-only planners and commission-only planners. A fee-only financial planner, who works only on a fee basis, sells no financial products for which he or she receives a commission. Such

---

[2]Institute of Certified Financial Planners, 9725 East Hampden Ave., Suite 33, Denver, Colorado 80231 (303) 751-7600.

[3]5775 Peachtree Dunwoody Rd., Suite 120C, Atlanta, Georgia 30342.

a financial planner may charge an hourly fee, ranging from $50.00 to $125.00, or a flat annual fee, payable monthly, semi-annually, or annually. The annual fee will be based on the complexity of your affairs and/or a percentage of your income or net worth. In any case, expect to pay from $500 to $10,000 or more, depending on these factors.

Fee-only planners are more frequently hired by the wealthy. It takes several hours to do financial planning for even a relatively simple set of financial circumstances; this translates to $500–$1,250. In addition, much of what a fee-only planner recommends requires relatively large amounts of cash to implement: trusts, tax shelters, and retirement plans, for example. However, really good fee-only planners make or save more money for you than their fee represents; some guarantee that they will.

Fee-only planners frequently complain that a carefully designed financial plan can be ruined unless they select the products their clients buy. So in addition to planning, the financial planner should also locate, assess, and recommend specific products to his client.

Commission-only planners work for the commissions on any products necessary to implement a financial plan. They do not usually prepare written financial plans and will not usually coordinate them with your other advisors. They normally work out the plan, present it verbally, perhaps with working papers or an outline, and equip you with information so that you can coordinate the activities of the others yourself.

A commission-only financial planner may be a good solution for many people, and I do know some very fine financial planners who are compensated in this way. Don't expect to get too much technical help from a commission-only planner, however. It's not that they are not capable—in many cases they are—it's simply a matter of economics. They really can't afford to give you too much time for what the commissions pay.

Commission-only planners frequently complain that they can't afford to design a good financial plan for what they earn in commission, once the plan is implemented.

In our firm, financial planners receive fees and commissions. To those who insist that one cannot remain objective and receive commissions, I can only respond that we have been in business a long time.

Regardless of how your planner is compensated, be sure to discuss the arrangement so you both know what you can expect.

One last point. When you have made your selection, listen to your planner. Don't ask your Uncle Joe or Sister Sue or your next door neighbor for advice to second guess your professional consultant. Do your homework in selecting your planner—then rely on that individual. Talk over all your financial decisions with your financial planner and don't make any financial transactions without the benefit of his/her thinking. A good financial planner will be an invaluable help to you in achieving your financial goals.

Personal Benefits That Can Be Paid with Corporate Dollars

One of the first things a new client asks is, "which of my personal expenses can I have my business pay and take a business deduction?" This is a very valid question. In fact, one of your major motivations for incorporating will likely be to increase the number and amount of such items.

There are several categories of benefits that are based on their impact on personal taxation. For example, your salary is certainly a benefit to you, is deductible by your corporation, but is fully taxable to you personally. Your life insurance is fully deductible by your corporation, but a portion is tax free and the remaining portion is tax-favored to you. Contributions to a retirement plan on your behalf are fully deductible by your corporation.

This chapter lists benefits your business can buy for you and/or your employees, explaining the tax ramifications to you, your employees, and your corporation.

INSURANCE

Life Insurance

The first fringe benefit you will want to provide is life insurance. Your corporation can provide group, term life insurance for you and take a deduction for the full amount of premiums paid. The only limitation is that, like any business expense, it must be "ordinary and necessary."

The first $50,000 of coverage is provided tax free (the premium does not represent taxable income) as long as the coverage is provided under a nondiscriminatory plan. The cost in excess of that figure (less amount you may contribute) must be included in your gross income.

The taxable cost is determined by referring to the Uniform Premium table contained in Internal Revenue Code Section 1.79-3(d)(2). These rates are:

Five-Year Age Bracket	Costs per $1,000 of Protection for One-Month Period
Under 30	8¢
30 to 34	10¢
35 to 39	14¢
40 to 44	23¢
45 to 49	40¢
50 to 54	68¢
55 to 59	$1.10
60 to 64	$1.63

These costs per thousand bear no relationship to the actual premiums paid for the coverage.

To see how the table works, assume you are 37 years old and have $300,000 of insurance provided by your corporation. Your taxable income is $420.00 a year. (14¢ × 12 months = $1.68 yr × $250 (000) = $420.00) The first $50,000 is tax free. You therefore have taxable income of $420.00 regardless of the actual premium cost.

Nondiscrimination Requirements

TEFRA has enacted new nondiscrimination requirements in order for key employees to obtain the income tax exclusion on the "cost" of the first $50,000 of coverage.

A plan will not be considered discriminatory as long as it meets the following eligibility-to-participate and amount-of-benefits standards. Eligibility requirements must allow for the following participation:

1. The plan must benefit at least 70% of all employees.
2. Of the participating employees, at least 85% must not be key employees.

Certain groups of employees can be excluded from consideration in applying the eligibility-to-participate standards.

The amount-of-benefits standard states that all benefits available to participants who are key employees must be made available to all other participants. The level of benefits, though, will not be considered discriminatory if they bear a uniform relationship to compensation.

Retired Lives Reserve

Retired lives reserve (RLR) is a fund established by your corporation for the purpose of providing premium payments for postretirement, group, term insurance for employees. Contributions to the reserve fund are not taxable personally to the employee. Under federal code section 79 (b)(1), the value of the group term life insurance coverage provided after retirement is also exempt from personal taxation.

Your corporation is permitted to deduct premiums paid for RLR if conditions are met assuring that the fund is used to provide insurance for retired employees and that contributions are reasonable.

Disability Insurance

Disability income insurance is, to me, one of the most critical elements in a good financial plan. For most of us, our financial objectives are achievable provided we stay healthy and able to work. Disability plans are designed to replace your earnings if you become ill or disabled. I always recommend that my clients buy the maximum coverage available, between 40% and 60% of their predisability earnings.

I also recommend that they buy a noncancelable, guaranteed renewable policy, which assures that it cannot be canceled and that the premium cannot be raised above the fees cited in the policy. The policy's definition of disability should be: inability by reason of sickness or injury to perform the duties of your normal occupation. Such a policy is the most expensive.

Choose a policy payable for life or until age 65, if payment for life is unavailable. To keep the premium manageable, choose a longer elimination period. The elimination period is roughly akin to a deductible, in that it defines the amount of time that elapses after your disability or illness before you can start collecting.

The payment of premiums on your disability policy can be deducted by your corporation, but you should think seriously about this course of action because if you receive disability-insurance proceeds from a policy purchased by your company, the portion of the proceeds taxable to you is the portion attributable to the corporation's contributions to the premium. This portion is the amount bearing the same ratio to the amount received as the premium paid by the employer bears to the total premiums paid.[1]

For example, your company pays two-thirds of your premium. You

---

[1]Internal Revenue Regulation 1.105-1(c)(4)(d).

pay the remaining one-third by payroll deduction. The annual premium is $240, of which your company pays $160. If you are disabled and begin collecting disability benefits from the policy, two-thirds of the proceeds is taxable and the remaining one-third is excludable.[2]

If you meet the special provisions of federal code section 105, you can exclude up to $5,200 per year. However, the exclusion is reduced dollar for dollar by the amount that your adjusted gross income, including your disability payments, exceeds $15,000 a year.

My recommendation is to pay disability premiums from after-tax personal income and receive the benefits tax-free. Considering that you can only buy about half your present income as a benefit, I believe this is a better approach.

Health Insurance

Few things are as potentially able to wreck your family's financial well-being as a serious illness or accident. You should therefore install an extremely good health-insurance plan. The tax benefits are:

1. Your corporation can deduct premium payments, if each employee is named as beneficiary.
2. Premium payments do not represent taxable income to you or other covered employees.
3. Any benefits received are normally tax free.

Premiums will, of course, be a function of the age and sex distribution of your employees. If the cost of a really good policy is more than you can afford, I suggest you set up the plan and have your employees pay part of the cost. They will be better off—the premiums on a group policy will be less than on an individual policy—and your company will still pay some portion of the premiums. You, personally, will be better off for the same reasons.

Medical Reimbursement Plan

As an individual, you can deduct medical expenses only to the extent they exceed 5% of adjusted gross income. (If you're unsure how to define adjusted gross income, see Appendix B). This limit can prevent you from deducting a large amount of medical expenses. For example, if your adjusted gross income is $80,000, you can deduct only medical expenses that exceed $4,000 ($80,000 × 5%). The first $4,000 of medical expense you incur is lost to you

---

[2]Internal Revenue Code Section 104 (a)(3).

as a deduction. In the 50% tax bracket, that means you must pay an extra $2,000 in income taxes.

You can avoid losing these deductions with a medical reimbursement plan, with which your company can pay these expenses and take a full deduction without being subject to the 5% limitation.

Prior to 1979, a company could adopt a medical reimbursement plan limited to key executives, stockholders, corporate officers, and their families. These plans paid for the medical expenses incurred by these selected individuals with corporate funds. The payments were completely deductible by the corporation and the benefits received completely tax free for the individuals. It was a sure bet that IRS would challenge that practice!

Although there was some fear that the challenge eliminated the benefits of a medical reimbursement plan, the benefit is still available to you. It is still tax free if your plan does not discriminate in favor of officers, stockholders, or highly paid employees.

A distinction between self-insured and insured plans was among the changes created by the 1979 challenge.

Self-Insured Plans

Self-insured plans are just what the term implies: plans in which your company pays your expenses or reimburses you (and other eligible employees) without insurance coverage.

Nondiscriminatory Plans

Code section 105(b) makes it clear that self-insured medical reimbursement plans may not discriminate in favor of employees who are officers, or shareholders, or are highly paid. It sets forth the following eligibility requirements:

1. The plan must benefit either 70% or more of all employees *or*
2. Must benefit 80% of the 70% eligible who are actually members, *or*
3. Must benefit employees who qualify under a classification determined by the employer that is found by the Secretary of the Treasury not to be discriminatory in favor of highly compensated participants.

In determining eligibility requirements, the following employees may be excluded:

1. Employees with less than three years of service.
2. Employees under age 25.

3. Part-time or seasonal workers (those who customarily work less than 35 hours per week or less than nine months per year).
4. Employees who are members of a collective bargaining unit (union members whose accident and health benefits were the subject of good faith bargaining).
5. Employees who are nonresident aliens who receive no earned income from the employer from sources within the United States.

A medical reimbursement plan is considered nondiscriminatory only if the same benefits are provided for all participants. For example, the benefits provided cannot be a function of such factors as compensation or length of service. You may, however, coordinate benefits with other plans or by public benefits such as Medicare and still have a nondiscriminatory plan.

Discriminatory Plans

The distinction is important because, under a discriminatory plan, a portion of the reimbursement is personally taxable to the "highly compensated." Highly compensated individuals include:

1. The five highest-paid officers;
2. Shareholders who own more than 10% of the employer's stock;
3. Individuals who are among the highest-paid 25% of all employees and who are not excludable under the eligibility standards.[3]

If the benefits are available only to the highly compensated and not made available to a broad cross-section of employees, any and all reimbursement received by the "highly compensated" is fully taxable to them personally.

If the plan provides benefits for employees generally, but is still defined as a discriminatory plan, the "highly compensated" will be held personally taxable on some portion of the benefit. The amount of the tax liability depends on whether the nature of the discrimination is relative to benefits or coverage. Some examples will demonstrate how the numbers work.

Assume your plan covers all employees for medical, but provides dental only for the highly compensated. Any reimbursement for dental received by the highly compensated is taxable income.

Assume your plan covers all employees, but has an $8,000 limit for the highly compensated and a $2,000 limit for all other participants.

---

[3]Internal Revenue Code section 105(b)(5).

Any reimbursement received by the highly compensated in excess of $2,000 is taxable personally.

Both of these examples relate to plans that are discriminatory as to benefits.

Where the plan is discriminatory as to coverage, taxable income is computed on the basis of coverage provided for the highly compensated (as a group) and the other employees covered under the plan (as a group). The taxable portion of benefits is determined by multiplying the benefit received by a fraction whose numerator is the total amount reimbursed during the plan year to *all* the highly compensated and whose denominator is the total amount reimbursed during the same period to all participants.

For example, a discriminatory self-insured plan reimburses you for $4,500 of medical expenses during the year. During the same period, the plan pays $50,000 in reimbursements to all other participants, of which $30,000 is paid to the highly compensated. Your taxable income from the benefit is calculated as follows:

$$\$4,500 \times \frac{\$30,000}{\$50,000} = \$2,700$$

In short, you receive a $4,500 reimbursement, of which you must claim $2,700 as taxable.

Insured Plan

The problem posed by a discriminatory plan can be avoided by setting up an insured plan. Benefits provided by a licensed insurance company under a group policy are exempt from the nondiscrimination requirements. The rationale, I suspect, is that underwriting considerations would tend to minimize or even eliminate discrimination. Some companies make a specialty of insured medical reimbursement plans.

If you choose ultimately not to install medical reimbursement, remember that you can still pay for medical examinations. These expenses are fully deductible by your corporation and are not taxable income to you or any employees availing themselves of the benefit.

Liability Insurance for Officers and Directors

Generally, expenses for liability insurance are not taxable to the officers or directors and are deductible by the corporation. If you pay this insurance plus a small fee you can obtain very fine people to sit on your board. The amount of very valuable business advice and guidance available to you in this manner makes the insurance a real bargain.

AUTOMOBILE EXPENSES

You may deduct transportation expenses for your business or profession whether or not you are away from home. Remember, however, that commuting expenses between your home and usual place of business are not deductible.

If your corporation owns the car you drive, you should report as taxable compensation the value of the personal use of the car. The corporation may take the full deduction as determined by depreciation; general cost of operation, gas and oil, maintenance, lubrication, repairs, antifreeze, tools, motor club memberships, and insurance; state and local taxes; and casualty and theft losses. Even though you incur a tax liability for the personal use of the car, its nominal amount normally makes a corporate-owned car a worthwhile benefit. In calculating the deduction (either personally or for the corporation), you may use either actual expenses attributable to the business use of the car or the federal standard mileage allowance.

The standard mileage allowance is 20¢ per mile for the first 15,000 miles and 11¢ per mile thereafter. If your car is fully depreciated, the standard mileage allowance is only 11¢ a mile for all business use of the car.

While the standard mileage allowance simplifies record keeping—it requires only recording of odometer readings—you may find that given the costs of operating a car, the actual expenses may give you a greater deduction. Remember, it's either/or. If you take the standard mileage allowance, the only additional deductions allowed are parking fees, highway tolls, and interest on the car-purchase loan.

LEGAL EXPENSES

The Federal Tax Reform Act of 1976 provided a new fringe benefit: the Group Legal Services Plan. The plan was effective for tax years between 1976 and 1982; the Economic Recovery Act of 1981 extended the plan until 1984. The basics of the plan are very simple:

1. The cost of prepaid legal-service plans for you and other eligible employees is fully deductible as a business expense.
2. The value of legal services is not personally taxable to the recipient.
3. The contribution your business makes to provide the legal service does not represent taxable income.

In order to qualify for special tax treatment, your plan must meet the following requirements:

1. It must be in writing.

2. The key district director of internal revenue must be notified on form 1024.

3. Only employees, their spouses, and/or dependents may be beneficiaries of the tax-free plan.

4. Coverage must be limited to personal legal problems.

5. All eligible employees must be given thorough explanations so that they understand exactly what legal services are covered by the plan.

6. Payments must not be in the form of direct reimbursement to employees. The law firm retained to provide these services should be paid directly. The plan may be funded through a tax-exempt organization, trust, or insurance company, in which case that organization should be paid directly by your company.

Your plan should not discriminate in favor of the highly compensated, corporate officers, or shareholders, but you are allowed to limit the plan to a class of employees. If you do this, then all employees in that class must be eligible.

To retain its tax-free status, your plan must place a limit on the owner(s) of your company: No more than 25% of the amount contributed by the employer is to be used on behalf of individuals, their spouses, or dependents who own more than 5% of the outstanding stock of the firm.

EMPLOYEE DEATH BENEFIT EXCLUSION

Under federal tax code section 101(b), amounts up to $5,000 paid to the beneficiaries or the estate of an employee, or former employee, are exempt from income taxation if (1) they were paid by or on behalf of the employer, and (2) were paid because of the death of the employee. The exclusion can be used against distributions from retirement plans or it may be an additional death benefit. If given as an additional death benefit, amounts up to $5,000 are tax deductible to the corporation.

EDUCATIONAL ASSISTANCE

Traditionally, the IRS has allowed a deduction for education that "improves or maintains" skills or is "job-related." The Revenue Act of 1978 expanded this educational allowance, providing that amounts paid by or incurred by your business for educational assistance to you and your employees are excluded from personal taxation and are deductible by your business.

The educational assistance must be provided through a program that meets certain nondiscrimination tests and other requirements:

1. No more than 5% of the benefits may be paid to shareholders, officers, highly compensated individuals, or dependents of these.
2. The plan may require successful completion of a course or attainment of a certain grade in determining availability of benefits.
3. The program will not be considered discriminatory merely because it is used more by one class of employees than by others.

Because of the limitation on the use by officers and stockholders, the benefit is obviously not one designed to be personally beneficial to the principals. It may, however, have merit as a management tool, facilitating promotion from within and enabling good employees to become better. The requirement of completion of the course with a certain grade minimizes abuse of the program.

SCHOLARSHIPS FOR CHILDREN OF EMPLOYEES

Along these same lines, many companies have become interested in offering company-sponsored programs to children of their employees. Indeed, the tax ramifications are attractive. Grants providing scholarship aid for full-time study leading to a degree are normally deductible by the company. The deduction is limited, however, by the corporate charitable contribution (10% of taxable income).

The grant may be excluded from personal taxation by the recipient if the following conditions are met:

1. The grant is supported by a contribution to a tax-exempt educational institution or foundation.
2. The grant isn't restricted to named individuals.
3. The class or group of eligible beneficiaries is broad enough to meet IRS standards.
4. The primary purpose of the grant is to further the education of the recipient as an individual.

In order to award the scholarships exclusively to the employees' children, with no competitive criteria being required, some companies have established an educational benefit trust (EBT). The trust can be funded as desired. It pays taxes on its earnings (at trust rates).

Scholarship contributions are deductible as a legitimate fringe benefit in the year paid to the children, but the benefit is fully taxable to the employee. The IRS takes this position on the grounds that the employees "have allowed a portion of their earnings to be paid to their children."

To achieve any tax advantages, an EBT has to be constructed in such a way that it becomes useless to the participants.

FINANCIAL COUNSELING

Expenses paid or incurred for financial counseling are deductible by your corporation and are not taxable to you if the counseling concerns tax advice, the preparation of tax returns, or investment advice.

MOVING EXPENSES

If your business becomes (or has become) successful to the point that you need branches or units in other cities, you may feel that transferring some of your personnel is better than hiring new people at the new location.

Federal code section 217 provides that corporate reimbursement of qualified employee moving expenses is not taxable to the employee and is deductible by the corporation. The statute specifies that five categories of expenses are allowable as a deduction from gross income when incurred by the transferring of employees:

1. Expenses of moving household goods and personal effects from the former residence to the new residence
2. Expenses of traveling (including meals and lodging) from the former residence to the new residence
3. Expenses of traveling (including meals and lodging) from the former residence to the new residence and returning, for the principal purpose of searching for a new residence
4. Expenses of meals and lodging while occupying temporary quarters in the new place of work during any period of thirty consecutive days after obtaining employment
5. Expenses that constitute "qualified sale, purchase, or lease expenses" relating to the disposal of the employee's former residence and the acquisition of the new residence in the new place of work.

BARGAIN PURCHASES AND FREE MERCHANDISE

As a matter of law, you (or your employees) have taxable income if you buy (or permit employees to buy) property from your company at a bargain price or if the business donates the property to you or other employees. As a matter of practice, however, many firms allow employees to buy goods at a discount, and the administrative burden of collecting the tax seems to prohibit strict enforcement. Even assuming strict adherence, bargain purchases can still be advantageous.

Let's assume your business owns a car with a "Blue Book" retail of $12,500, and a wholesale value of $8,500. You decide to buy the car from the business for $8,500. There is a serious question of whether the purchase results in any taxable income to you, but even if it does, it is in the amount of the "bargain element": $4,000. Assuming you're in the 50% tax bracket, that's an extra $2,000, so you still have a $12,500 car for $10,500. Your corporation takes a tax deduction for the "bargain element," so both you and the corporation come out ahead.

GIFTS TO EMPLOYEES

Under federal tax code section 102, gifts to an individual are not taxable. For a corporation, however, an annual gift of cash to an individual is deductible if it does not exceed $25, with three exceptions. These are:

1. Advertising items on which your company name is permanently printed and which cost $4.00 or less. The items should be distributed by your company to your clientele or the public. You can send any number of such items to the same individual each year—the $25.00 limit does not apply.
2. Business materials given to your customers to aid them in the promotion of your product or services.
3. Gifts awarded to employees because of some merit achievement or length of service, if they cost less than $100.

CHARITABLE CONTRIBUTIONS

If your personal tax situation does not benefit much from itemizing—for example, your house is paid for, you have few medical expenses, or you show no losses or interest write-off from loans—you may find it advantageous to have your corporation make charitable contributions on your behalf. Your corporation can make a gift to your favorite charity, which is not taxable to you, and the corporation can take the deduction.

MEMBERSHIPS IN BUSINESS, PROFESSIONAL, SOCIAL, AND ATHLETIC CLUBS

Membership expenses in business and professional clubs are not taxable to the employee and are deductible to your corporation. The same taxation prevails with social and athletic clubs if these memberships are used primarily to further your corporation's business. Any personal use by you and/or your employees, however, is taxable to each of you personally.

DEPENDENT-CARE ASSISTANCE

The Economic Recovery Tax Act of 1981 created a new fringe benefit for dependent-care assistance. Although code section 129 does not address the issue of deductibility, the presumption is that the cost of dependent-care assistance is deductible by your company. The value of the benefit is not included in the employee's gross income; the benefit must be provided under a written plan and must be nondiscriminatory.

You, as employer, can set up the classification of employees who may benefit, but this classification must meet IRS approval. The plan does not discriminate in favor of owners or their dependents, officers, or the highly compensated or their dependents.

Not more than 25% of the total dependent-care assistance provided during the year may be provided for shareholders or owners (or their spouses or dependents) owning 5% or more of the stock, capital, or profits of the employer. The plan can provide dependent care either in-house or by third persons.

TRAVEL AND ENTERTAINMENT

One of the most frustrating areas of business expense is travel and entertainment. It is one that IRS looks at very hard during an audit, and an area where substantiation requirements are very clear and very stringent.

Federal code section 274(d) states that "no deduction should be allowed for any expenditure for travel, entertainment, or a gift unless the taxpayer substantiates the following elements for each such expenditure: amount, time and place of travel and entertainment, business purpose, and business relationship."

The same section indicates that a diary or account book containing that information should be adequate to establish that the expense was incurred. But to prove that the expense was actually paid, you need either a bill marked "paid" or a cancelled check. A diary serves to substantiate amounts less than $25.

Travel and entertainment expenses are deductible only "if they are ordinary and necessary expenses of carrying on your trade or business and can be proved. . . ." Moreover, they must be directly related to or associated with the active conduct of your trade or business.

SPOUSE'S TRAVEL EXPENSES

The only condition under which your spouse's travel expenses are deductible is if his/her presence has a bona fide business purpose. If your spouse frequently performs business chores at home or if you can demonstrate that in your spouse's absence you would have to hire someone else to perform those business-related services, you stand a better chance of getting the deduction.

If this is not a valid stance, then you can still deduct your full expenses as if you were alone. For example, if the double-room rate at the hotel is $75 and the single rate is $50, you can deduct the full single rate of $50.

RETIREMENT PLANS

Retirement plans are among the most valuable of all fringe benefits because they permit you to contribute and deduct large percentages of your income to a retirement trust and to have 100% of everything earned by the money contributed to build capital for you.

Pension and profit-sharing plans come in a wide variety, but all qualified plans provide common tax elements. They include:

1. Immediate income-tax deductions by the corporation.
2. No current income tax to the employee, even though she/he may have a vested (nonforfeitable) interest in the employer contribution.
3. No current income tax on earnings and income on investments to the retirement trust unless the income is unrelated to the trust's exempt purpose of accumulating retirement funds.
4. Special ten-year averaging for computing the tax on distributions that are made in a lump sum.
5. Special annuity taxation for distributions made in installments.
6. No tax on lump-sum distributions "rolled over" by a participant into an Individual Retirement Account (IRA).
7. No tax to a participant's spouse, who, upon receiving a lump-sum distribution at the participant's death, rolls it over into an IRS Rollover Account.
8. No gift tax on a gift of a participant's interest in the plan (except to the extent of his/her own contributions).

As I said earlier, there is a wide range of plans. We will be exploring in detail the characteristics of each and the factors that go into retirement plan design in Chapter 8.

INTEREST-FREE LOANS

One of the most exciting opportunities available to you as a principal in a closely held corporation is the opportunity to use your corporation as a bank, that is, grant yourself an interest-free loan from the corporation.

The IRS has long contended that the economic benefit of such a loan should be treated as taxable income, but the federal tax court in a landmark case decided against the Service on this point. Although the service has announced its nonacquiescence, the tax court continues to adhere to the J.S. Dean case.[4]

If a tax-free, interest-free loan appeals to you, structure it carefully so that it is clearly a loan. Observe the following precautions:

1. Be sure you have a written, formal, loan agreement. Have it notarized and include a repayment schedule.
2. Carry the loan on your corporate books as a receivable.
3. List the loan on corporate tax returns and financial statements.
4. Put up collateral, such as real estate, insurance policies, and bank accounts.
5. Don't make loans in proportion to stock ownership.
6. Be sure to demonstrate ability to repay. A disallowance is likely to rest on the fact that it is a loan that no credit institution would grant.

For the most part, the courts have been liberal in upholding the tax-free, interest-free loan. But don't go too far: A quote from a court of appeals opinion may provide some guidance:

> Whereas withdrawal(s) of reasonable amounts are countenanced as a loan if other loan factors are present, excessive and continuous diversion of corporate funds into the controlling shareholder's pocket takes on a different character. There is a principle of too much; phrased colloquially when a pig becomes a hog, it is slaughtered.[5]

In this case, the shareholder failed to develop or demonstrate a plan to repay the loan, and his ability to repay the loan was significantly doubtful.

In considering which (if any) of these benefit programs you want to install, I would suggest, as a point of departure, that you make a list of the items comprising your personal budget. Go down the list, checking off those items that the firm can provide. Then determine whether employee costs offset your tax savings. If employee costs more or less negate your tax saving,

---

[4]See J.S. Dean, 35TC 1083, CCH Dec. 24, 742 (1961).

[5]R. Dolesc, CA-10, 79-2 USTC 9540, 605 F. 2d 1146 (1979).

is the benefit, viewed as a management tool, still desirable? If employee costs are nominal to nil, by all means, install all of these benefits! (See Table 4–1.)

If you want to explore the possibility of a full range of employee benefits, I suggest you employ a certified financial planner who specializes in professional and/or small business corporations (see Chapter 3).

TABLE 4–1
Checklist of Employee Benefits

Employee Benefits Deductible by Corporation	Taxation to Employee				
	Fully Taxable	Partially Taxable	Tax Free	Tax Favored	Tax Deferred
Life Insurance			Premiums on first $50,000 of coverage	Premiums on coverage in excess of $50,000	
Disability Income	Depends on ratio of payments by business and employee				
Medical Reimbursement		If self-insured and discriminatory	If nondis-criminatory or insured		
Medical Examinations			✔		
Automobile	Personal use		Business use		
Legal Service Plan			If nondis-criminatory		
Employee Death Benefit Exclusion			✔		
Educational Assistance			✔		
Scholarships for Children of Employees	To employee if no com-petitive cri-teria required		If properly structured		
Financial Counseling			✔		
Moving Expense			✔		
Bargain Purchases and Free Merchandise		✔			

TABLE 4–1 (continued)
Checklist of Employee Benefits

Employee Benefits Deductible by Corporation	Taxation to Employee				
	Fully Taxable	Partially Taxable	Tax Free	Tax Favored	Tax Deferred
Gifts from Company			If less than $25.00; $100.00 if because of merit		
Charitable Contributions			✔		
Officers' and Directors' Liability Insurance			✔		
Club Memberships	Personal use		Business use		
Dependent Care Assistance			✔		
Travel and Entertainment	If personal		If business related		
Spouse's Travel	If personal		If bona fide business purpose can be established		
Retirement Plans				✔	✔
Interest-Free Loans			✔		

5

Getting Money
Out of Your Corporation

A legitimate complaint by business owners is that distribution by dividends is subject to double taxation, once at the corporate level and again at the individual level.

Fortunately, there are several attractive alternatives to dividends for getting money out of your corporation. This chapter will focus on those alternatives.

This discussion will not include getting money out of your business through redemption of stock or by selling your business. While this is certainly one way to get money out, it is a specialized transaction that should be undertaken only with the aid of a highly competent advisor.

SALARY AND/OR BONUS

One of the most obvious ways to get money out of your corporation is by paying yourself a big salary and/or bonus. Initially this appears to be an excellent solution: clean, easy, and no double taxation. However, there are problems associated with this solution.

Reasonable Compensation

For one thing, the IRS has an animal called "reasonable compensation," defined as "only such amount as would ordinarily be paid for like services by like enterprises under like circumstances."

There is no single factor that determines whether or not your compensation is reasonable, but the courts have addressed the following factors:

1. What the job itself pays in similar firms;
2. The shareholder's special abilities;
3. How unique such abilities are;
4. How the shareholder's salary compares with salaries of employees in the business doing similar jobs;
5. Stockholder compensation during past years in the business;
6. How large and complex the business is;
7. The demands of the job itself;
8. The percentage of business gross and net the salary represents.

The list is by no means exhaustive, but I think you can get some feel for what goes into "reasonable compensation."

The distinction between reasonable and unreasonable is important because salaries in excess of "reasonable" are treated as dividends. The deduction for the excess is denied to the corporation, and you're back to square one with double taxation.

Minutes

I think minutes can do you a lot of good in this regard. Use your minutes to reflect compensation levels in similar jobs and similar circumstances and to record all that the job involves—hours, training, special skills, activities performed, and so forth. They should also formalize board of director approval. In addition, have an employment agreement with your firm detailing the arrangements between you and your corporation.

Oswald Bylaw

Another consideration is the so-called "Oswald Bylaws"[1], which is written into the corporate bylaws.

This requirement legally obligates stockholders to reimburse the corporation for any compensation found to be excessive. It binds the board of

---

[1]Oswald, 49 TC 645, 1969; Rev. Rul. 60-115, CB 1969-1,50.

directors to collect the reimbursement, provided, of course, that the stockholder has signed an agreement legally binding under local law.

If the bylaw has been provided and the shareholder has signed an agreement, IRS rulings allow the executive who has to reimburse the company to deduct such repayment.

TAX BRACKETS

In addition to considering the problem of unreasonable compensation when taking money out of your corporation through salary, you must also keep in mind your personal and corporate tax brackets. You should attempt to have all income taxed in the lower bracket up to the point that the brackets are about equal.

Let's assume, for example, that your corporation has profits (not counting your salary) of $200,000. If you take it all as salary, you are in the 50% tax bracket and your corporation is at zero. If you take none as salary, your corporation is in the 46% tax bracket and you are at zero. If you split it up, you take $100,000 at 50% and $100,000 at 46%.

Some alternatives include the following:

		Personal Tax	Corporate[1] Tax	Combined Tax
Salary	$ 50,000	$12,014		
Corporate Profits	$150,000		$48,750	$60,764
Salary	$100,000	$34,190		
Corporate Profits	$100,000		$25,750	$59,940
Salary	$ 70,000	$20,414		
Corporate Profits	$130,000		$39,550	$59,964
Salary	$130,000	$49,002		
Corporate Profits	$ 70,000		$14,250	$63,252
Salary	$ 60,000	$16,014		
Corporate Profits	$140,000		$44,150	$60,164

[1]1983 Tax Rates

So, your taxes can vary from a high of $63,252 to a low of $59,940, with a possible saving of $3,312. I grant you it's not a fortune, but remember, you didn't have to do anything or spend anything to get it. Remember, also that if you have a 10% gross-to-net ratio (you realize as profits 10% of your gross) you gross an additional *$62,000* to have an after corporate tax return of $3,300.00.

Gross	$62,000
Gross/Net 10%	6,200
Corporate Tax	46%
Corporate after tax net	3,348

RETIREMENT PLAN

Salary and bonus are not the only forms of compensation you have. One very good form of compensation is a retirement plan contribution. (See Chapter 8 for more details.)

Retirement plans not only do what they are designed to do: facilitate the accumulation of capital for your retirement years—but they are also the finest tax shelters available. They are one of the few ways to transfer money from your corporation to you in a way that is *fully taxable* by the corporation, but *not currently taxable* to you. Please give this possibility your most open-minded consideration.

FRINGE BENEFITS

Another way to take compensation is through fringe benefits, which are tax deductible by your corporation and either tax free or tax favored to you. (See Chapter 4.)

OTHER METHODS OF OBTAINING MONEY

Let's make the pleasant assumption that you have gone through your budget sheet, set up all the fringe benefits that are appropriate for you, set up your retirement plan, and still find that your corporation has money to disperse to you if only you could find some other ways to get it. Following is a list of those ways.

Stock Dividend

Stock dividends that are pro-rata distributions of common stock or rights to acquire common stock made to holders of common stock are not taxable to the shareholder. Because of this, they are often used to reduce the value of each share. If share value has become so high that it is impractical for shareholders to make transfers of stock to family members or to invite new shareholders to the firm, a stock dividend is a painless way to reduce the value.

Property Dividends

If your corporation owns appreciated property, consider taking this property as a dividend. You will be personally taxed on the fair market value at distribution, but your corporation doesn't incur a capital gains tax on the appreciation.

There are four exceptions to the general rule that the corporation may not be taxed on a dividend distribution of appreciated property. The corporation *may* be taxed when:

1. The corporation has taken depreciation deductions on the property.
2. The property consists of installment sale obligations.
3. The property is subject to investment credit recapture.
4. The property consists of inventory reported under the last in-first out method.

Let's assume that in your corporate stock portfolio (see Chapter 7) you have a stock that you bought for $25 per share which is now selling for $150/share. You decide to take that stock as a property dividend, and sell it. The results are:

$$\begin{array}{rl} \$150 & \text{taxable income} \\ \underline{@50\%} & \text{tax bracket} \\ \$\ 75 & \text{net after tax proceeds} \end{array}$$

The sale by you results in no capital gains because your basis is $150.

Contrast that with having the corporation sell and disperse the proceeds to you:

$$\begin{array}{rl} \$150 & \text{sale price} \\ \underline{-\ 25} & \text{basis} \\ \$125 & \text{long-term capital gain} \\ \underline{\times\ 28\%} & \text{corporate capital gain tax} \\ \$\ 35 & \text{corporate tax} \end{array}$$

$$\begin{array}{rl} \$150 & \text{sale proceeds} \\ \underline{-\ 35} & \text{corporate tax} \\ \$115 & \text{net proceeds to be distributed} \\ \underline{\times\ 50\%} & \text{personal tax} \\ 57.50 & \text{net after tax proceeds} \end{array}$$

Just as gains are not recognized at the corporate level, neither are losses. Therefore, property on which your corporation has a loss should not be distributed as a property dividend. Instead, the corporation should sell, recognize the loss, and disperse the proceeds.

Deferred Compensation

Deferred compensation can be an extremely good alternative to currently taxable income. In the simplest possible terms it is a nonqualified plan represented by an agreement between selected employees and the business whereby a portion of the employee's current income is deferred until some future date. The future period is frequently, but not necessarily, the retirement of the employee.

A nonqualified deferred compensation contract is a good way to benefit key employees to the exclusion of the broad base of employees. This discriminatory approach cannot be used with qualified deferred compensation plans (such as profit-sharing plans).

A deferred compensation contract binds the company to pay the participating employee at some future time for work currently being performed. The major advantage to the participating employee, of course, is that it lowers the current income tax bill by postponing recognition of income. Yet, from the corporation's point of view, the deduction for compensation is also deferred.

A deferred compensation plan may be funded or unfunded. With a funded plan, the corporation segregates assets to meet the obligation for compensation at a later date. Deferred compensation is deductible to the corporation in the year that the employee includes the compensation in gross income.

With an unfunded deferred compensation plan, the company does not set aside assets to pay the obligation, but, of course, it has a contractual commitment to pay.

With a funded plan, the corporation does segregate assets, but the title of the assets remains in the company's name. They are available to satisfy corporate creditors.

A funded plan gives the company an added advantage at distribution. Suppose the company places $100,000 into the deferred compensation plan. At distribution, there is a corporate expense of $100,000. But suppose the plan grows to $200,000. If the plan calls for the entire amount to be paid out, the corporation has a deduction for $200,000. If the plan does not call for payment of the earnings, the corporation pays out $100,000, writes off $100,000 and keeps the additional $100,000 as an asset.

Increasing numbers of deferred compensation plans are tied to phantom stock arrangements. (See Chapter 6.) In this instance, deferred compensation is treated as if it were invested in the company's stock. The account is credited with the equivalent of dividends being paid to the stockholders. When the participating employee begins receiving the payout, the deferred compensation is based on the value of the company at that point, plus, of course, the build-up of "dividends."

This idea appeals to employees who feel that they can be (or have been) instrumental in increasing the company's value and appreciate an opportunity to participate in that growth.

From your point of view as shareholder, deferred compensation has good applicability if your income is greater than your current need, since this lowers your current income tax. From the corporate point of view, deferred compensation should be considered for companies where cash flow is more critical than corporate tax.

Deferred compensation should also be considered if it will help you attract or hold valuable people in your organization, even if corporate taxes increase some.

One last point: If most of your fringe benefits, retirement plan contributions especially, are geared for cash compensation, deferred compensation may adversely affect these benefits. It is possible to modify other plans to define compensation in a way that includes salary reduction amounts. You should seek highly competent professional help to achieve these results.

Leasing to the Corporation

If you own real or personal property that may be used by your business, both you and the business may benefit if you lease the property to the business. The advantages are fairly straightforward:

1. Your business gets a deduction for the rent paid.
2. You will receive rent payments.
3. You may take depreciation deductions on the property rented to your business.

There are several points to consider in dealing with your controlled corporation. For one thing, don't offer your business a "bargain rent." If it appears that you are willing to forego a profit, your depreciation allowance may be disallowed. Also, be sure to make rent payments an absolute requirement as a condition for the continued use and occupancy of the property.

In short, the lease arrangements should be those that you would be willing to make in an arm's length transaction with a stranger. You should try to fix a "fair" rental. You may want to have an independent appraiser make that determination, especially if there is a significant amount of money involved. You should also consider escalator clauses in the lease and/or rents, based on some percentage of business gross income.

Federal code section 109 contains a provision that I think can be particularly useful to you. It provides that if the lease is of vacant land and the corporation places permanent improvements on the land, the improvements become the lessor's at the end of the lease term. *The added value will not be taxable to the lessor.* Work out details with your professional planning team. This is definitely not a do-it-yourself project!

Remember that if your leased property is retained and becomes a part of your estate, the basis for your heirs will be stepped up to fair market value at your death. The effect is for the capital gains to be "forgiven."

Sale-Leaseback

It may be that there is property in your business (such as real estate, equipment, or machinery) that would lend itself nicely to a lease arrangement between you, personally, and the business. If you hadn't arranged at the onset of your business to own such property personally, it may be possible to do so now through a sale-lease back arrangement.

The term "sale-leaseback" is very descriptive of the transaction. The owner of property sells to an investor-buyer with the agreement that the seller will lease back the property. The seller then has the use of the property and a deduction for rent. The buyer has rental income and depreciation deductions. The buyer who financed the purchase also has interest deductions.

Let's go through an example so you can see exactly how it works. Assume the following. Success, Inc. owns a building and land that it bought ten years ago for $500,000. The building and land are now worth $750,000. The building was allocated at $350,000; land at $150,000. The corporation had taken a total of $140,000 of depreciation.

Success, Inc. sells the property to Mr. Senior, a stockholder, for $750,000 and takes a 20-year leaseback. The rental is agreed to be equivalent to a 20-year amortization of the $750,000 at 11%. This is an annual rental of $94,185. (See table in Appendix D.)

Because of the anti-churning rules prescribed by the Treasury Department as part of the Economic Recovery Tax Act of 1981, let's assume Mr. Senior has to use the same recovery period and method of depreciation that Success, Inc. used. Assume that $525,000 of the value is allocable to the building.

The results are:

1. Success, Inc. has the use of the property for 20 years at a fixed rental. Mr. Senior might have negotiated a flat rental plus a percentage of gross and/or a cost-of-living increase.
2. Success, Inc. has cash of $750,000 to finance other business growth.
3. The full rental of $94,185 is deductible as opposed to the $14,000 of depreciation it has been deducting.
4. Mr. Senior has rent flows of $94,185 each year and depreciation of about $21,000. (The depreciation schedule is assured to be straight-

line for 25 years.) This may or may not give him a positive cash flow depending on the financing he arranged to purchase the property.

If Mr. Senior owns 80% or more of Success, Inc. stock, the gain on the sale of the building is considered ordinary income. Gain on the sale of the land is still capital gain. Notice also, that for the purpose of this rule Mr. Senior's stock includes stock owned by Mrs. Senior, minor children, and minor grandchildren.

You should be careful when making sales of property at a loss. Losses on sales to a shareholder owning more than 50% of the stock of the selling corporation are disallowed as deductions.

For purposes of the sale-leaseback rule, IRS really reaches for ownership. The stockholder is considered to own stock owned by his/her spouse, children, grandchildren, brothers, sisters, parents, trustees, partnerships, and other corporations in which s/he is a shareholder, if that corporation owns stock in the selling corporation.

If your business sells to you, you will not have the problem of possibly losing use of the property at the end of the lease term. If you have entered into a sale-leaseback with an investor outside of your business, this is a point worthy of consideration.

One option is to have some sort of recapture provision in the lease. These arrangements are fairly common, but you must be very careful when setting the recapture price, for if the agreement sets this price too low, the transaction may not hold up as a sale, and your rent deductions will be lost. The best approach is probably to set the option price to the fair market value of the property at the time the option to repurchase is exercised.

One last point. Mr. Senior did not get a "bargain" on the sale price. If a stockholder pays less than fair market price for property, the difference between fair market value and the purchase price may be considered a dividend. In fact, the principal in a corporation should always be alert to the many ways that money taken from the corporation may be considered a dividend.

Gift-Leaseback

The gift-leaseback arrangement is used basically as a family income-splitting device. The normal procedure is for an individual who owns property used in a business or practice to give such property to children or other family members, either outright or through a trust.

I should warn you that the IRS has taken the position that the typical gift-leaseback transaction via a short-term trust is a sham and lacks business purpose. They contend that the degree of control the settlor-lessee retains over the property is tantamount to retention of an "equity" interest in the property. The result, they contend, is that a rental deduction should not be allowed.[2]

If a gift-leaseback is done through a trust, it is normally a short-term reversionary trust (refer to Chapter 9) lasting more than ten years or for the life of the beneficiary, whichever is shorter. The trust, in turn, leases the property back at fair rental value. The desired results are:

1. To provide the beneficiaries of the trust with a source of income at low (maybe even zero) tax rates;
2. To create rent deductions for the business or practice. In effect, these are deductions of payments made to family members;
3. To reacquire property when the trust terminates.

If it all sounds too good to be true, that's exactly how the IRS feels. The service continues to challenge this practice and has taken a "litigate, don't settle" position.

If you are in circuits other than the fourth and fifth, and want to try a gift-leaseback, they have held if the following conditions are met:

1. As donor, you must not maintain substantially the same control over the property that you had before the transfer;
2. The leaseback should be in writing and require a reasonable rental;
3. The leaseback (as distinguished from the gift) must have a bona fide business purpose (an all but insurmountable obstacle in the second, fourth, fifth, and sixth circuits);
4. You, as donor, must maintain an equity interest in the trust.

The tax court states that the requirement to relinquish control is usually met through transfer to an independent trustee who has the right and opportunity to negotiate regarding the leaseback and who acts for the primary benefit of the beneficiaries rather than the grantor.[3]

An independent trustee is an important factor. The eighth circuit's opinion in Quinlivan suggests that, "if no independent trustee is present, then the existence of a gift brings into question whether there is, in fact,

---

[2]Since the IRS took its position against gift-leasebacks in 1954, and has not backed down since, it has enjoyed some success in the fourth and fifth circuit courts but has had defeats in the third, seventh, eighth, and ninth circuits.

[3]C. J. Mathews, 61 TC12, CCH Dec. 32, 161-reversed by the Fifth Circuit (75-2 USTC 9734, 520 F2d 323, cert.den. 424 US967).

any 'requirement' that the rent be paid, and also suggests the possibility of a disqualifying equity."[4]

It seems clear that the IRS is committed to eliminating the gift-leaseback, and I can only caution that if you decide to try it, do so with great care and seek out the very best professional guidance.

Selling to Your Corporation

The rules regarding sales to a corporation by a shareholder or related parties are, to say the least, not very favorable to the shareholder. Generally, if you sell property to your corporation at a fair price, you recognize gain on the sale and are taxed under the normal rules governing such transactions. However, this is not universally true. You should be aware that:

1. If the price your corporation pays is greater than the fair market price, the difference between the fair market price and the "excessive" price may be treated as a dividend. The result, of course, is taxable income to you and not deduction to the corporation.

2. If you own 80% or more of the value of the outstanding stock of the corporation, you and the corporation are considered "related persons." Ownership by your spouse is attributed to you for purposes of this rule. A sale of *depreciable* property between "related persons" causes gains to be treated as ordinary income (federal code section 1239).

3. If you own more than 50% of the value of the outstanding stock, any loss in a sale to your corporation is disallowed. Constructive ownership rules are basically those of federal code section 318. These rules leave undepreciated property to be sold at a fair market value or as depreciable property, if having the gain taxed as ordinary income does not negate the advantage of the sale otherwise.

Lending to Your Corporation

Lending to your corporation has the following results:

1. You can enjoy yields on your loan, which match or exceed money market yields.

2. Your corporation has additional cash.

---

[4]R. R. Quinlivan, 37 + CM 346, CCH Dec. 34, 992 (M), TC Memo. 1978–1970, aff'd CA-8, 79-1 USTC 9396).

This transaction is fairly straightforward, but there is one point of which to be aware. Be sure to arrange the loan in such a way that there is no question that it is a true loan and not an equity investment. The reason is obvious. A true loan results in your corporation paying you deductible interest; equity results in your receiving nondeductible dividends.

The treasury has issued final regulations designed to guide you in setting up an advance as a loan.[5] Your financial planner can help you comply.

Borrowing From Your Corporation

One of the most exciting opportunities available to you as a principal in a closely held corporation is the opportunity to use your corporation as a bank for purposes of making yourself an interest-free loan.

The IRS has long contended that this economic benefit should be treated as taxable income, but the federal tax court decided against the service on this point.[6] Although the service has announced its nonacquiescence to the ruling of this landmark case, the tax court continues to adhere to it.

If the idea appeals to you, carefully structure the loan so that it is clearly a loan and observe the following precautions:

1. Be sure you have a written formal loan agreement. Have it notarized and include a repayment schedule.
2. Carry the loan on your corporate books as a receivable.
3. List the loan on corporate tax returns and financial statements.
4. Put up collateral, such as real estate, insurance policies, and bank accounts.
5. Don't make loans in proportion to stock ownership.
6. Be sure to demonstrate ability to repay. A disallowance is likely to rest on the fact that it was a loan that no credit institution would grant.

For the most part, the courts have been liberal in upholding the tax-free, interest-free loan. But don't go too far: A quote from a court of appeals opinion may provide some guidance:

---

[5]Reg. 1.385.2.

[6]J. S. Dean, 35TC 1083, CCH Dec. 24, 742 (1961).

Whereas withdrawal(s) of reasonable amounts are countenanced as a loan if other loan factors are present, excessive and continuous diversion of corporate funds into the controlling shareholder's pocket takes on a different character. There is a principle of too much; phrased colloquially, when a pig becomes a hog, it is slaughtered.[7]

In this case, the shareholder failed to develop or demonstrate a plan to repay the loan, and his ability to repay the loan was significantly doubtful.

---

[7]R. Dolesc, CA-10, 79-2 USTC 9540, 605 F. 2d 1146 (1979).

ESOP and Other Stock Option Plans

Suppose I told you that your company could take a bank loan, put the money to work in your company, and take a *deduction* for the *full amount* of *repayment* of *principal* and *interest*. Interested? Well, that's what can happen with an employee stock ownership plan (ESOP).

Before I explain how this act of magic works, let's look at what an ESOP is. Pension reform law defines an ESOP as an individual account plan that is a stock plan or a stock bonus plan and money-purchase plan pension plan (qualified under Section 407 of the Internal Revenue Code) that invests primarily in employer securities the employer's stocks and marketable obligations.[1]

The ESOPs are designed to benefit participating employees, but employee ownership depends on the vesting schedule adopted by your company. You may select any vesting schedule available to other qualified plans. (See Chapter 8 for more on vesting schedules.)

The core of an ESOP is a *stock bonus plan*. The IRS regulations define this plan as one that provides benefits and has contribution limits similar to those of a profit-sharing plan, with two exceptions. They are:

1. An employee's contribution to a stock bonus plan is not dependent on profits.

---

[1]ERISA Section 407(d)(6).

2. Benefits must be distributed in the stock of the employer company.

In other respects, stock bonus and profit-sharing plans are almost identical.

To get a clear concept of an ESOP, think of it as a profit-sharing plan designed to invest primarily in employer stock, but which must distribute benefits to employees in that stock. The ESOP may receive cash or company stock as a contribution from the company and may purchase stock from the company or from other shareholders.

HOW AN ESOP WORKS

An ESOP arrangement initially involves three steps:

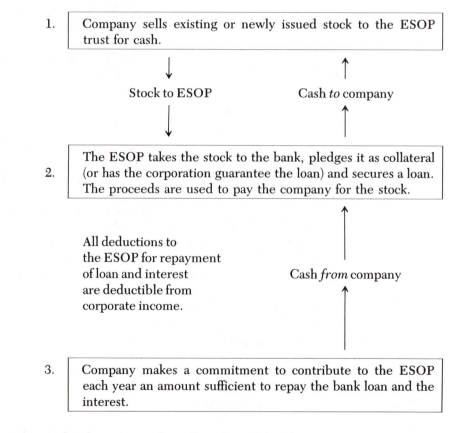

1. | Company sells existing or newly issued stock to the ESOP trust for cash.

Stock to ESOP   Cash *to* company

2. | The ESOP takes the stock to the bank, pledges it as collateral (or has the corporation guarantee the loan) and secures a loan. The proceeds are used to pay the company for the stock.

All deductions to
the ESOP for repayment
of loan and interest
are deductible from
corporate income.

Cash *from* company

3. | Company makes a commitment to contribute to the ESOP each year an amount sufficient to repay the bank loan and the interest.

Let's take an example. When the ESOP of Success, Inc., was established, the trust borrowed $600,000 from the bank and bought 20,000 shares of Success, Inc., stock. As required, the shares were deposited with the

ESOP trustee. They were allocated to individual employee-participant accounts and will eventually be distributed to them.

The $600,000 was borrowed for five years at 16%. The annual payment is $175,091. Success, Inc., took the $600,000 and bought equipment, which could be depreciated in five years.

Assume Success, Inc., needs to buy a piece of equipment. Let's trace the purchase through the profit and loss statements, assuming three alternatives: no qualified plan, a profit-sharing plan, and an ESOP.

	No Plan	Profit Sharing Plan	ESOP Plan
Gross Receipts	11,000,000	11,000,000	11,000,000
Expenses:			
General and Administrative	9,000,000	9,000,000	9,000,000
Depreciation	120,000	120,000	120,000
P/S and ESOP		175,000	175,000
Taxable Income	1,880,000	1,705,000	1,705,000
Corporate Tax	844,550	764,050	764,050
	1,035,450	940,950	940,950
Cash Available:			
After Tax Retained Earnings	1,035,450	940,950	940,950
Plus Cash from ESOP	—0—	—0—	175,000
	1,035,450	940,950	1,115,950

The numbers are even more dramatic than they appear at first. The reason? With no plan, principal on the bank note must be repaid from $1,035,450 after-tax dollars. With a PS plan, the principal must be repaid from the $940,950 after-tax dollars. But with the ESOP, $1,115,950 is available for further business expansion, since the *$175,000 of deductible contribution will be used to repay the bank loan*!

WHERE AN ESOP IS APPROPRIATE

An ESOP is appropriate for a business that:

1. Is a regular corporation, since no shareholders of a Subchapter S corporation can form a trust.
2. Is operating at a profit.
3. Is fairly stable in terms of profit and doesn't fluctuate to any meaningful degree from year to year.

4. Stays consistently in a high federal income tax bracket.

5. Has a reasonably substantial net worth.

6. Is relatively free of debt.

7. Is in an industry that is not declining or depressed.

8. Has a payroll of $200,000 or greater that does not fluctuate substantially.

9. Is well established, with a history of consistent earnings.

10. Is not largely dependent for its profits on one person's efforts.

Now let's look at the advantages to your employees. Later we'll look at the advantages to the company.

ADVANTAGES TO EMPLOYEES

One advantage is that the ESOP encourages companies to make larger contributions to it than they might to a profit-sharing or pension plan. The obvious result is greater participant accumulation in an ESOP than in other plans.

Remember that an ESOP purchases stock from existing stockholders or directly from the company. If the ESOP purchases directly from the company, the cash flow increases. This should increase company earnings, and thus the value of the stock.

The employee benefits in two fundamental ways:

1. He or she receives direct reward for effort. The more productive employees are, the greater the value of their holdings of company stock through the ESOP.

2. Because ESOPs increase company cash flow, management is motivated to contribute more to the plan.

Tax Treatment

The employee also receives very favorable tax treatment on the distributions.

Income tax

If an employee who participated in the plan for at least five years reaches age 59½ or more, leaves the company, or dies, and his or her entire interest is distributed:

1. The receipt of the stock is tax free if the employee's contributions were used to acquire the stock.

2. Any appreciation on the stock is untaxed until the stock is sold.
3. The taxable portion attributable to participants before 1974 may be taxed as capital gain.
4. The taxable portion attributable to participation after 1973 is taxed as ordinary income, but the taxes may be computed under a special ten-year averaging rule. Although the employee gets his/her entire distribution in a lump sum, the tax treatment is as if the distribution were received in ten annual payments.
5. Employees may elect to treat the entire distribution as ordinary income under the ten-year averaging rule.
6. A future sale of the stocks at a gain is taxed at capital gains rates. (The ESOP itself provides a market for the stock.)

Estate tax

If the employee dies before benefits are distributed:

1. Only contributions made by the employee are subject to estate tax.
2. Employer contributions are not subject to estate tax provided they are not distributed to the beneficiaries in a lump sum.
3. If the beneficiaries prefer lump-sum distribution and waive capital gains and/or ten-year income-averaging tax treatment, then the distribution may avoid estate tax.
4. The distribution is subject to estate tax if the beneficiary is the employee's estate.

If the employee dies after the stock has been distributed out before it has been sold, the stock is subject to estate tax.

Converting Stock

Another advantage to employees is that a leveraged ESOP (the kind that borrows money to buy company stock) or a tax-credit ESOP (a TRASOP) may be required to purchase stock distributed to a participant. If the securities are not readily tradable on an established market, the price is determined by a fair-valuation formula.

The flip side of this requirement is not true: the IRS normally views a requirement that employees resell their distribution, either to the corporation or to the ESOP, as an effort to violate the spirit of the law. From a practical point of view, however, the employee will probably welcome an opportunity to convert stock to cash, and the corporation and/or the ESOP probably represents the most convenient market.

An employee can be required to offer stock to the company and/or the

ESOP before offering it to a third party. The company or the ESOP cannot offer a price less than fair market value or less than a third party would. These requirements give the employee the best of all possible worlds: stock in a growing business, given to him by the company; with a ready market. Any employee who understands the ESOP will love it! Remember, you, too, are an employee of your corporation.

ADVANTAGES TO EMPLOYER

But how about your interest as a principal? Do you, as an employer, come out as well as the employee in a list of advantages? Think for a moment of your most common problems, those that surface over and over again.

As a CFP who works with business owners and also as a principal in a closely held business, I would list:

1. Motivating employees
2. Generating cash for expansion
3. Generating deductions to lower the corporate tax (preferably of the noncash variety, for example, amortization and depreciation)
4. Having a market for closely held stock.

An ESOP can help with almost every item.

Motivating Employees

The proverbial "piece of the action" is among the strongest of all motivations. At first blush, it would appear that sharing compensation programs would accomplish the same thing. But with an ESOP, the employee not only benefits from increased profits but also from increases in business worth. Employees become beneficiaries of capital expansion as well as of profit improvement.

Generating Cash for Expansion

There's not much more I can say on this particular point. The description of an ESOP demonstrates how it generates cash through loans that can be repaid with pretax dollars. In addition to loan proceeds, there are substantial tax savings that also create additional cash.

Generating Deductions to Lower the Corporate Tax, Preferably of the Noncash Variety

Anybody who pays taxes loves deductions you can take without having to spend cash. Depreciation, amortization, and depletion are three examples.

Contribution to an ESOP is another. Although you do contribute cash to repay loans, the loan proceeds are given over to the company. In effect, you don't give up cash, you get cash—the repayment of which is fully tax deductible.

Having a Market for Closely Held Stocks

As a principal in a closely held business, a good portion of what you own is probably in the stock of your business. That's great while you're active in the business and/or don't need any cash from your stock, but what happens if you leave the business, retire, or die?

Business owners frequently feel they have jobs they can't quit. But an ESOP, by providing a market for their stock, mitigates this concern. If you wish, you can slowly and systematically sell out to employees who have a significant interest in maintaining the profitability and viability of the firm. You can arrange for the ESOP to buy your shares in the event of your death. The ESOP then buys life insurance on your life to raise funds for the purchase of your shares (from your heirs) and the premiums are paid by the ESOP from deductible corporate contributions.

VALUATION OF SHARES

When the ESOP buys company stock, how is the price of the stock determined? Valuation of shares of a closely held business is always difficult. When shares are not traded on an established market, what factors can be considered to establish value?

Recent sales are useful, theoretically representing what a willing buyer would pay a willing seller, but if these are intrafamily sales, the IRS is going to be suspicious. Was there some donative intent when pricing the stock? Or was the price too high to establish value for a charitable contribution later on?

It would be more reassuring to the principals of closely held corporations if the IRS issued a formula to solve this problem but unfortunately, no such animal exists. The IRS has, however, issued some guidelines.[2]

Here is a list of the factors the IRS considers important when valuing shares in a closely held corporation, together with a brief comment on each factor.

1. *Nature and history of the business.* In assessing this factor, consideration is given to the business' rate of growth, stability of earnings, diversity, and any facts inherent in the nature of the business that may affect its worth.

---

[2]Rev. Rul. 59-60(CB 1959-1,237).

2. *Economic outlook in general and condition of the industry in particular.* Here the IRS considers the company's relative ability to compete. How does the company rank in the industry? One of the things to be considered here is the relative importance of one person to the firm. Is there a key person so critical to the success of the business that the absence of that person through death, disability, or retirement will damage the ability of the firm to compete? If so, a strong key-man life insurance policy should be placed on that person's life to give management a "breather" to continue running the business. Another factor considered here is the securities market. If the market is depressed, it will be reflected in the valuation of your stock.

3. *Book value and financial condition of the business.* For this step, at least two years of financial statements should be considered. In addition to the balance sheet and the income statement, you need supplemental schedules calculating: ratio of current assets to current liabilities; book value of fixed assets; working capital; long-term indebtedness; capital structure; and net worth.

   When a valuation has come before the tax courts because of income, estate, or gift tax, the courts have consistently rejected the argument that book value and market value are the same. The courts have also examined:

   a. *Depreciation or cost recovery schedules.* These schedules help determine the cost, age, and an approximate remaining life on depreciable assets. These schedules also aid in determining future needs for capital assets.

   b. *Analysis of retained earnings.* Where did they come from, why are they being held, and what is their relationship to dividends?

   c. *Financial statements of subsidiaries.* These are prepared separately from the consolidated statements.

   d. *Investments owned by the company and their fair market value.*

   e. *Capital structure.* What kind of stock is outstanding? What is the ratio of debt to equity? If preferred stock is outstanding, what are the dividend and liquidation rights? If debt is outstanding, what are the maturity dates, what interest is being paid, are any assets pledged?

4. *Earning capacity of the company.* A detailed study of profit and loss statements for the previous five years is used to assess earning capacity. Factors studied include trends of earnings, nonrecurring items of income or expense, the relationship of fixed expenses to gross income, rates and amounts of dividends, and interest on preferred stocks and bonds.

   In this category, the compensation of principals and officers may be adjusted. If the business is doing well, principals and officers may be "overpaid" relative to what a nonshareholder with the same abilities and responsibilities would be paid. The earnings are adjusted up in this case. On the other hand, the business may be "underpaying" its officers and principals; in this case, earnings are adjusted down.

Earnings are also adjusted for any interest-free loans outstanding. Once some reasonable figure for earnings has been determined, a multiplier for capitalization must be determined. This is roughly equivalent to the price-earnings ratio (P/E) on publicly traded funds. If there is a publicly traded firm very similar to yours, its P/E makes a reasonable capitalization multiplier. Multipliers ranging from 5 to 20 have been applied to adjusted earnings (see Chapter 7).

5. *Dividend-paying capacity*. The courts have traditionally stressed capacity as determined by earnings, rather than the dividend-paying record. This is probably valid, since in a closely held business the principals prefer compensation to dividends. The dividend-paying record reflects this preference.

6. *Goodwill or other intangible value:* Goodwill is a much misunderstood term. As a general rule, the value of goodwill depends on the excess of net earnings over and above a fair return on net tangible assets. In addition to this value, elements of goodwill include a good reputation for the business and ownership of brand or trade names.

7. *Sales of the stock and size of the block to be valued*. Only sales at "armslength" transactions are deemed meaningful.

8. *The market price of similar corporations*. If similar businesses are being traded, the market price for each serves as a guideline.

Valuation of shares for sale to an ESOP involves some additional special factors. The courts have allowed discounts of from 10% to more than 50% because of the lack of a market for shares of closely held corporations, especially of minority interests. Because an ESOP literally creates a market for the stock, the value is increased accordingly.

The ESOP regulations issued in 1977 by the IRS and the Department of Labor require that for company stocks purchased with an ESOP loan participants must be given the right to "put" their vested shares back to the company upon their withdrawal from the plan. A "put" is the right, but not the obligation, to sell. Furthermore, the company has the opportunity, but not the right, to demand to buy it. This "put" right generally improves the marketability of shares and thereby increases their value.

Management's past policies regarding repurchase of shares from former participants should be considered. It's not uncommon for management to give former participants a put option even in cases where the option is not required by law. A history of offering such puts increases the value of the shares.

It will be obvious to the astute reader that the company's financial condition is important in the consideration of ESOPs to assure that adequate funds are available to buy back stock from former participants. Future put options should also be considered to determine future financial strength.

NOT A "DO IT YOURSELF" PROJECT

Company stock should be appraised when shares are sold or contributed to an ESOP or when an annual report of plan assets is given to participants. The close of the fiscal year is a good time for a valuation. At that time, all transactions with the ESOP can be combined and executed at one value.

An independent appraiser is not required by ESOP regulations; the only requirement is that "valuations must be made in good faith and based on all relevant factors for determining the fair market value of securities." There are, however, very serious risks involved when the company attempts to value the stock without using an appraiser. For example, if the IRS disputes the value of the shares involved in an ESOP transaction, a fiduciary may be held personally liable for any losses or for any profit gained on the transaction.

It is therefore advisable to retain an independent appraiser. The ESOP regulations state, "a determination of fair market value based on at least an annual appraisal independently arrived at by a person who customarily makes such appraisals and who is independent of any party to a transaction . . . will be deemed to be a good faith determination of value."

Many practitioners use the analogy of a good valuation being good insurance—don't buy a cut-rate "policy."

VOTING OF STOCK IN THE ESOP

A common and very valid question a business owner may ask when considering an ESOP is: "How is the stock voted?" Frequently in closely held corporations there is a carefully developed and preserved balance of voting power that everyone is reluctant to disturb.

Typically, what happens is this. The company's board of directors appoints an administrative committee that directs the trustee (who holds legal title to the stock) in the voting of company stock. It is expected that the committee will vote in the best interest of the participants and, indeed, should have a consistent record of voting in their best interest.

While this doesn't give management total control over voting of the stock owned by the ESOP, it does tend to assure management that the ESOP stock won't control management.

It is possible for the company to pass voting rights through the ESOP to the participants. With a tax-credit ESOP or a leveraged ESOP (the kind that borrows money to buy company stock), voting rights *must* be passed through to the participants.

CONTRIBUTION LIMITS

Remember, all contributions are deductible. Units of contribution are:

1. Fifteen percent of compensation of covered employees, *plus*
2. An additional 10% if the ESOP is in the form of a money purchase pension plan.
3. Twenty-five percent of aggregate employee compensation if the contributions are applied by the plan to make principal payments on a loan that was secured to buy employee securities.[3]
4. Unlimited contributions if the contributions are applied to pay interest on the loan.
5. The normal dollar limits on an employee's account in a defined contribution plan is the lessor of $30,000 or 25% of compensation. This rule applies to defined contribution ESOP. There is an exception, however. The permissible dollar amount may be doubled if the additional amount consists only of employer securities. This double contribution is disallowed if more than one-third of the employer contributions to the plan for a year are allocated to employees who are officers and stockholders.

   The double contribution is also disallowed if compensation to officers and stockholders exceeds twice the amount of the dollar limitation ordinarily applicable to the annual addition to participants' accounts. At this writing, that would be compensation in excess of $90,950.00.

TRASOPS: Tax-Credit ESOPs

An extra .5% of the compensation of covered employees is allowed as an income tax credit for 1983 and 1984. For 1985, 1986, and 1987, the percentage will be .75%. There will be no tax credit for ESOP contributions after 1987.

The credit is disallowed if more than one-third of the employer's

---

[3]Items 3 and 4 were created by an amendment to ERTA 1981.

contributions to the plan for a year are allocated to employees who are officers or stockholders owning more than 10% of the company stock. In calculating the 10%, stock held by qualified plans on behalf of the employee/stockholder is not considered. The credit is also disallowed if the compensation of officers and employee/stockholders exceeds $90,950 a year.

The total amount of tax liability that can be offset by contributions to an ESOP is $25,000 plus 90% of tax liability over $25,000. Unused credits can be carried back three years and forward ten.

COSTS

An ESOP is significantly more costly than, for example, a pension and profit-sharing plan. There is some consensus among practitioners that you should have at least $200,000 of covered payroll to justify an ESOP, although some practitioners set the number higher or lower.

STOCK OPTIONS

Suppose ESOPs are wrong for you for a variety of reasons, but you like the idea of motivating your people through "a piece of the action" and you like paying them in a way that gives them some tax advantages. What other choices do you have?

For one, you can give them stock options. There are two types: nonqualified stock options and qualified stock options, called incentive stock options (ISOs). Phantom stock is an interesting compromise though not really a stock option.

Nonqualified Stock Options

Nonqualified stock options are nearly a no-loss situation for an employee. Such options grant a selected executive or executives the right to buy a specified amount of company stock at a specified price or within a specified range, within a certain time period. The option can be at or below fair market value. If the value of the stock increases, the executive exercises the option and has a gain. If the value of the stock does not increase, the executive does not exercise the option, but has really lost nothing, except maybe some extra effort spent trying to increase the value of the stock.

It's a straightforward business transaction. But what about the tax treatment?

1. If the option value is readily ascertainable at the time the option is *granted*, the difference in the value and the option price is considered a "bargain" and taxed accordingly. The bargain element is

taxable to the executive as ordinary income and is deductible by the company.

2. Appreciation occurring after the grant is issued is taxed as capital gains when realized.

3. If the option value is *not* readily ascertainable, there are no tax consequences to either the executive or the company at the time the option is *granted*.

4. When the option is *exercised*, the difference between the fair market value and the option price is considered the bargain element and taxed as ordinary income to the executive and is deductible by the corporation.

5. If at the time of exercise, the company makes the executive an interest-free or low-interest loan, the "interest bargain" is currently held by the courts not to result in taxable income to the executive. The IRS has filed a nonacquiescence to this court ruling, however.

Incentive Stock Options

Incentive stock options (ISOs) are a creation of the Economic Recovery Tax of 1981 which added Section 422A to the Internal Revenue Code. The Act basically restores the tax advantages of "qualified stock options" that Congress abolished with the Tax Reform Act of 1976.

The business aspect of ISOs is just like that of a nonqualified stock option: Selected executives are given the right to buy a specified number of shares of the company at a specified price or within a specified range, within a certain time period. The employee is taxed neither at the time of grant nor at the time of exercise if:

1. The option holder is an employee from the date the option is granted until three months before the date of exercise. Employees leaving because of disability may exercise within 12 months of leaving.

2. The employee holds the stock for two years after the date of the grant of the option or one year after the date of the exercise of the option.

The employer company receives no tax deduction for the incentive stock option.

The conditions that must be satisfied to "qualify" ISOs are:

1. The option must be granted under a plan approved by the stockholders within 12 months before or after adoption.

2. The option must be granted within ten years of the date of adoption or the date of approval.

3. The term of the option may not exceed ten years.

4. The option price must equal or exceed the value of the stock.

5. The option, by its terms, must be nontransferable other than at death and must be exercisable during the employee's lifetime only by him/her.

6. The employee must not, immediately before the option is granted, own more than ten percent of the combined voting power of the employer or its parent or subsidiary.

7. The option, by its terms, is not to be exercisable while there is outstanding any incentive stock option that was granted to the employee at an earlier time.

8. The maximum value of stock for which any employee may be granted option in any calendar year under the plan generally should not exceed $100,000.

The taxation of incentive stock options gives the employee significant tax savings compared to taxation of nonqualified options.

TEFRA makes the bargain element of an ISO a tax preferred item except in the case of an early disposition of the stock acquired though the exercise of the option.

Phantom Stock

Well, that's all well and good, you're saying to yourself. But you're a diehard. You don't want to let any of your stock go to anyone for any reason. If that's you, consider phantom stock, which is not really a stock option but is an interesting compromise between your employees' desires to share in the success of the business and your desire not to give up any stock.

Did you ever just follow a stock—not invest in it, just follow it and it made you money, on paper? That's how phantom stock works, except that your employees follow the stock in your company and if it makes money—on paper—you pay them what it makes. It's an interesting idea for business owners who think having a "piece of the action" will motivate their people but who don't want to let any stock go. It also answers the employee's dilemma about where to get money to exercise a stock option.

The actual mechanics and calculations of phantom stock differ from firm to firm, but the technique generally works like this. Selected executives are credited with a share of the firm's increase in value. Since no shares are actually issued, there are no problems about voting, dividends, redemption rights, and so forth. The executives selected are given phantom-stock contracts that assure they will benefit from the increase in the firm's worth. The increase may be defined as an increase in book value or be tied to a formula that determines annual stock value when book value is inappropriate.

Although the executive doesn't enjoy all the privileges of being a stockholder, she or he does not have to invest any cash and will benefit personally from increases in the firm's long-term success. Some firms even create "dividends" and credit the executive's account.

Phantom stock (and its "dividends") frequently tie the employee to a reasonable covenant not to establish a business competitive with the employer if the employee leaves.

For purposes of making money in the stock, the employee has the benefit of stock ownership, yet you as employer don't have to give up any stock.

7

Your Tax-Sheltered Investment Program

One of the major objectives of the incorporated professional or principal of a closely held corporation is wealth building. One of the most effective means of wealth building through your corporation is to retain and invest corporate surplus.

I want to explore with you the advantages of investing retained earnings and to point out some factors that will be a part of your investment decision making, but first let's review where these funds come from.

To begin, let's take a sample income statement for Success, Inc.

Success, Inc.
Income Statement
For the Year Ending December 31, 1982

Revenues		$1,500,000
Expenses		
Rent	$200,000	
Salaries	600,000	
Advertising	150,000	
Supplies	45,000	
Employee benefit programs	150,000	
Total Expenses		1,145,000

Income before income tax	$ 355,000
Income tax expense	$ 143,550
Net income	$ 211,450

Once you get to the net income figure, you have two options: You can retain some or all of the $211,450 in the corporation or you can pay some or all of it as dividends. Your decision would be reflected in your statement of retained earnings.

Success, Inc.
Statement of Retained Earnings
For the Year Ending December 31, 1982

Retained earnings, January 1, 1982	$ 88,550
Net income	211,450
Dividends	(50,000)
Retained earnings, December 31, 1982	$250,000

As the statement reveals, you elected to distribute $50,000 as a dividend and retain the balance. These earnings, combined with accumulated earnings to this point, brings you to a balance of $250,000 in retained earnings.

Now that you can see clearly the nature and origin of these funds, let's look at your investment alternatives. One is, of course, to use these funds to expand the business. This might entail buying a new plant and equipment or hiring and training new staff. Or you might prefer to make investments in real estate, securities, or art and antiques for your office.

If you aren't going to invest the funds to expand or improve your business, however, I would encourage you to invest in a portfolio of dividend paying stocks. The reason can be found on the corporate tax return itself (see pages 157–160). Look at line 29, item (b) "Special Deductions"; then look at Schedule C on page 161. As you can see, 85% of the dividends received from domestic corporations and 59.13% of certain preferred stock of public utilities are exempt from taxation.

Let's repeat the example from Chapter 1 to refresh your memory about how dramatic the tax advantage of dividend paying stock can be. Assume that you have $250,000 invested in a portfolio of dividend-producing stocks and are earning 10%. In the first column, it is assumed that you are holding these stocks personally and are in the 50% tax bracket. In the second column, it is assumed that your corporation holds the stocks and is in the

Form **1120**

Department of the Treasury
Internal Revenue Service

U.S. Corporation Income Tax Return

For calendar year 1982 or other tax year beginning ...., 1982, ending ...., 19..........

▶ For Paperwork Reduction Act Notice, see page 1 of the instructions

OMB No. 1545-0123

1982

Check if a—			
A. Consolidated return ☐	Use IRS label. Otherwise please print or type.	Name	**D.** Employer identification number
B. Personal Holding Co. ☐		Number and street	**E.** Date incorporated
C. Business Code No. (See page 9 of Instructions)		City or town, State, and ZIP code	**F.** Total assets (see Specific Instructions) $

Gross Income

1 (a) Gross receipts or sales $ .... (b) Less returns and allowances $ .... Balance ▶	**1(c)**	
2 Cost of goods sold (Schedule A) and/or operations (attach schedule)	**2**	
3 Gross profit (subtract line 2 from line 1(c))	**3**	
4 Dividends (Schedule C)	**4**	
5 Interest	**5**	
6 Gross rents	**6**	
7 Gross royalties	**7**	
8 Capital gain net income (attach separate Schedule D)	**8**	
9 Net gain or (loss) from Form 4797, line 11(a), Part II (attach Form 4797)	**9**	
10 Other income (see instructions—attach schedule)	**10**	
11 TOTAL income—Add lines 3 through 10	**11**	

Deductions

12 Compensation of officers (Schedule E)	**12**	
13 (a) Salaries and wages .... 13(b) Less jobs credit .... Balance ▶	**13(c)**	
14 Repairs (see instructions)	**14**	
15 Bad debts (Schedule F if reserve method is used)	**15**	
16 Rents	**16**	
17 Taxes	**17**	
18 Interest	**18**	
19 Contributions (not over 10% of line 30 adjusted per instructions)	**19**	
20 Depreciation (attach Form 4562)	**20**		
21 Less depreciation claimed in Schedule A and elsewhere on return . **21(a)** ( )	**21(b)**	
22 Depletion	**22**	
23 Advertising	**23**	
24 Pension, profit-sharing, etc. plans (see instructions)	**24**	
25 Employee benefit programs (see instructions)	**25**	
26 Other deductions (attach schedule)	**26**	
27 TOTAL deductions—Add lines 12 through 26	**27**	
28 Taxable income before net operating loss deduction and special deductions (subtract line 27 from line 11) . .	**28**	
29 **Less:** (a) Net operating loss deduction (see instructions—attach schedule) . **29(a)**		
(b) Special deductions (Schedule C) . . . . **29(b)**	**29**	
30 Taxable income (subtract line 29 from line 28)	**30**	

Tax

31 TOTAL TAX (Schedule J)	**31**	
32 Credits: (a) Overpayment from 1981 allowed as a credit . .		
(b) 1982 estimated tax payments		
(c) Less refund of 1982 estimated tax applied for on Form 4466 . ( )		
(d) Tax deposited: Form 7004 .... Form 7005 (attach) .... Total ▶		
(e) Credit from regulated investment companies (attach Form 2439)		
(f) Federal tax on special fuels and oils (attach Form 4136)	**32**	
33 TAX DUE (subtract line 32 from line 31—If line 32 is greater than line 31, skip line 33 and go to line 34). See instruction C3 for depositary method of payment	**33**	
(Check ▶ ☐ if Form 2220 is attached. See instruction D.) ▶ $		
34 OVERPAYMENT (subtract line 31 from line 32)	**34**	
35 Enter amount of line 34 you want: **Credited to 1983 estimated tax** ▶ **Refunded** ▶	**35**	

Please Sign Here

Under penalties of perjury, I declare that I have examined this return, including accompanying schedules and statements, and to the best of my knowledge and belief, it is true, correct, and complete. Declaration of preparer (other than taxpayer) is based on all information of which preparer has any knowledge.

Signature of officer	Date	Title

Paid Preparer's Use Only

Preparer's signature ▶	Date	Check if self-employed ☐	Preparer's social security no.
Firm's name (or yours, if self-employed) and address ▶		E.I. No. ▶	
		ZIP code ▶	

363-121-1

Figure 7–1. Form 1120.

Schedule A Cost of Goods Sold (See instructions for Schedule A)

1 Inventory at beginning of year . . . . _____
2 Merchandise bought for manufacture or sale . . . . _____
3 Salaries and wages . . . . _____
4 Other costs (attach schedule) . . . . _____
5 Total—Add lines 1 through 4 . . . . _____
6 Inventory at end of year . . . . _____
7 Cost of goods sold—Subtract line 6 from line 5. Enter here and on line 2, page 1 . . . . _____
8 (a) Check all methods used for valuing closing inventory:
    (i) ☐ Cost
    (ii) ☐ Lower of cost or market as described in Regulations section 1.471–4 (see instructions)
    (iii) ☐ Writedown of "subnormal" goods as described in Regulations section 1.471–2(c) (see instructions)
    (iv) ☐ Other (Specify method used and attach explanation) ▶ _____
  (b) Check if the LIFO inventory method was adopted this tax year for any goods (If checked, attach Form 970.) . . . . . ☐
  (c) If the LIFO inventory method was used for this tax year, enter percentage (or amounts) of closing inventory computed under LIFO . . . . |____
  (d) If you are engaged in manufacturing, did you value your inventory using the full absorption method (Regulations section 1.471–11)? . . . . ☐ Yes ☐ No
  (e) Was there any substantial change in determining quantities, cost, or valuations between opening and closing inventory? . . . ☐ Yes ☐ No
    If "Yes," attach explanation.

Schedule C Dividends and Special Deductions (See instructions for Schedule C)

	(A) Dividends received	(B) %	(C) Special deductions: multiply (A) × (B)
1 Domestic corporations subject to 85% deduction		85	
2 Certain preferred stock of public utilities		59.13	
3 Foreign corporations subject to 85% deduction		85	
4 Wholly-owned foreign subsidiaries subject to 100% deduction (section 245(b)) .		100	
5 Total—Add lines 1 through 4. See instructions for limitation	/////	/////	
6 Affiliated groups subject to the 100% deduction (section 243(a)(3))		100	/////
7 Other dividends from foreign corporations not included in lines 3 and 4			/////
8 Income from controlled foreign corporations under subpart F (attach Forms 5471) .			/////
9 Foreign dividend gross-up (section 78)			/////
10 DISC or former DISC dividends not included in line 1 (section 246(d))			/////
11 Other dividends			/////
12 Deduction for dividends paid on certain preferred stock of public utilities (see instructions)	/////	/////	
13 Total dividends—Add lines 1 through 11. Enter here and on line 4, page 1 ⟶		/////	/////
14 Total deductions—Add lines 5, 6 and 12. Enter here and on line 29(b), page 1 ⟶			

Schedule E Compensation of Officers (See instruction for line 12) Complete Schedule E only if your total receipts (line 1(a), plus lines 4 through 10, of page 1, Form 1120) are $150,000 or more.

1. Name of officer	2. Social security number	3. Time devoted to business	Percent of corporation stock owned		6. Amount of compensation	7. Expense account allowances
			4. Common	5. Preferred		
						/////
						/////
Total compensation of officers—Enter here and on line 12, page 1						

Schedule F Bad Debts—Reserve Method (See instruction for line 15)

1. Year	2. Trade notes and accounts receivable outstanding at end of year	3. Sales on account	Amount added to reserve		6. Amount charged against reserve	7. Reserve for bad debts at end of year
			4. Current year's provision	5. Recoveries		
1977						
1978						
1979						
1980						
1981						
1982						

363-121-1

Figure 7–1 (continued).

Schedule J Tax Computation (See instructions for Schedule J on page 7)

Note: **Fiscal year corporations,** see *instructions on page 10. If you are not a member of a controlled group of corporations (sections 1561 and 1563), omit lines 1 and 2, and enter on line 3, the amount from line 44, Part III, of the fiscal year worksheet provided on page 11 of the instructions.*

Calendar year corporations, see instructions for Schedule J on page 7. If you are not a member of a controlled group of corporations (sections 1561 and 1563), omit lines 1 and 2, and start with line 3.

1 Check if you are a member of a controlled group (see sections 1561 and 1563) . . . . ▶ ☐

2 If line 1 is checked, see instructions and enter your portion of the $25,000 amount in each taxable income bracket:

    (i) $.............................. *(ii)* $.............................. *(iii)* $.............................. *(iv)* $..............................

3 Income tax (see instructions to figure the tax; enter this tax or alternative tax from Schedule D, whichever is less). Check if from Schedule D ▶ ☐ . . . .

4 **(a)** Foreign tax credit (attach Form 1118) . . . .

   (b) Investment credit (attach Form 3468) . . . .

   (c) Jobs credit (attach Form 5884) . . . .

   (d) Employee stock ownership credit (applies only to fiscal year 1982–83 corporations—see instructions) . . . .

   (e) Research credit (attach Form 6765) . . . .

   (f) Possessions tax credit (attach Form 5735) . . . .

   (g) Alcohol fuel credit (attach Form 6478) . . . .

   (h) Credit for fuel produced from a nonconventional source (see instructions) . .

5 Total—Add lines 4(a) through 4(h) . . . .

6 Subtract line 5 from line 3 . . . .

7 Personal holding company tax (attach Schedule PH (Form 1120)) . . . .

8 Tax from recomputing prior-year investment credit (attach Form 4255) . . . .

9 Minimum tax on tax preference items (see instructions—attach Form 4626) . . . . . .

10 Total tax—Add lines 6 through 9. Enter here and on line 31, page 1 . . . .

Additional Information (See page 8 of instructions) | Yes | No

G Did you claim a deduction for expenses connected with:

  (1) Entertainment facility (boat, resort, ranch, etc.)? . . . .

  (2) Living accommodations (except employees on business)? . .

  (3) Employees attending conventions or meetings outside the North American area? (See section 274(h)) . . . . .

  (4) Employees' families at conventions or meetings? . . .

    If ''Yes,'' were any of these conventions or meetings outside the North American area? (See section 274(h)) . . . . .

  (5) Employee or family vacations not reported on Form W–2? . .

H (1) Did you at the end of the tax year own, directly or indirectly, 50% or more of the voting stock of a domestic corporation? (For rules of attribution, see section 267(c).) . . .

    If ''Yes,'' attach a schedule showing: (a) name, address, and identifying number; (b) percentage owned; (c) taxable income or (loss) (e.g., if a Form 1120: from Form 1120, line 28, page 1) of such corporation for the tax year ending with or within your tax year; (d) highest amount owed by you to such corporation during the year; and (e) highest amount owed to you by such corporation during the year.

  (2) Did any individual, partnership, corporation, estate or trust at the end of the tax year own, directly or indirectly, 50% or more of your voting stock? (For rules of attribution, see section 267(c).) If ''Yes,'' complete (a) through (e) . . . . .

    (a) Attach a schedule showing name, address, and identifying number.

    (b) Enter percentage owned ▶ ....

    (c) Was the owner of such voting stock a person other than a U.S. person? (See instructions) . . . .

    If ''Yes,'' enter owner's country ▶ ....

    (d) Enter highest amount owed by you to such owner during the year ▶ ....

    (e) Enter highest amount owed to you by such owner during the year ▶ ....

(Note: For purposes of H(1) and H(2), "highest amount owed" includes loans and accounts receivable/payable.)

I Refer to page 9 of instructions and state the principal:

  Business activity ....

  Product or service ....

J Were you a U.S. shareholder of any controlled foreign corporation? (See sections 951 and 957.) If ''Yes,'' attach Form 5471 for each such corporation . . . .

K At any time during the tax year, did you have an interest in or a signature or other authority over a bank account, securities account, or other financial account in a foreign country (see instructions)? . . . .

L Were you the grantor of, or transferor to, a foreign trust which existed during the current tax year, whether or not you have any beneficial interest in it? . . . .

  If ''Yes,'' you may have to file Forms 3520, 3520–A or 926.

M During this tax year, did you pay dividends (other than stock dividends and distributions in exchange for stock) in excess of your current and accumulated earnings and profits? (See sections 301 and 316) . . . .

  If ''Yes,'' file Form 5452. If this is a consolidated return, answer here for parent corporation and on Form 851, Affiliations Schedule, for each subsidiary.

N During this tax year was any part of your tax accounting records maintained on a computerized system? . . . .

363–121–1

Figure 7–1 (continued).

159

Schedule L | **Balance Sheets**

	Beginning of tax year		End of tax year	
ASSETS	(A)	(B)	(C)	(D)
1 Cash				
2 Trade notes and accounts receivable				
(a) Less allowance for bad debts				
3 Inventories				
4 Federal and State government obligations . . .				
5 Other current assets (attach schedule)				
6 Loans to stockholders				
7 Mortgage and real estate loans				
8 Other investments (attach schedule)				
9 Buildings and other depreciable assets				
(a) Less accumulated depreciation				
10 Depletable assets				
(a) Less accumulated depletion				
11 Land (net of any amortization)				
12 Intangible assets (amortizable only)				
(a) Less accumulated amortization				
13 Other assets (attach schedule)				
14 Total assets				
LIABILITIES AND STOCKHOLDERS' EQUITY				
15 Accounts payable				
16 Mtges, notes, bonds payable in less than 1 year . .				
17 Other current liabilities (attach schedule) . . .				
18 Loans from stockholders				
19 Mtges, notes, bonds payable in 1 year or more . .				
20 Other liabilities (attach schedule)				
21 Capital stock: (a) Preferred stock . . .				
(b) Common stock . . .				
22 Paid-in or capital surplus				
23 Retained earnings—Appropriated (attach sch.) . .				
24 Retained earnings—Unappropriated				
25 Less cost of treasury stock	( )		( )	
26 Total liabilities and stockholders' equity				

Schedule M–1 | **Reconciliation of Income Per Books With Income Per Return** Do not complete this schedule if your total assets (line 14, column (D), above) are less than $25,000.

1 Net income per books		7 Income recorded on books this year not included in this return (itemize)
2 Federal income tax		(a) Tax-exempt interest $..............
3 Excess of capital losses over capital gains		
4 Income subject to tax not recorded on books this year (itemize)............		
		8 Deductions in this tax return not charged against book income this year (itemize)
5 Expenses recorded on books this year not deducted in this return (itemize)		(a) Depreciation . . . $..............
(a) Depreciation . . . . . $..............		(b) Contributions carryover . $..............
(b) Contributions carryover . . $..............		
		9 Total of lines 7 and 8 . . . .
6 Total of lines 1 through 5		10 Income (line 28, page 1)—line 6 less 9 . .

Schedule M–2 | **Analysis of Unappropriated Retained Earnings Per Books (line 24 above)** Do not complete this schedule if your total assets (line 14, column (D), above) are less than $25,000.

1 Balance at beginning of year		5 Distributions: (a) Cash . . . . . .
2 Net income per books		(b) Stock . . . . .
3 Other increases (itemize)................		(c) Property . . . . .
		6 Other decreases (itemize)................
		7 Total of lines 5 and 6 . . . .
4 Total of lines 1, 2, and 3		8 Balance at end of year (line 4 less 7) . . .

Figure 7–1 (continued).

Schedule C	Dividends and Special Deductions (See instructions for Schedule C)			
		(A) Dividends received	(B) %	(C) Special deductions: multiply (A) × (B)
1	Domestic corporations subject to 85% deduction		85	
2	Certain preferred stock of public utilities.		59.13	
3	Foreign corporations subject to 85% deduction		85	
4	Wholly-owned foreign subsidiaries subject to 100% deduction (section 245(b)) .		100	
5	Total—Add lines 1 through 4. See instructions for limitation			
6	Affiliated groups subject to the 100% deduction (section 243(a)(3))		100	
7	Other dividends from foreign corporations not included in lines 3 and 4			
8	Income from controlled foreign corporations under subpart F (attach Forms 5471) .			
9	Foreign dividend gross-up (section 78)			
10	DISC or former DISC dividends not included in line 1 (section 246(d))			
11	Other dividends			
12	Deduction for dividends paid on certain preferred stock of public utilities (see instructions)			
13	Total dividends—Add lines 1 through 11. Enter here and on line 4, page 1 			
14	Total deductions—Add lines 5, 6 and 12. Enter here and on line 29(b), page 1			

Figure 7–2. Schedule C.

46% tax bracket. Obviously, we are assuming maximum tax brackets for both you and your corporation.

	Personal Investment 50% Tax Bracket	Corporate Investment 46% Tax Bracket
Investment of $250,000 at 10% dividend rate equals	$25,000	$25,000
Less exclusion: 85% corporate exclusion married filing joint—personal exclusion	200	21,250
Taxable income	$24,800	$ 3,750
Times the tax rate	50%	46%
Income tax liability	12,400	1,725
Amount of taxes saved		10,675
Percentage saved		86%

Wow! That's so dramatic that you want to retain and invest much more money.

Does the IRS object to your retaining and investing more than $250,000? It depends. When your corporation accumulates earnings and profits, you run the risk of the accumulated earnings penalty.

THE ACCUMULATED EARNINGS PENALTY

The accumulated earnings penalty is pretty stiff: 27½% of the first $100,000 and 38½% on any excess. This tax is purely punitive and is an addition to the regular corporate tax. It is not imposed on any corporation that does not accumulate over $250,000 ($150,000 for personal service corporations). Accumulated earnings over these amounts are subject to the tax.

Unless. . . . even if your accumulation exceeds $250,000, you can avoid the penalty if you can demonstrate "reasonably anticipated needs of the business." The funds do not have to be reinvested in the business immediately; but you must have definite future needs that are spelled out in some detail and documented in your corporate minutes.

The tax courts have found accumulations reasonable when they were to be used for:

1. Business expansion
2. Mergers
3. Acquisitions
4. Purchase of land and/or building
5. Reserve against the threat of strike
6. Future operating costs when expansion is expected to create short-term operating losses
7. Future purchases of goods in bulk to avoid financing
8. Reserve by recession-sensitive firms against future slumps

You should be prepared to document large excess accumulations with complete minutes, reports, articles, correspondence, and anything that will back up your contention that you have a legitimate business need for the accumulated funds.

Let's assume at this point that you've accumulated some funds and feel you're in no danger of the accumulated earnings penalty, but you're not quite sure what to do with the money until the business needs it.

I'm going to take the liberty of confining my remarks to selecting dividend-producing investments. You can, however, choose from the full spectrum of investments. You are limited to those "a prudent man" would use if you have stockholders to account to; if not, you can invest in almost anything. Remember, however, that these are corporate assets. They should be paid for with a corporate check and insured in the corporate name. The title (if applicable) should be in the corporate name. Investments in art, antiques, and so forth must be on corporate territory—don't take the art home to hang.

DIVIDEND-PRODUCING INVESTMENTS

Let's look now at choosing dividend-producing investments.

Mutual Funds

If your corporate portfolio is $50,000 or less, I would suggest you consider investing through a mutual fund. In simple terms, this is a means of pooling the investment funds of many people who share the same investment goal. A mutual fund is not so much an investment as it is a *means of investing*. Full-time, professional investment managers are employed by the mutual fund to select the finest investments available within the investment objective of its participants.

Services of the Mutual Fund

In the last few years, mutual fund assets have grown to the incredible total of more than $250 billion. The number of shareholders is somewhere in the neighborhood of about 18 million. One of the reasons for this dramatic growth is the range of customer services and advantages that mutual funds offer. A simple listing of these services and advantages would include:

1. Diversification
2. Automatic reinvestment
3. Ease of dollar-cost averaging
4. Matching personal financial objectives to your investment program
5. Exchange privileges
6. Professional management for your heirs in the event of your death
7. Record keeping
8. Withdrawal plans
9. Retirement plans

Let's look at each of these points in detail.

Diversification

The Investment Company Act of 1940 assures you of diversification by providing that a mutual fund may not have more than 5% of its assets in any one company or own more than 10% of the outstanding shares in any one company. The regulation guarantees your investment in at least 20 companies. In reality, most funds hold 100–150 different stocks across industry groups.

Automatic Reinvestment

Mutual-fund investment accounts can be opened with a fairly small amount of money. Some funds have no minimum; others have minimums of $1,000 or more. You can add to your account in amounts ranging from $25 to $100. Taking the time and making the commitment for the initial investment is the easiest part for most of us. It's disciplining ourselves to add to the account that is difficult.

Automatic reinvestment helps you in this respect because your dividends and capital gains are automatically used to buy more shares of the fund. Not only is this a more efficient way to use dividends and capital gains, it accelerates the compounding effect of your account.

Ease of Dollar-Cost Averaging

When you buy mutual-fund shares, you invest a fixed dollar amount and buy fractional shares. For example, suppose you wanted to buy $500 worth of a fund selling for $10.42 a share. You would write a check for an even $500 and would then own 47.9846 shares.

Let's assume you've decided to put $500 monthly into the mutual fund you've selected for your retained-earnings account. You can write a check each month to the mutual fund for this amount or authorize a bank to automatically draft your account for the purchase.

Dollar-cost averaging, which basically means you buy in both up and down markets consistently so as to average out your cost, takes advantage of the only sure thing about the stock market: that it fluctuates.

Ease of Matching Personal Financial Objectives to Your Investment Program

Mutual funds are highly regulated investments. A fund must describe its investment objective in its prospectus, and it cannot change its objective without the consent of the shareholders. Funds almost never change their objective because they are usually part of a family of funds with each "member" being a different type of fund. If management wants a different financial objective, it establishes a new fund with this objective, rather than trying to convince shareholders to change the objective of the existing fund.

A mutual fund's objective is considered so important that many informational services categorize the funds by their objectives. Such categories would include: growth, growth-plus-income, balanced income, bond funds, specialty funds, international funds, and option-income funds.

Categorization, combined with the funds' commitment to their financial objective, makes it possible to match your objective to a mutual fund very closely.

Exchange Privilege

Suppose, however, your investment objective changes. If your mutual fund is part of a family of funds, you can simply exchange your fund for another in the family. This can be done by phone or mail. Some funds charge a $5.00 fee. Although there is no commission on the trade, please note that the IRS considers this transaction a sale so you do owe capital-gains tax.

If you have a loss, but still have confidence in your fund, you can establish the loss by exchanging your fund for another, waiting at least 31 days (to be sure IRS won't call it a "wash sale"), and then moving back to your original position.

Professional Management for Your Heirs in the Event of Your Death

In some families, only one member excels at investing. If this is the case in your family, consider taking positions in some good mutual funds for your spouse's benefit. That way your spouse won't be concerned with trying to match your performance in the event of your death. The professional management team provided by the mutual fund will be at work for your family, and your family can add to the account as future liquidations of investments are made.

Record Keeping

Mutual funds shine their brightest where record keeping is concerned. You will receive statements routinely, but, in addition, you will get federal tax form 1099 at the end of the year showing exactly how much capital gains and/or dividends were paid to you during the year. Many funds send this statement on a form that tells you exactly where on your personal income-tax return to report the income!

To have a complete record of your mutual-fund account, you need only keep the last statement for each year. You will not need to keep up with certificates either, since these can be held for you by the mutual fund's transfer agent.

Withdrawal Plans

A withdrawal plan works very simply. You complete and mail a withdrawal application to the transfer agent. Describe the amount and frequency of the checks you would like to receive from the fund. You will receive a status report of your account with your check. If earnings (dividends and capital gains) are not enough to pay your requested amount, then the fund will begin sending you a portion of your original investment. You can change or stop the arrangement anytime you wish.

Now let's combine a few of the things we've learned.

Suppose you set up a deferred-compensation program for yourself. (Remember these can be totally discriminatory, so you can have one only for yourself if you wish.) Each month you put the funds into a mutual fund with a strong dividend-paying orientation. Be sure to keep the title in the corporate name. Remember that deferred compensation is a legitimate need for accumulated earnings, so the total value of the account will not create a retained-earnings problem.

When you decide to retire, you may authorize the withdrawal for just enough to use up the account in 5, 10, or 15 years, whatever you find appropriate in keeping with your personal income needs and income-tax bracket at retirement.

Retirement Plans

The IRS has qualified most mutual funds for use in IRAs, Keoghs, and corporate pension and profit-sharing plans.

Suppose you pick an average mutual fund. The industry average for the last five years for common-stock mutual funds is a 79% increase in value when capital gains and dividends are reinvested. That's 15.8% per year annualized. Think of those earnings compounding free from current income taxation!

To quote the national syndicated columnist George Wheeler, "The best idea for anyone with a decade or more before retirement, and especially for the young with several decades, would be a substantial commitment to mutual funds investing in common stocks."

What you should look for is a mutual fund invested primarily in dividend-producing common stocks. The dividends will be 85% excluded from taxation, and the balance of the earnings will be in the form of long-term capital gains. Your corporation will have a 28% maximum tax on these gains.

Mutual funds that invest in money-market instruments are money-market mutual funds. The earnings on these funds, while excellent in the last few years, are interest and not eligible for the dividend exclusion.

Bond mutual funds invest in government obligations, corporate notes, and/or money-market instruments. These funds are considered quite conservative, but the earnings are interest and therefore not eligible for the dividend exclusion.

Your financial planner can, of course, help you select the best mutual fund, but here are some factors to consider.

Load vs. No-load Mutual Funds

In the past few years, the theme song of many financial writers has been, "Don't buy a mutual fund with a sales charge—buy only no-load funds."

Indeed, there are many fine no-load funds, but don't lose sight of the fact that there are also many fine load funds.

I don't think you should make your decision solely on the basis of the load. If you find the right fund, with a good performance record and a good management team, buy it. Concern yourself with what it pays, not with what it costs. I own shares in three mutual funds—two of which are load funds. They have performed so well that the load has been immaterial.

Size of Fund

The size of the fund can be important in your determining whether its investment objectives can be achieved. Since a large fund can buy a more diversified portfolio and grow in a more orderly way, the objective of a stable income is more likely to be realized with a larger fund.

Structure of Management

One of the things we are very careful to avoid in our recommendations to clients is a mutual fund managed pretty much by one person. We like to see a strong management team, backed by a staff of analysts, each of whom is a specialist in some field such as oils, automotives, and utilities.

The Investment Record

Mutual funds have nowhere to hide—there are a number of services that track the investment record of mutual funds. You should study these records, but be careful of simply picking up a simple comparison, such as last year's percentage gain of one fund over another. Remember that mutual funds are not intended for speculation; they are a means to make relatively long-term investments. Look at relative performance over a one-year, five-year, and ten-year period, then consider the market environment during each of these periods. I prefer funds with more stable growth patterns during good markets and bad. Some funds are characterized by volatile upswings in a bull market, making their performance look excellent during this period.

The problem is that they have an equally volatile downswing when the market turns. Look for a fund that can enjoy good growth in an up market, but can hold its own in a down market.

Your financial planner can provide you with material describing mutual-fund performance. There are also several services that chart the performance of mutual funds individually and by industry. The most common are:

1. The mutual fund section in the back of Standard & Poor's *Stock Guide*

2. *Wiesenberger Investment Service* reports
3. Lipper Analytical Services: *Mutual Fund Performance Analysis*
4. United Mutual Fund Selector

Some things to look for in these reports are:

1. Total return (percentage increase on the original investment)
2. Capital-gain distributions
3. Dividends
4. Increases in the worth of each share

Age of Fund

Generally, I prefer a fund that has been in existence more than five years because I like to be able to assess its performance in up markets and down. Age gives management time to season and time for its investment philosophies to jell.

Makeup of the Portfolio

Points to consider are:

1. The number of holdings in the portfolio
2. The fields in which the fund is invested
3. The size of firms in which the fund is invested
4. The age of firms in which the fund is invested
5. What percentage of the portfolio is in cash

The Time Factor

From time-to-time when I talk about mutual funds someone asks me whether they aren't primarily for the unsophisticated—the so-called "little guys" who don't know enough about choosing stock market investments for themselves and so resort to mutual funds. Absolutely not!

For our clients a mutual fund is chosen over individual stocks because of time. It takes a great deal of time to choose good stock-market investments. Many people feel that they simply can't take that much time away from their own career demands. Some folks say, "I let my broker handle my portfolio." Well, that brings you back to square one because if you're going to let someone else do it, why not use a mutual fund where you get a great deal of diversification, highly competent management, and constant supervision of the portfolio? Even the most conscientious broker can't give your portfolio constant attention unless the size of the portfolio makes you an extremely important customer.

Choosing Individual Stocks

"O.K.," you're saying, "but I still want to choose a few stocks for myself." Entire volumes, indeed libraries, have been written on the subject of choosing stocks. A full treatment is beyond the scope of this book since we are primarily interested in choosing high-dividend-paying stocks.

For our purposes, we want to look at two major categories of securities: common and preferred stock. Common stock falls into two categories: growth and income stocks.

Growth Stocks

Growth stocks are issued by corporations that plow back most (in some cases all) of their profits to finance growth in the hope that this business expansion will result in increases in the market price of the stock.

Income Stocks

Income stocks are issued by corporations that pay out a large portion of their profits as dividends to the stockholders. If you buy common stocks, you will probably prefer the income stocks. However, it would be unfair not to point out that any profit you make on a growth stock is treated as capital gain. If you have owned the stock at least one year, only 40% of your gain is taxable.

Preferred Stock

Preferred stock is a hybrid with characteristics of bonds and common stock. Like bonds, preferred stock pays a fixed income, but it is paid from profits and is not a required payment. Preferred stocks, as hybrids, have neither the guarantees of bonds nor the appreciation potential of common stock.

Because preferred stocks are fixed income securities, the market price tends to move in reverse relation to the interest—up when interest rates drop and down when interest rates increase.

The word *preferred* does not mean these stocks are better—it only means that preferred stockholders are paid their dividends before common stockholders. In other words, preferred stockholders are "preferred" as to dividends.

Many financial advisors dislike preferred stock because there is no appreciation potential. This is definitely a valid point, and if you can find good common stock with a reasonable P/E and a competitive dividend (relative to other income-producing assets) you are probably better off than with preferred.

Price/Earnings Ratio

The P/E is a sort of value yardstick, figured as per-share earnings divided by the market price. To understand the P/E ratio, let's take some really simple examples. Suppose you take $100 to your bank, and the bank tells you that, with your $100, the bank can earn $5. It's important that it is understood that the $5 is bank earnings and not earnings to the depositor on the $100 deposit. The P/E ratio deals with what the company *earns*, not with what it pays out to its shareholders.

The arithmetic involved is:

$$\frac{\text{Price}}{\text{Earnings}} = \frac{\$100}{\$5} = \$20$$

The bank would have a P/E of 20.

The true significance of the ratio, however, is in the reciprocal. This is calculated by dividing the P/E into 100. The resulting number is the earnings yield. In our example:

$$\frac{100}{20} = 5\%$$

Now let's look at why you will probably prefer stocks with lower P/Es. Let's assume that the following year you go to the same bank to make an investment of another $100. The bank manager tells you that because of some new activities, the bank can earn $10.00 with your $100. The P/E is now 10:

$$\frac{\text{Price}}{\text{Earnings}} = \frac{\$100}{\$10} = 10$$

The reciprocal is:

$$\frac{10}{100} = 10\%$$

With a P/E of 20—earnings of 5%.

With a P/E of 10—earnings of 10%.

See why the lower P/E is more desirable?

Now let's put this in the context of stock selection. Assume that interest rates are about 13%. To duplicate that in a stock would dictate a P/E of 7½.

$$\frac{100}{7.7} = 13\%$$

So you will prefer P/Es of 5–9.

If you go to a P/E of 9, that means the company is earning only 11¼%. This is still acceptable since you lose so little of it to taxation.

Book Value

Here we are considering book value as a measure of what the company's assets could be sold for if its directors decided to cease operations.

Suppose the company you were considering had net assets worth $20 million and $1 million shares of stock outstanding. Its book value would be $20 a share. If the company went out of business, you could reasonably expect to get about $20 for every share you owned. If you paid $20 you would break even and if you paid less, you'd make a profit on the liquidation. It's easy to see why I suggest you pay an amount as close to book value as possible. Some excellent stocks even sell below book value from time to time!

Let's look now at the steps involved in selecting your income-producing stocks.

1. Get a copy of the *Wall Street Journal, Barrons,* or the *Financial Weekly.* (A list of publications and addresses is at the end of the chapter.) Go to the stock table where you will find lists of stocks with information about their yield (in percentage), dividend (in amount), P/E ratio, volume of sales, and price. You are looking for stocks with a dividend of 8%–9% or greater. This will eliminate a large number on the list. You should look for stocks with fairly low P/Es. Price-earnings ratios of 5 to 9 are reasonable in the market environment that prevails at this writing.

2. After using the criteria in number 1 to develop a manageable list, look up the book values of each prospect. You will prefer book values as close to the price of the stock as possible. They are normally expressed as a percentage. *Barrons* and the *Financial Weekly* both publish book values.

3. Since each new criterion eliminates large numbers of stocks, you probably now have a fairly small workable list. Now let's begin to apply some subjective criteria. This is where your good business sense takes over. Ask yourself the following questions:

   a. What business is the firm in?

   b. Is it recession sensitive? Inflation sensitive?

   c. How does that fit in with the current economic environment?

   d. Do they have foreign subsidiaries?

   e. Are they politically vulnerable?

   f. What is the general state of their industry?

To answer these questions and others you may think of, start by asking for a copy of each prospects' latest annual report. Also ask for its "10-K," which the Securities and Exchange Commission (SEC) requires and which includes a description of the company's business; a summary of its operations; a list of its properties; a list of its parent and subsidiary companies; any legal proceedings pending against the company; and increases and decreases in the company's outstanding securities, the number of shareholders, and remuneration of officers.

Once you get to the point of seriously considering the purchase of a stock, you may want to call and talk to management. Don't think this is presumptuous on your part. Most firms of any size have someone paid to take your call—in some cases there are staffs of people who will be pleased to hear their stock survived your rigorous elimination process and will want to provide you with information about their company.

Okay, you've done all your homework: checked dividends, P/Es, and book values. You've talked to management. You've finally found the stock you want and have owned it for a while. It's doing nicely and you feel just fine about the whole process.

Except . . . the stock is up. And now the agony begins. Should you hold and wait for more profit or should you sell? I've often said that knowing what and when to buy is twice as easy as knowing when to sell. But really, it's not that difficult.

A few general guidelines may help. First, don't get married to a stock. Believe me, the stock doesn't know you sold it and doesn't take your decision personally. Second, remember the famous dictum usually attributed to Bernard Baruch: Nobody ever went broke taking a profit. So don't be heartsick if you make some money because you didn't make it all. There are worse things than selling too soon. Third, reapply the rules you used to select your stocks. Would they still survive your elimination process? No? Then sell. If you wouldn't buy them, don't hold them. Replace the stock with one that fits your criteria.

If your stock goes down, make sure you've got as much information as possible. Start by calling the company and ask for its reason why the stock went down. It may be that a large block was dropped on the market by an estate or an institutional trader. If it's down because earnings are off, or for some reason as fundamental as the earnings, you may as well take your lumps and get out. Don't let losses ride. Better to get the money at work in a·more rewarding environment.

The Greed-And-Fear Syndrome

Be careful not to fall into a greed-and-fear syndrome. This situation arises when investors get out of a depressed or falling market because of their fears that it will never recover, and conversely they invest in a rising market because of their greed. Many market analysts attribute the giant stock market swings to this phenomenon.

I believe that smart, thorough people can make money in any market. I believe that we will probably have another great bull market in the 1980's. But I also believe that you should ignore "the market" regardless of whether it's up or down. If that sounds like sheer nonsense, let me explain why. For one thing, you don't (and can't) buy "the market." It is not for sale, and your problem is not how "the market" is doing, but how *your stocks* are doing.

When you invest according to the guidelines you've established, you're not really investing in "the market": You're investing in carefully chosen companies. The market you're concerned with now is *their* market. Can your chosen company's stock continue to pay dividends at a rate acceptable to you and hold its market price stable or cause it to increase?

Don't let "the market" be anything but a mechanism for the buying and selling of shares of carefully selected firms.

Make some profits in your own company, invest in a good mutual fund or a few good dividend-producing stocks, and let Uncle Sam help you compound faster through the 85% exclusion.

RECOMMENDED PUBLICATIONS

Following is a list of publications that provide valuable information to help you in setting up your investment program.

The Wall Street Journal
200 Burnett Road
Chicopee, Massachusetts 01021

Excellent for business news. It has the daily stock tables with the P/E ratios, but you will need another publication for statistical profiles.

Barron's
The Dow Jones Business & Financial Weekly
200 Burnett Road
Chicopee, Massachusetts 01021

Strong suit is details of the latest quarterly or interim earnings. Doesn't show book value.

The Financial Weekly
P.O. Box 26991
Richmond, Virginia 23261

Lists earnings, P/E ratios, and book values. Doesn't have daily quotes, and has very little news. Tells you almost everything you need to know to get past the "numbers" selection process. This one is my favorite.

Standard & Poor's
345 Hudson Street
New York, New York 10014

Monthly stock guide. Gives a fairly detailed picture of each company's market performance going back several years, P/E ratios, a few book values.

Value Line Investment Survey
Arnold Bernhard & Co., Inc.
711 Third Avenue
New York, New York 10017

Gives both an analysis of stocks and an interpretation of opinion as to their future performance.

Wiesenberger Investment Service
Warren, Gorham & Lamont, Inc.
210 South Street
Boston, Massachusetts 02111

Mutual-fund rating service giving performance by time periods.

Lipper Analytical Services: Mutual Fund Performance Analysis
Lipper Analytical Dist.
74 Trinity Place
New York, New York 10006

United Mutual Fund Selector
United Business Service Company
210 Newbury Street
Boston, Massachusetts 02116

Money Magazine
Time, Inc.
3435 Wilshire Blvd.
Los Angeles, California 90010

Forbes Magazine
60 Fifth Avenue
New York, New York 10011

Retirement Plans

Retirement plans are certainly among the best tax shelters available to the self-employed, and the primary focus of this chapter will be on retirement plans. However, it's important to understand the fundamentals of retirement *planning* before we move on to retirement *plans*, so I'd like to begin by taking you through those fundamentals.

RETIREMENT PLANNING

First, determine exactly what your retirement income needs are in *today's* dollars using the budget worksheet in the appendix. Don't get carried away by eliminating expenses at retirement. For example, clients often point out to me that by the time they retire, their house will be fully paid for. That's true, but remember that you will also have a 20- to 30-year-old house by then. Roofs and air conditioners need replacing, and you might go on a remodeling binge. Your children may be grown and through college, but if they move away and have children you may find your travel expenses to visit the grandchildren every once in a while nearly equals tuition.

My observation after many years as a financial planner is that the amount you spend at retirement doesn't change that drastically. The *nature* of your spending will change, but the amount remains rather stable, *in today's dollars*.

To see the results of 8% inflation on your retirement planning, let's look at an example. Then I'll show you how to do your own projections at whatever inflation rate you think is appropriate for you. Table 8–1 shows the number of future dollars needed annually to duplicate the purchasing power of various levels of today's dollars at 8% inflation.

Let's assume that you are 45 years old, plan to work until age 65, and want to have a retirement income equal to $50,000 in today's dollars. Look at the table. Notice that $50,000 in today's dollars 20 years from now translates to $233,045 annually in future dollars.

TABLE 8–1
Future Dollars Needed to Duplicate Today's Purchasing Power
(8% Inflation Rate)

Today's Dollars Needed Annually	Years from Now					
	5	10	15	20	25	30
20,000	29,386	43,178	63,442	93,218	136,968	201,252
30,000	44,079	64,767	95,163	139,827	205,452	301,878
40,000	58,772	86,356	126,884	186,436	273,936	402,504
50,000	73,465	107,945	158,605	233,045	342,420	503,130
60,000	88,158	129,534	190,326	279,654	410,904	603,756
70,000	102,851	151,123	222,047	326,263	479,388	704,382
80,000	117,544	172,712	253,768	372,872	547,872	805,008
90,000	132,237	194,301	285,489	419,481	616,356	905,634
100,000	146,930	215,890	317,210	466,090	684,840	1,006,260

Now let's get down to work. You've worked through your budget. You know with some accuracy what your retirement income projection should be. Now you want to know exactly what you need to do to achieve these goals.

Following is a worksheet with a space for you to fill in your own numbers and my example of the 45-year-old who plans to work 20 years. I'm going to be taking you through compound interest tables. (See Appendix D.) These tables are frequently intimidating simply because there are so many members congregated on a page. But, please, please don't take one look and skip this section. This is a critical step toward getting a handle on your retirement planning, and compound interest tables are not difficult to work with. If you can operate a business at a profit, you can master these tables with just a few minutes of concentrated effort.

	Example	*You*
1. Future dollars needed annually to duplicate the purchasing power of ($50,000) $ _____ of todays dollars at 8% inflation is ($50,000 × 4.6609)	$233,045	_____
2. Capital required to produce $233,045 _____ annually at 12% yield is	$1,942,041	_____
3. Minus the value of current capital assets (excluding the home) projected at 12% for _____ years ($ _____ ($50,000) × _____ ((.6462)=)	$ 482,310	_____
4. Additional capital to be accumuluated by retirement.	$1,459,731	_____
5. Annual savings required to accumulate at 12% per year for _____ (20) years ($1,459,731 × .0138 =)	$ 20,144	_____

Step One. To determine the amount of future dollars you will need annually at the inflation rate you have determined to be appropriate for you, go to the table labeled "Future Worth of One Dollar at Compound Interest" in Appendix D.

Let's assume you think 10% is likely to be the inflation rate, that your annual needs in today's dollars are $65,000, and you plan to work 20 more years. Go to the column labeled 10% and run your finger down to 20 years. You will see the factor 6.7274. Multiply that times $65,000. The result $437,281 is how much you will need annually in 20 years to buy what you can buy today with $65,000 if inflation is 10%.

Step Two. To determine the amount of capital that will be required to generate your income, divide the future dollars needed annually by whatever yield you think is appropriate considering your personal risk tolerance. For my example, I've used 12%. As you can see, if you want to generate $233,045 a year in income and your capital base throws off 12% yield, you need $1,942,041. If you are extremely conservative, you may want to use a lower yield assumption than 12%.

Step Three. You probably already have some investments and/or savings. What we want to do now is determine the value of these assets when you retire. The analysis of course, assumes you do not take the earnings (interest, rent, dividends), as current income, but rather allow the asset to compound with the earnings. Do not include your home in this step since that will not be available to produce current income. For my example, I've assumed $50,000 has been invested and is compounding at 12%.

Look now at the table in Appendix D again. Go to the column labeled 12% and run down the column to 20 years. You'll see the number 9.6462. Multiply $50,000 times 9.6462. The result, $482,310, is the future value of your $50,000 *if allowed to compound.* (More detailed instructions are on the table.)

You may need to do several calculations for maximum accuracy. For example, you may own a piece of rural property that is appreciating by 5%–6% a year, a mutual fund that averages out at 12%, and commercial real estate growing at 15% or more. Each item should be figured separately if your assets are growing at disparate rates.

Step Four: Subtract the number in Step 3 from the number in Step 2. The result will be the additional capital you need to accumulate by retirement.

Step Five: Determine how much you need to save/invest each year to reach this figure.

In our example, Step 4 is $1,459.731.

Assume you can keep your money at work at 12%. Go now to the table labeled "Annual Savings Per $1 Needed at Various Interest Rates To Obtain a Predetermined Amount of Capital" in Appendix D. (Accountants call this sinking fund factors.) Go to the column labeled 12% and run your finger down the column labeled 20 years. You'll see the factor 0.0138. Multiply that number times $1,459,731. The result, $20,144, is how much you need to save annually to have an additional $1,459,731 in 20 years.

Let's suppose now you're saying to yourself, *"No way.* I can't save that kind of money each year." You can save $10,000, however. Do you wonder what $10,000 each year will grow to if kept at work at 12%?

For the answer to this question, go back to table labeled "Future Worth of One Dollar Periodically Deposited at Compound Interest." Go to the column labeled 12% and down to 20 years. You will see the factor 72.0524. Multiply $10,000 × 72.0524. The result, $720,524, is how much $10,000 invested *each year* for 20 years at 12% will be worth at the end of 20 years.

QUALIFIED RETIREMENT PLANS

The best way to work toward these goals is through a qualified retirement plan. A qualified retirement plan is a plan that qualifies for tax exemptions under provisions of the Internal Revenue Code and regulations of the Commissioner of Internal Revenue and the Secretary of Labor.

Although unqualified plans have merit also, this chapter includes some descriptions of all the major types of qualified retirement plans. We described unqualified plans in Chapter 5.

A qualified plan usually refers to a pension, profit sharing, stock bonus, annuity, or bond purchase plan that satisfies the requirements of federal code section 401, 403, or 405.

Tax Advantages

Although there are some fairly vigorous requirements to qualify a plan, a simple list of tax advantages may provide enough motivation. Remember that you are an employee and your corporation is the employer.

1. Your company may deduct currently every dollar contributed to a retirement plan up to the statutory limit. This deduction is not affected by whether or not an employee's interest is forfeitable.

2. Employees pay no tax on contributions made on their behalf to a qualified plan. This is true even if the employee has a vested (nonforfeitable) interest. An employee will pay taxes when benefits are distributed.

3. There is no current income on the earnings and income on investments to the retirement trust fund (unless it has unrelated business income).

4. Very favorable tax treatment is allowed on distributions made to employees in a lump sum.

5. Distributions made in installments are allowed special annuity taxation.

6. Lump-sum distributions may be "rolled over" by a participant into an IRA, and taxes further deferred.

7. Lump-sum distributions of benefits attributable to employer (company) contributions escape estate tax to a maximum of $100,000 of distribution if the beneficiary is other than the participant's estate and irrevocably elects not to use the ten-year averaging and partial capital-gains treatment for purposes of computing the income tax due on the distribution. Distributions to a surviving spouse qualify for the marital deduction (refer to Chapter 9).

8. No estate tax is levied on annuity or other payments up to a maximum of $100,000 made under the plan to the beneficiary of the participant.

9. If a participant irrevocably designates a beneficiary to receive death benefits under the plan, the participant has not made a gift that is subject to gift taxes.

This is a pretty impressive list of tax advantages—hopefully enough to persuade you to read on and seriously consider the use of a qualified retirement plan.

Nontax Advantages

In addition to providing a way for you to get money out of your business in a tax-favored manner, a qualified retirement plan offers some nontax advantages. Many of my clients feel that a retirement plan is helpful to them in attracting and retaining more talented and competent staff. As we consider some aspects of plan design you will see how employees who don't make a meaningful contribution to your business do not benefit from the plan to any real degree, but those who help you make money are rewarded.

EMPLOYEE RETIREMENT INCOME SECURITY ACT PLAN (ERISA)

There was a time when retirement plans were horribly abused. Employers installed retirement plans that literally never benefited employees. The Pension Reform Act of 1974 made sweeping changes in the entire area of pension, annuity, profit-sharing, stock bonus, and employee welfare plans.[1] The purpose of the act was to protect employees from pension-fund abuses.

ERISA sets rigid standards of fiduciary responsibility, imposes restrictions on certain kinds of investments, and penalizes specifically prohibited transactions.

ERISA created detailed requirements on plan registration. It requires disclosures relative to plan operations to the Internal Revenue Service, the Department of Labor, and to plan participants and their beneficiaries.

The Act also established a mandatory system of plan termination insurance, designed to protect participants in a pension plan against loss of benefits in the event that an insured plan should be terminated. It also provided for a new type of tax-favored individual retirement savings program (IRA), which was expanded twice: once by the Revenue Act of 1978 and again by the Economic Recovery Tax Act of 1981.

Basic Requirements under ERISA

ERISA makes no requirement that an employer provide any employee benefits. However, if an employer elects to provide employee benefits, ERISA's demands must be met.

The requirements of ERISA fall into two categories: labor law provisions and tax law provisions.

The basic requirements of all qualified plans are:

---

[1]This act is also called the Employee Retirement Income Security Act of 1974 (ERISA).

1. Participation
2. Coverage
3. Vesting
4. Funding
5. Limitations on contributions and benefits
6. Termination insurance
7. Tax-free rollover
8. Fiduciary responsibility and prohibited transactions. Additional, more stringent rules in these areas are applicable to "top-heavy" plans. A top-heavy plan is basically a plan that is unusually favorable to officers and/or key employees. Favorability is spelled out in The Tax Equity and Fiscal Responsibility Act of 1982.

Participation

Generally, an employee who is at least 25 years old and has at least one year of service with the employer must be included in a plan.

There are three exceptions: (1) a plan may set a three-year waiting period if 100% immediate vesting for participants is provided; (2) a defined-benefit plan (a plan that aims at fixed benefits at retirement) may exclude an employee who is within five years of attaining normal retirement age under the plan; and (3) part-time workers, defined as those who have worked less than 1,000 hours per year.

An hour is defined as each hour for which an employee is paid directly or indirectly by the employer for performance of duties or other reasons. Paid vacations, holidays, sickness, disability, and layoffs all count.

Coverage

A qualified plan must cover either

1. Seventy percent or more of all employees, or 80% of all those eligible, if 70% or more of all employees are eligible to benefit under the plan, or
2. All employees under a classification that does not discriminate in favor of employees who are shareholders or other highly compensated individuals.

In applying the 70% and 80% tests, employees who have not satisfied the age or service requirements may be excluded. Employees excluded because of maximum age requirements must be counted. Seasonal and part-time employees do not have to be either included in the plan or counted for the 70% and 80% test.

Employees covered by a collective bargaining unit may be excluded when applying the percentage rule, provided retirement benefits have been the subject of good-faith bargaining under which a pension plan was bargained for but rejected. They do not have to be counted for either the 70% and 80% rule or the antidiscrimination rule.

Let's assume your company has 100 employees, 25 of whom are ineligible for the company's plan because they do not work at least 1,000 hours a year or have not served the stipulated number of years. That leaves 75 employees who must be considered for the purpose of the percentage test.

Now assume that an additional 15 employees are ineligible for any of the reasons just cited. Sixty of the remaining 75 employees would be covered by the plan and the coverage requirement be satisfied:

Number of employees who must be counted for the 70% test	75
Times 70%	
Equals: number of employees who must be covered if the plan is to qualify	53
Number of employees covered	60

If the plan requires employee contributions, only 80% of the 60 eligible employees—or 48 employees—need to participate in the plan to qualify it.

In terms of meeting the provision that a plan must not discriminate, employees of a controlled group of corporations (or a commonly controlled partnership or sole proprietorship) are considered employees of a single employer. This makes it impossible for an employer to avoid the coverage and antidiscrimination rules by operating his business through separate entities rather than a single entity.

Vesting

To "vest" an employee's benefits means that the employee has nonforfeitable ownership in such benefits even though s/he terminates employment. In short, vesting answers the question of when the benefits are actually the employee's. An employee's own contributions to a plan are never forfeitable. Employer contributions, however, may be forfeitable up to the point they become "vested," depending on the terms of the plan and ERISA requirements.

Vesting is another area in which the plan may not discriminate in favor of employees who are officers, shareholders, or highly compensated individuals.

To protect employees who have served long periods of time with a company and are still in danger of losing their accumulated benefits because they quit their job or were discharged, a government-approved plan must provide for some schedule of vesting benefits over the employee's working career.

Before 1974, there was no express regulation of provisions of the law that required vesting of employer contributions when employees terminated employment prior to retirement. Then ERISA took steps to formalize the vesting schedule to be used under private retirement plans. The law is now quite specific about the minimum vesting requirements that must be met in order to qualify a plan.

The IRS has a dual concern regarding vesting:

1. Does the plan satisfy one of the three vesting schedules provided by ERISA?
2. Does the plan's vesting schedule satisfy the general nondiscrimination requirement?

Of the three alternative statutory vesting schedules, none provides less than 50% vesting after 10 years of service and 100% vesting after 15 years of service. The three vesting schedules provided by ERISA are:

1. *Ten-year vesting.* This requirement provides that accrued benefits from employer contributions be 100% vested after ten years of service.
2. *Five-fifteen-year rule.* This is a graded standard under which employees must be at least 25% vested in their accrued benefits derived from employer contributions after five years of covered service and 50% vested after ten years of service. In addition, they must receive vested benefits at the rate of 10% per year for each year of service thereafter, culminating in 100% vesting after 15 years of service. The statutory schedule is:

Years of Service	Nonforfeitable Percentage
5	25
6	30
7	35
8	40
9	45
10	50
11	60
12	70
13	80
14	90
15 or more	100

3. *Rule of 45.* The third minimum vesting schedule provides that employees who have completed at least five years of service and

whose age plus years of service equals or exceeds 45 must have at least 50% nonforfeitable rights to their benefits.

The formula applies as follows:

If years of service equal or exceed	And sum of age and service equals or exceeds	Then the nonforfeitable percentage is
5	45	50
6	47	60
7	49	70
8	51	80
9	53	90
10	55	100

ERISA provided that even if a plan conforms to one of the above three vesting schedules, the IRS could compel more rapid vesting if there was a "pattern of abuse" such as firing employees before they became vested or if there was evidence that the plan operated to favor highly compensated employees.

Funding

"Funding" designates contributions that are made to a plan in order to accumulate a reserve from which to pay its future benefits.

Plans that are covered by the funding rules must set up a "funding standard account" to help the employer and the government administer minimum funding rules. It also assures that an employer who has funded more than the minimum amount required will be credited for the excess and for interest earned on the excess. Conversely, of course, those employers who have paid too little are charged with interest on the underfunding.

The minimum amount that an employer is required to contribute annually to a plan is the sum of:

1. *Normal costs of the plan*. These are the current contributions in keeping with the plan's provisions.

2. *Amounts necessary to amortize past-service costs*. Past-service costs are payments for costs of an employee's services prior to adoption of the pension plan. These costs are normally amortized over 30 years, although under some circumstances they can be amortized over 40 years. A plan does not have to provide for past-service funding. The interest rate used in determining the amortization schedule is the one used when funding rules first apply (normally quite low).

3. *Experienced losses and gains.* This term is quite descriptive. As costs and gains and losses on investments are greater or less than projected, current funding adjusts to reflect these variances. Depending on the nature of the increases or decreases, they may be amortized over 15 years or less.

Not every retirement plan is subject to minimum funding standards. A list of the types of plans that are exempt includes:

1. Profit-sharing or stock-bonus plans
2. Plans that are basically supplemental, providing benefits in excess of the limitations of the Internal Revenue Code, Section 412(b).
3. Plans to which only employees contribute after the date of enactment.
4. Any IRA plans
5. Plans funded exclusively by qualified insurance contracts or group insurance, if the plan has the same characteristics as individual insurance.
6. Certain pension trusts[2]
7. Federal, state, and local government plans
8. Deferred compensation plans that are unfunded and maintained for the primary benefit of highly compensated employees
9. Church plans. A church may elect to have its plan covered. Once made, the election is irrevocable.
10. Plans of certain fraternal societies, if they cover only members, not employees, and the employer of the plan participants doesn't contribute.

Limitations on Contributions and Benefits

The regulations established ceilings on what can be contributed to a retirement and the maximum benefit from a retirement.

Termination Insurance

Certain kinds of plans are required to pay for plan-termination insurance, to insure participants and their beneficiaries against loss of benefits should there be complete or partial termination of the plan. The insurer is the Pension Benefit Guaranty Corporation (PBGC). A solvent employer is liable for reimbursement to PBGC up to an amount equal to 30% of his/her net worth.

---

[2]Covered by code section 501 (c)(18) and created before June 25, 1959.

Tax-free Rollover

The ERISA provides for portability of retirement funds by providing tax-free transfers from fund to fund.

Fiduciary Responsibility and Prohibited Transactions

An individual or business entity is considered a fiduciary to the extent that:

1. Discretionary authority or control can be exercised by the person or entity,
2. The individual or entity receives a fee or other compensation in exchange for investment advice, or
3. The individual or entity has responsibility or authority over administration of the plan.

Individuals or entities who are considered fiduciaries by these descriptions are expressly prohibited from allowing the plans to engage, directly or indirectly, in the following transactions with a "party-in-interest":

1. Selling, leasing, or exchanging property
2. Acquiring security or real property for the plan from any employer if the aggregate fair market value of such property would exceed 10% of the plan's total assets after its acquisition.
3. Furnishing goods, services, or facilities
4. Using assets of the plan for the benefit of a party-in-interest.
5. Transferring assets of the plan to a party-in-interest.
6. Lending money or otherwise extending credit to a party-in-interest.

The Internal Revenue Code refers to a party-in-interest as a "disqualified person" and defines it as:

1. A fiduciary, counsel, or employee of the plan.
2. An individual or business entity providing services to the plan.
3. An employer, if any of the employees are covered by the plan.
4. An owner, direct or indirect, of 50% or more of the:
   a. Combined voting power of all classes of stock entitled to vote or the total shares of all classes of stock of a corporation.
   b. Capital interest or the profit interest of a partnership, or
   c. Beneficial interest of a trust or union corporated enterprise, which is an employer or an employee organization described in (3) or (4) above.

5. A relative (spouse, ancestor, lineal descendant, or spouse of a lineal descendant) of an individual described in the first four entries above.

6. An employee organization, if any of its members is covered by the plan.

There are some exceptions to the prohibited transaction rules. They deal primarily with common-sense needs. For example, the plan can rent office space to house the operation of the plan for a reasonable rent from a party-in-interest. The plan can buy services from parties-in-interest at reasonable compensation. Plan participants can borrow from the plan if loans are adequately secured, made available on a nondiscriminatory basis in accordance with plan provisions, and bear a reasonable rate of interest.

TOP-HEAVY PLANS

The Tax Equity and Fiscal Responsibility Act of 1982 (TEFRA) established additional qualification requirements for plans considered "top heavy." The qualifications are effective for tax years beginning after 1983. A plan is considered "top heavy" if:

1. In a defined benefit plan the present value of the accumulated benefits for key employees exceeds 60% of the total value of such benefits for all employees, or

2. In a defined contribution plan the total account balances of key employees exceeds 60% of the total balances of all plan employees. "Top heaviness" is determined annually as of the last day of the preceding plan year.

Key Employees

A "key employee" is defined by TEFRA as any participant in an employer plan who, at any time during the plan year or any of the four preceding plan years, is:

1. An officer

2. One of ten employees owning directly or indirectly the largest interests in the employer

3. A five-percent-or-greater owner of the employer company

4. A more-than-one-percent owner earning more than $150,000 a year. No more than 50 employees may be treated as officers for these purposes.

A plan held to be "top heavy" must meet more demanding criteria to remain tax qualified. The additional requirements are in three areas:

1. *Vesting*. The plan may either provide

   a. Full vesting after 3 years of service, or

   b. Six-year graduated vesting (that is, 20% after two years and 20% a year for the following four years)

2. *Includable Compensation*. For earned income on which benefits or contributions are based for the group, there is a $200,000 per year limit. The limit will be subjected to cost-of-living adjustments beginning in 1986.[3]

3. *Minimum Benefits/Contributions for Nonkey Employees*. These must be provided on a nonintegrated basis. In the case of a defined benefit plan, the benefit accrued must be at least 2% but is not required to exceed 20% of compensation per year of service. Compensation in this case is the average for the five highest consecutive years.

In the case of a defined contribution plan, the contribution must be not less than three percent of the participant's compensation.

TYPES OF PLANS

Now that we've looked at some of the fundamentals of retirement plans, let's look at the different types of plans and their characteristics. We will be looking at:

1. Defined contribution plans that include profit-sharing and money purchase pension plans
2. Defined benefit plans
3. Target benefit plans
4. Thrift plans
5. Keogh plans
6. Individual retirement accounts (IRA)
7. Simplified employee pension plans (SEPP)

Defined Contribution Plans

A defined contribution plan, as the term implies, defines the contribution to be made to the retirement plan. Since a pension plan must have definitely

---

[3]Internal Revenue Code Section 415 limits.

determinable benefits, the defined contribution plan makes an actuarial projection to determine the benefits an employee will receive at retirement based on annual contributions to which the employer is committed.

The two major types of defined contribution plans are the money purchase pension plan and the profit-sharing plan.

Money Purchase Pension Plan

The money purchase pension plan fixes the employer's (the company's) contribution by a predetermined formula. An employee's benefit depends upon the length of time the employee worked while covered under the plan and the amount of money contributed on his/her behalf each year.

The contribution formula can be expressed in several different ways:

1. *Flat amount formula*. This provides that a set amount of money is contributed to the plan on behalf of the participating employee each year. This formula is fairly unpopular, even though it's very simple, because it does not reflect an employee's income or length of service.

2. *Flat percentage of earnings formula*. This formula fixes the percentage of income contributed annually to the plan on behalf of the employee.

The contribution may be fixed as a combination of these two formulas.

3. *Unit benefit formula*. A "unit" of benefit, which may be expressed as a percentage of compensation or a flat dollar amount, is credited for each year of service.

Maximum deductible contribution is the *lesser of* 25% of the participants' compensation or $30,000 per year.

Profit-Sharing Plan

The other major type of defined contribution plan is a profit-sharing plan. The name of this plan is highly descriptive. Each year the employer contributes a portion of the company's profits to the retirement plan trust.

One of several benefit formulas may be used to determine the employer's annual contribution or your board of directors may determine it. If you prefer a formula, you may want to consider either a flat percentage of profits or some modification. The two most popular modifications are:

1. Percentage of profits above a minimum level; for example, ten percent of all profits in excess of $50,000.

2. Increasing contributions as profits increase; for example, 10% of the first $50,000 of profit; plus 15% of the second $50,000, plus 20% of the third $50,000, and so forth, to the maximum deductible contribution.

The contributions of both a money purchase and profit-sharing plan must be allocated to each employee's account. In fact, these plans are often called "individual accounts plans."

The formula will determine an employee's allocation on the money purchase plan. The profit-sharing contribution may be allocated according to income, length of service, or by allocating to each employee that portion of the employer's contribution represented by the same ratio that such employee's salary bears to the total payroll of all participants under the plan. The critical factor is that the allocation formula must not discriminate in favor of stockholders, officers, or more highly compensated employees.

If you refer to the vesting schedules allowed by ERISA, you will recognize that some employees will be leaving the plan before being fully vested. When employees leave, their funds are "forfeited," to the extent they are not vested. Such forfeited funds are used to reduce corporate contributions to a money purchase plan. With a profit-sharing plan, the forfeited funds are added to the account of the remaining participants. The net result is, of course, to increase the accounts of all plan survivors, *including you*.

Investment gains and losses work exactly the same way: they increase or decrease account balances.

These plans can be integrated with Social Security.

The maximum deductible contribution for a profit-sharing plan is the same as a money purchase plan. These plans are frequently combined, and the typical split is 10%–15% in money purchase; 10%–15% in profit sharing. You can determine the respective percentages yourself, but in combination they must not exceed the lesser of 25% of each participant's compensation or $30,000 a year.

Voluntary Contribution

Voluntary contributions are just what they sound like—contributions that are not required and that do not affect the level of employer contributions.

Participants in money purchase and profit-sharing plans may contribute up to ten percent of their compensation, in addition to contributions made on their behalf by the company.

Voluntary contributions are not tax deductible, but any income earned by the investment of voluntary contributions accumulates tax-free until withdrawn or distributed.

Defined Benefit Plan

A defined benefit plan takes a different approach. This plan defines what you may take out of the plan rather than what you put into it. Once your benefit (at retirement) has been defined, an actuary determines what you must contribute each year to meet the defined goal.

The benefit formulas are similar to those for defined contribution plans: flat amount formula, flat percentage of earnings formula, and unit benefit formula. For example, the flat amount formula with defined contribution states that $X a year will be contributed on behalf of each participant. With defined benefit, the formula states that $X a month (or year) will be provided at retirement.

With the flat percentage of earnings formula, the formula provides that a set percentage of preretirement income will be provided at retirement.

The unit benefit formula provides that a certain percentage of salary for each year of service will be provided to the employee at retirement.

The maximum deductible contribution is then defined as that amount needed to fund the predetermined benefit.

You are allowed to fund the lesser of $90,000 or 100% of average compensation for three highest consecutive years.

Since the thrust of a defined benefit plan is to have a predetermined amount of money in your account when you retire, it probably won't surprise you to learn that forfeited funds are used to reduce corporate contributions. In keeping with this objective, corporate contributions are also adjusted to reflect investment gains and losses.

Defined benefit plans may also be integrated with Social Security and are subject to the vesting requirements discussed earlier, as well as all other ERISA requirements.

Target Benefit Plans

Target benefit plans are a hybrid of defined benefit plans and money purchase plans. Contributions must accumulate a set pool of capital to provide a specified benefit for participants at retirement. In this regard a target benefit resembles a defined benefit plan. A significant departure, however, is that a target benefit does not promise to deliver benefits but simply sets the benefit as a "target." The ultimate benefit depends largely on the investment experience of the plan. In this respect, a target benefit plan resembles a money purchase or a profit-sharing plan.

The limits on annual deductible contributions are determined as though the plan were a defined contribution plan. Contributions are the lesser of $30,000 or as needed to fund a benefit equal to 100% of earned income at retirement, but they may not exceed $30,000 per account per year.

Contributions and their earnings and losses are allocated to the separate accounts of the participants. This is similar to a profit-sharing or money purchase plan and differs from a defined benefit plan.

Thrift Plans

Thrift plans are hybrids of pension, profit-sharing, and stock-bonus plans. They may resemble profit-sharing plans by making employer contributions contingent on current profits or accumulated earnings; they resemble ESOPs by allowing employer securities as an investment; and they resemble pension plans by making employer contributions mandatory.

Thrift plans (sometimes called "savings" plans) may or may not be tax qualified, but in either case are subject to ERISA's fiduciary and reporting requirements. If tax qualified, they must also satisfy the participation requirements of ERISA.

Although thrift plans come in a variety of forms, they all work fundamentally the same. Participating employees contribute a percentage of their compensation to the plan, and the employer makes a contribution to the account in some fixed ratio to the employee's contribution.

For those thrift plans that are tax qualified, an employer may deduct his contribution for income-tax purposes. The employee does not claim this contribution as part of currently taxable income.

Contributions made by the employee, however, must be made with after-tax dollars (no deduction is allowed). Earnings on the contributions of both employee and employer are free from current income tax; consequently, plan assets grow considerably faster than if part of the earnings had to be used to pay income tax.

Withdrawals and distributions are treated in the same way as those from a pension, profit-sharing, and stock-bonus plan.

Typically, employees are required to contribute a percentage of their compensation in order to participate in the plan. This tempted some employers to set the percentage so high that many lower-paid employees were effectively eliminated, since they simply could not afford to commit that much of their compensation.

The IRS has ruled that requiring employee contributions of up to 6% of compensation is *not* discriminatory. An employer can rebut the presumption that higher percentage requirements are discriminatory by proving that the paid employees do participate.[4] This ruling is based on the specific prohibition that tax-qualified plans may not discriminate in favor of officers, shareholder employees, and the highly compensated.

---

[4]Revenue Ruling 59-185, 1959-1 CB86.

Individual Retirement Account

An individual retirement account (IRA) is a retirement plan established, as the term indicates, by individuals rather than businesses. If a business establishes an IRA, it is called a simplified employee pension plan (SEPP).

The Economic Recovery Tax Act of 1981 provided that, beginning in 1982, any individual with earned income can contribute the lesser of 100% of compensation or $2,000 a year to an IRA. Contributions are fully deductible, and earnings on the contributions grow free of current income tax until withdrawn.

An IRA may be used *in addition* to any other retirement plan in which you may be a participant.

If your spouse has earned income, your spouse may also contribute and deduct the lesser of $2,000 or 15% of earned income. If your spouse has no earned income, you can set up a subaccount for him/her in your IRA account and take an additional $250 deduction. With subaccounts, each spouse has right of survivorship in the other's subaccount.

You *may* begin withdrawing at age 59½, but distributions *must* begin no later than the end of the tax year in which you reach age 70½. If you withdraw funds from an IRA before reaching age 59½, you incur a penalty of ten percent on the amount required to be included in your gross income and the entire amount in the account. In addition, the amount distributed must be included in gross income. Withdrawals by death or disability are exempt from the penalty.

Clients sometimes observe that, among a number of employees, only a few are really deserving of extra consideration. An IRA is a good way to do something extra for them. You can give those employees that you wish to favor a bonus to be used to establish an IRA. If you prefer, you can set up an IRA only for yourself and not cover any employees.

Distributions from an IRA are taxed as ordinary income when received. You are entitled to general income averaging but not the more generous ten-year averaging allowed in distributions from other retirement plans.

You can set up an IRA either by participating in a prototype plan established by banks, insurance companies, trade or professional associations, mutual funds, or others; or by adopting a model trust or custodial account.[5] You will require a qualified trustee or custodian for the latter, but this allows you more freedom in choosing your investments, since a variety of investments, rather than those of the prototype, may be used. Your financial planner can refer you to firms that will establish a custodian account for you.

Effective with tax year 1982, participants in qualified thrift plans could

---

[5]Based on Form 5305, Individual Retirement Trust Account, and Form 5305-A, Individual Retirement Custodial Account.

either make tax deductible contributions to the thrift plan *instead* of IRA contributions or nondeductible contributions to the thrift plan *plus* deductible contributions to their own IRA. To be allowed this choice, the thrift plan must meet the following requirements:

1. The thrift plan must be a qualified plan
2. The plan must permit voluntary contributions
3. The employee must pay the contribution in cash
4. The employee must not designate the contribution as nondeductible

Simplified Employee Pension Plan

A simplified employee pension plan (SEPP) is basically a company IRA subject to special rules.

The ERTA raised the maximum allowable tax deductible contribution from the lesser of $7,500 or 15% of compensation to the lesser of $15,000 or 15% of compensation.

The TEFRA of 1982 raised the allowable tax deductible contributions from the lesser of $15,000 or 15% of compensation to the lesser of 15% of compensation or $20,000 in 1983, $25,000 in 1984, and $30,000 in 1985.

Maximum compensation which may be taken into account in determining permitted annual benefit accruals is $100,000 in 1982, $133,000 in 1983, $167,000 in 1984, and $200,000 in 1985.

Beginning in 1986, post-1984 limits are adjusted for cost of living.

The SEPP was designed to provide several advantages to a company considering a retirement plan including:

1. Lower start-up and administrative costs than for a regular pension and profit-sharing plan. This is to be possible through simplified record keeping and reporting required by the Labor Department.
2. Portability of benefits. This is made possible because participants who terminate their employment take their benefits with them in the form of an IRA. Since lump-sum distributions from regular retirement plans can be rolled over to other qualified plans or to a rollover IRA, this advantage is frequently exaggerated.
3. Reduced fiduciary responsibility of the employer, since SEPP participants choose their own investment vehicle when they establish an IRA.

The SEPP, however, has a number of disadvantages that may negate the advantages. The most significant disadvantages are:

1. The SEPP requires inclusion of part-time or seasonal employees. The effect of this requirement is to dilute the benefits of full-time and/or long-term employees to provide benefits for part-time or seasonal employees.

2. All contributions to a participant's IRA are fully (100%) vested. The effect of this requirement is that an employee takes immediate ownership of company contributions. Corporate pension and profit-sharing plans allow several years before employees have full ownership.

3. A SEPP requires that all eligible employees participate in the plan. Any employee who has reached age 25 and has performed services for the employer for the current calendar year and at least three of the five preceding calendar years is eligible. If an eligible employee refuses to participate, for whatever reason, all other eligible employees are denied the benefits of the SEPP.

4. A SEPP requires that eligible employees who terminate during the first year of employment must agree to open an IRA. As an employer, you are burdened with the responsibility they open an IRA so that your SEPP can continue. If an employee refuses to establish an IRA, the SEPP cannot be continued.

Distributions from a SEPP are the same as for an IRA. Installments must be made at least annually, but may be at shorter intervals. Payments should extend over the participant's lifetime. Married participants may extend payments over their spouse's lifetime, if desired.

Keogh

Keogh plans, sometimes called HR-10 plans, are available to sole proprietors and partners but cannot be used by business owners who incorporate.

The Tax Equity and Fiscal Responsibility Act of 1982 focused, in the pension area, on creating parity between retirement plans for the self-employed and corporate retirement plans. Some of the special rules for Keogh plans that were repealed:

1. Set lower limits on contributions/benefits for the self-employed,
2. Prevented some plans from limiting coverage to a cross section of employees,
3. Restricted integration with Social Security

Some rules, previously applicable only to corporate qualified plans, now relate to Keoghs. The rules explained for top-heavy plans may, in some instances, apply to Keogh plans as well.

THE MECHANICS OF SETTING UP A RETIREMENT PLAN

Business owners are frequently uneasy about the mechanics of establishing their retirement plans, but the burden on you is much less than you might suppose.

Your certified financial planner provides the liaison between you and the other professionals and entities involved in the design, installation, and administration of your retirement plan. For now, let's concentrate on the steps involved in establishing and qualifying your plan.

First, it is your responsibility to have your board of directors approve the establishment of a retirement plan. This approval takes the form of a resolution indicating intention to establish the plan.

The next step is to secure a trust agreement or corporate master/prototype plan. This is the document outlining the provisions of the plan and the privileges and obligations of the employer, the participants, and the trustee. The document may be secured from a number of sources:

1. A company specializing in document preparation
2. The plan sponsor (such as a mutual fund or insurance company) or
3. The plan administrator. Your attorney may draw up a document for you if your needs are highly specialized.

After the documents have been secured, you, as the employer, are responsible for enrolling your employees. This step also includes announcement of the plan. The financial planners at our firm like to do this with the client (or even for the client), reviewing with each employee the summary plan description and benefit statement. We feel that the employer is giving the employees a valuable fringe benefit, and this should be communicated. Since a major motivation on the part of many clients in establishing a retirement plan is to reward those employees who have been instrumental in the success of the business, it is critical that the employees understand how they are being rewarded.

Once the employees are enrolled, the plan is submitted to the Internal Revenue Service for approval. The approval is to insure the favorable tax treatment afforded qualified plans. This step may be done by the plan administrator, the attorney, or the CPA.

The last step is for the administrator, attorney, or CPA to file a description of the plan with the Department of Labor and to provide it with a copy of the summary plan description that was given to the participants.

That's it! Now you have a retirement plan.

INTEGRATING A PLAN WITH SOCIAL SECURITY

As an employer, you are making contributions to a pension plan on behalf of your employees: Social Security. Pension plan regulations recognize this fact and allow an employer to offset contributions to a private pension plan with Social Security contributions.

Integration allows you, as employer, to provide highly compensated employees (including yourself) a larger portion of the total plan benefits without breaking the rules against discrimination.

The rules to integration are highly complex and are set out in detail by the IRS. Your financial planner, working with a highly skilled pension plan designer, can determine whether integration serves your best interests.

INVESTMENTS IN RETIREMENT PLANS

After setting up the plan, the next step you have is the happy one of deciding on the investments to go into the plan.

Background

As mentioned earlier, ERISA established specific standards for investment of retirement funds. The trustee, investment manager, or other responsible parties must abide by these standards. Highlights of the standards are:

1. *Prudent man rule*. ERISA charges a fiduciary with the responsibility to act "with the care, skill, prudence, and diligence under the circumstances then prevailing that a prudent man acting in a like capacity and familiar with such matters would use in the conduct of an enterprise of a like character and with like aims."

2. *Investment diversification*. The ERISA does not spell out formula for diversification, but rather requires that diversification be adequate to minimize the risk of large losses. The rule is frequently interpreted to imply diversification among different industries as well as geographical locations.

3. *Limitation on investments in employer's securities*. The fundamental rule is that pension plans may not invest more than ten percent of plan assets in the employer's securities. Defined contribution plans (profit-sharing, stock bonus, thrift plans, money-purchase plans, and ESOPs) may be exempted by specific provisions in the plan.

4. *Prohibited transactions*. Some transactions between the plan and "parties-in-interest" are specifically prohibited. These are detailed in the section "fiduciary responsibility."

Investment Opportunities

The list that follows highlights those more frequently chosen.

Cash Equivalents

You will probably want to keep some percentage of your retirement funds in what are frequently called "cash equivalents." Your choices include: certificates of deposit, government securities (treasury bills, bonds, and notes), and money-market mutual funds. Financial planners seem to be particularly partial to the money-market mutual funds, and your financial planner will help you select a good one.

Common Stocks

The selection of common stock for a retirement plan is much the same as selecting stocks to use the dividend-exclusion allowance. Chapter 7 has some guidelines, but a full treatment is beyond the scope of this book.

Remember that the earnings on investments in your retirement plan are free of current income tax. This will afford you the luxury of taking the safer path that more stable dividend-providing stocks provide.

Mutual Funds

Chapter 7 has guidelines on mutual-fund selection. As with common stocks, you will be primarily motivated by high income with a more stable fund.

Bonds

Until a few years ago the traditional bond market was fairly dull. In recent years, however, the bond market has become quite dynamic—a place where both large profits and losses have been made.

You may choose between high-yielding, long-term bonds that "lock-in" the yields for a long period of time, shorter-term bonds that yield a little less, and/or deep discount bonds that offer an opportunity to participate in any increase in bond prices.

Yield on bonds in recent years have been in the 11%–16% range. Pension plans have been aggressive purchasers of high-yielding corporate bonds.

Annuities

Annuities can best be described as a "tax advantaged savings account."

An annuity is a fully guaranteed deposit with an insurance company.

The earnings are also fixed and guaranteed. Income tax on the interest, however, is deferred until the interest is received.

Although annuities do pay a reasonably competitive rate of return and are allowed in retirement plans, I rarely recommend them for retirement plans since they are a shelter in and of themselves.

Limited Partnership

A limited partnership is a legal, nontaxable entity. By investing in a limited partnership, you limit liability to the amount of investment, and your retirement plan becomes a passive investor. A general partner assumes all liability as well as the responsibility for managing any business activity acquired by the limited partnership.

Income and expenses flow through the partnership to your retirement plan. For example, if you invest in a real estate limited partnership, your retirement plan will receive a pro-rata share of the rents.

The yields are attractive and highly competitive with other investments. Because each partnership is basically a business enterprise, it is difficult to quote averages, but yields of 12%–18% are not unusual. The minimum investment is $5,000.

There are limited partnerships that invest in real estate, equipment leases, oil and gas, and a variety of more "exotic" enterprises. There are some very fine limited partnerships specializing in investments for retirement plans.

Since limited partnerships are "pooling" arrangements, they do provide a great deal of diversification with relatively small amounts of money.

TERMINATING RETIREMENT PLANS

Qualified retirement plans can be terminated at the employer's discretion. The ERISA has set out specific guidelines for plan terminations. This is a highly complex transaction and should not be undertaken without expert advice.

9

Estate-Tax Planning and Your Corporation

An ulcer is just not the financial status symbol it used to be. There was a time when simply having an ulcer implied your financial success. Not any more. The new financial status symbols are needing tax shelters and worrying about estate-tax liability.

The estate-tax laws have been changed so frequently and so dramatically since 1976 that the only people I meet who are not confused about these taxes are those few who lead such sheltered lives that they don't even know there is such a tax.

BACKGROUND ON ESTATE TAX

Estate tax is a federal tax. It is normally paid by the executor(trix) of the estate on behalf of the estate. A similar tax, usually called an inheritance tax, is extracted by state governments. It is normally paid by heirs.

Shortly after the estate tax was created, it became obvious that it could be avoided simply by giving property away prior to death. Thus the gift tax was born. Prior to 1977, gift-tax rates were lower than estate-tax rates, and the tax was calculated separately. This meant that making lifetime gifts could save a lot of estate taxes.

The 1976 Tax Reform Act charged that, instead of having separate tax computations for estate and gifts taxes, the 1976 law created a unified tax rate on the total amount of an estate and any gifts made during the estate owner's life. Prior to 1976, there was a $30,000 lifetime exemption from gift tax, plus a $60,000 estate tax exemption. There was also a $3,000 per year per donee exemption.

The Economic Recovery Tax Act of 1981 (ERTA) maintains the same basic approach, i.e., the credit system, but is more generous with the credit and has also covered the brackets on the unified tax rate schedule.

With that brief background, let's take a look now at estate planning.

ESTATE PLANNING

Broadly defined, estate planning includes:

1. Lifetime planning designed to increase the size of your estate. Areas to be addressed include: current and future income-tax minimization, portfolio management, wealth accumulation, and budgeting.

2. Lifetime planning designed to minimize shrinkage of your estate and problems associated with continuity. This area of planning would be designed to:

   a. minimize estate (federal) taxes and inheritance (state) taxes;

   b. reduce probate and administrative costs;

   c. assist in business continuity;

   d. provide for charitable giving; and

   e. aid in the orderly distribution of your estate with professional management.

That sounds like a tall order! Let's start, as the song suggests, "at the very beginning."

THE PERSONAL INVENTORY

The "very beginning" for estate planning is with an inventory. The inventory that we use at Resource Management, Inc. has been reproduced as Appendix K. As you can see, it's very thorough.

After you've worked through the inventory, recap on the sheet provided.

Recap Sheet For Estate Tax Calculation

Assets	Community or joint	Separate husband	Separate wife
1. Passbook savings			
2. Certificates of deposit			
3. Credit union deposits			
4. Money-market mutual funds			
5. Bonds			
6. Government obligations			
7. Annuities			
8. Accounts receivable			
9. Personal property			
10. Life insurance			
11. Real estate			
12. Stocks and mutual funds (excluding closely held interest)			
13. Limited partnerships			
14. Value of closely held business interest			

The ERTA of 1981 provides that each spouse is to be treated as one-half owner of jointly held or community property regardless of which spouse paid for the property. On the death of the decedent, only one-half would be included in the estate.

Liabilities	Community or joint	Separate husband	Separate wife
Accounts and notes payable			
Mortgages in real estate			
Other			

Now we're ready to "guesstimate" your estate tax liability.

Tentative Tax on Husband's Death

One half of community or jointly
    owned property $ _____
Plus: husband's separate property   + _____
Equals: Gross estate   = _____

Less: (a) ½ of community or joint debts $ _____

     (b) husband's separate debts   _____

     (c) estimated administrative expense
        (10% of gross estate is reasonable)   _____

     (d) casualty and theft losses   _____   − $ _____

Equals: Adjusted gross estate $ _____

Less: Marital deduction $ _____

     Charitable bequests   _____

Equals: Taxable estate $ _____

Tentative tax (see table) $ _____

Less: Unicredit $ _____

     State death taxes   _____

Net estate tax to be paid $ _____

Sample Calculation of Estate Tax

To be sure you can work through the estate-tax calculation, let's do one example. Let's assume you get to "taxable estate" with the figure $975,000.00. The tax is calculated as follows:

On the first $750,000 the tax is	248,300
plus 39% of excess (975,000 − 750,000 × 39%)	87,750
	336,050
Minus unified credit	79,300
Taxes due	256,750

Okay, now you've got your inventory done and your tax calculated. If the number for net estate tax to be paid is greater than zero, you should read on, and work on!

Actually, working to reduce the estate-tax bill involves making some decisions that will affect your family. I always encourage my married clients to have long, very honest, spouse-to-spouse talks at this point. How do you both feel about making gifts to charity, providing for the kids, and so forth?

FAMILY INVOLVEMENT IN ESTATE PLANNING

Teach your heirs how to assess their investments, or at least teach them to select advisors who will help them. No matter how smart you are, you cannot manage the family estate effectively from the grave.

Talk to your family about your desires and theirs. What are each family member's preferences? Can they all be honored in the framework of good estate tax planning? If not, what's the trade off? Would you rather pay some tax and give your family more freedom? How do they feel?

In a family unit, one spouse frequently emerges as the "money manager" writing the bills and managing the family's investments. If you're the money manager in your family don't just assume your spouse can't do the job. Talk about what he or she might do without you. You might consider having him or her do the job under your supervision for a few weeks. If your spouse really hates the chore, figure out how you can obtain some professional help.

For investments, seek out a good CFP to work with you and your spouse. Ideally your CFP will be flexible enough to work with the spouse who loves to be heavily involved with the personal money management and the one who dislikes it. In fact, most CFPs are accustomed to a wide range of personal preferences regarding involvement.

DON'T MANAGE YOUR ESTATE FROM THE GRAVE

The point is, don't try to manage your family affairs from the grave. I deal with widows occasionally who say, "John told me never to sell the Acme Widget stock" and dutifully hang on while Acme drops from 27 to 3.

I had a client whose father told her to keep her bonds *no matter what*. So through a period of unprecedented inflation and high interest rates, they lost about 60% of their market value and virtually all of their purchasing power value. But she kept them.

WHAT ARE YOUR CHOICES?

Let's move on to your specific choices and how they may affect your survivors.

Marital Deduction

The first decision to make involves the marital deduction, which is a deduction from the adjusted gross estate granted to estates of married individuals.

The Tax Reform Act of 1976 provided for estate-tax marital deductions of the greater of $250,000 or one-half of the adjusted gross estate for property passing to the decedent's spouse. That same act provided an unlimited gift tax marital deduction on the first $100,000 of gifts to a spouse and a 50% deduction for gifts in excess of $200,000.

The Economic Recovery Tax Act of 1981 provides an unlimited gift and estate-tax marital deduction for gifts made and estates of decedents dying after 1981. The result is that all qualifying transfers between spouses (including community property) are allowed to pass free of gift and estate taxes.

Many practitioners interpret Congress' rationale to mean that since a husband and wife represent one economic unit for income taxes, they should also represent one economic unit for estate and gift taxes.

There is a potential pitfall here—the so-called stacking effect. Since estate tax is a progressive tax (higher rates of taxation applied to higher amounts to be taxed), the death of the second spouse could expose the estate to significantly higher taxes than if the two estates were divided and taxes were paid at lower rates on each.

The point is, don't assume that everything should pass to your spouse just because it can do so without tax. If there is a possibility that your spouse will also leave an estate on which taxes must be paid, you may want to consider transferring some of your estate to your children through a trust. If your estate is large enough, you may want to transfer enough to use your full personal exemption, in addition to the marital deduction.

Let's look at an example, assuming a family of husband, wife, and son. It's 1985 and the husband dies, leaving an estate of $1 million. He leaves everything to his wife. His estate taxes are calculated as follows:

Adjusted Gross Estate	$1,000,000
Less: Marital deduction	1,000,000
Tax	–0–

One year later the wife dies, leaving everything to her son. Assume the estate is still intact.

Adjusted Gross Estate	$1,000,000
Less: Marital deduction	–0–
Taxable estate	$1,000,000
Tentative tax:	
$248,300 plus 39% of excess over $750,000	$ 345,800
Less credit	155,800
Taxes due	$ 190,000

Now let's assume that when the husband dies he leaves $400,000 in trust for his son, and $600,000 to his wife. His taxes are calculated as follows:

Adjusted Gross Estate	$1,000,000
Less: Marital deduction	600,000
Taxable estate	$ 400,000

Tentative tax:

$70,800 plus 34% of excess over $250,000 $ 121,800

Minus: Credit   121,800

Taxes due   –0–

When the wife dies, she leaves everything to her son. Assume the estate is intact.

Adjusted Gross Estate $ 600,000

Less: Marital deduction   –0–

Taxable estate $ 600,000

Tentative tax:

$155,800 plus 37% of excess over $500,000 $ 192,800

Minus: Credit   155,800

Taxes due $ 37,000

Notice that if the husband leaves everything to his wife, his taxes are zero; hers are $190,000. When we changed the provisions of his will to leave enough to the son in trust to use the full exemption, combined estate taxes were $37,000! Quite a savings.

Terminable Interests

If you're really paying attention, you're thinking, "Why can't I leave my spouse income only on enough property to fully use my exemption and leave the remainder outright to my children? He or she would get the income for life and at his or her death my children get the property."

Well, you can—but that opens a can of worms called "terminable interests." Prior to the Economic Recovery Tax Act of 1981, "terminable interests" did not qualify for the marital deduction. The gift of an income interest to a spouse such as we just described, for example, with the remainder interest to a third party, would not have qualified for the marital deduction.

The ERTA of 1981 allows property transferred to the spouse, on which the spouse is entitled to all income for life, to qualify for the unlimited marital deduction *if* certain conditions are met.

1. The surviving spouse must be entitled to lifelong annual payment of income from the property.

2. If the interest is not in a trust, a qualifying life income interest in any other property should combine the interest with a power of appointment. This provision is more suggested than specified, and practitioners are not unanimous in their opinions.

3. There must be no power in anyone, including the spouse, to appoint

any part of the property to any person other than the spouse during the spouse's lifetime.

4. The interest will not be considered a qualified interest unless the donor spouse or his or her executor so elects.

Why would there be any question about the election of qualified income interest? Why would the executor(trix) pass up a deduction if one is available?

The answer is simple. If your spouse disposes of all or part of the qualifying income interest by gift, sale, or otherwise, or at death, the entire value of the property, reduced by any amount received by the spouse or depositor, is subject to the transfer tax. Notice the trap here: your spouse will have only a life-income interest, while the estate is taxed as if the full property interest were owned.

The method may still suit your purposes, however, if you feel very strongly about providing your spouse with life-income interest but being sure that a third party gets the property at the death of your spouse, for example, in the case of a second marriage with children from a first marriage. This method does not require a trust.

Use of a Trust

But a trust that pays your spouse income for life and leaves the remainder to your children might be a better idea.

With a trust, your executor(trix) can still elect to treat the amount placed in the trust as qualifying life-income interest (if your spouse is the beneficiary of the income stream), use the marital deduction and, in effect, defer estate taxes until your spouse's death.

Your estate is liable for estate taxes if you leave more to the trust than your estate tax credit eliminates.

There is no right or wrong way—work through your numbers and talk it over with your spouse. The "right" way is the way that suits your needs best.

For many of you, full use of the credit combined with the marital deduction will eliminate your estate tax liability. If it does, you've got a lot of company. It's been estimated that new laws will result in an exemption from federal estate and gift taxes for approximately 99.6% of estate.

For those of you who still have an estate-tax liability (if you can't use the marital deduction, you probably do), we'll go through some other tools for your consideration.

Current-Use Valuation

It may be that your estate includes real property used in a business or as a family farm that is more valuable in some alternative use.

Before the Tax Reform Act of 1976 was passed, all real property had to be included in a decedent's estate at its fair market value. The position of the IRS and the courts was that the value for purposes of estate-tax valuation was the "highest and best use" to which the land could be put. The actual use of the land was deemed immaterial. In many cases, income from the business or family farm was totally inadequate to pay estate taxes and the family farm or business was lost to the heirs.

Congress finally recognized the extent of this burden and enacted the current-use valuation. (This provision was previously called "special-use valuation.") The provision in code section 2032A permits the executor to elect to value qualifying property at its value *as a farm or in the business*.

In order to qualify for current-use valuation, the property and its owner must meet the following requirements:

1. The decedent must have been a United States citizen in residence at the time of death.
2. The value of the farm or business (including both the real and personal property, but reduced by debts attributable to them) must be at least 50% of the gross estate (reduced by debts and expenses).
3. At least 25% of the adjusted value of the gross estate must be "qualified" farm or closely held business real property.
4. The qualified real property must pass to a "qualified heir." A qualified heir is a member of the decedent's family. If a qualified heir transfers interests in qualified real property to a family member, the person acquiring the interest becomes a qualified heir with respect to that interest. A "member of the family" includes:

a. Ancestors

b. Spouse

c. Lineal descendants

d. Spouse's lineal descendants

e. Parents

f. Spouse of any lineal descendants described in (c) and (d)

Property may be passed to a discretionary trust and still qualify for current-use valuation if: no beneficiary has a present interest for gift tax purposes and the potential beneficiaries are qualified heirs.

5. The real property must have been owned by the decedent or a family member and used by the decedent or family member as a farm or closely held business for five of the eight years immediately preceding the decedent's death.

Property that qualifies for current-use valuation is any real property located in the United States that is devoted either to use as a farm or use in a trade or business other than farming. It is possible that property rented to a related person who conducts an active trade or business will qualify. Personal property used for farming purposes, in a trade, or business that passes to a qualified heir will also qualify.

Passive rental or investment property does not qualify—the property must be actively used in a trade or business.

INSTALLMENT PAYMENT OF ESTATE TAX

The next thing we'll want to look at is the extension of time for payment of the estate tax.

Law prior to passage of ERTA provided that payment of estate taxes attributable to business interests could be deferred under three separate provisions of the code that set out procedures for: (1) an automatic 14-year extension, (2) an automatic 10-year extension, and (3) a discretionary extension granted by the district director for up to 10 years.[1]

The ERTA repealed the 10-year extension and expanded the provisions of the 14-year extension.

For decedents dying after 1981, an executor can elect to pay the portion of the estate tax attributable to an interest in a closely held business over a 15-year period. The 15-year period includes a five-year deferral during which the estate pays interest only at a rate of 4% on the first one million dollars of the business and at the current rate (roughly prime) on the balance. The five-year deferral is followed by ten equal annual installments. To qualify, the value of the business interest must constitute 35% of your gross estate or 50% of the taxable estate.

INTEREST IN A CLOSELY HELD BUSINESS

Interest in a closely held business is defined as:

1. An interest as a proprietor in a trade or business
2. An interest as a partner in a partnership carrying on a trade or business if 20% or more of the capital interest is included in the gross estate or if the partnership has 15 or fewer partners
3. Stock in a corporation carrying on a trade or business, if 20% or more of the value of the voting stock is included in the gross estate or the corporation has 15 or fewer shareholders

---

[1]Internal Revenue Code Section 6166, 6166A.

If your family as well owns interest in the qualifying business, all stock and partnership interests owned by them are considered to be owned by you for the purpose of meeting the 20% tests. Family members whose interests are attributable to you include: brothers and sisters; spouse; ancestors; and linear descendants, that is children and grandchildren.

If you own interest in more than one closely held business, they will be treated as a single business for purposes of including the total value of *each* business in your gross estate.

The deferred payments become immediately due and payable if one-half or more of the value of the business is "distributed, sold, exchanged, or otherwise disposed of" or withdrawn, but there is no acceleration of deferred payments, however, if the transfer is made on death to a family member.

Let's do a little arithmetic now. To determine if your estate qualifies for installment treatment take the total value of business interest and divide by the gross estate minus amounts *allowable*[2] as deductions—funeral and administration expenses, debts and certain taxes, and code 2054 losses.[3] This is the adjusted gross estate. The result must be 35% or greater.

The crux of the problem, as you can see, is proper valuation of your business interest. There is a full treatment of this subject in Chapter 6.

Qualification for Deferred Payment

Do you qualify? If not, we'll look at some ways to bring your estate into qualification if desired. For those of you who do qualify, let's see how much tax can be paid in installments.

First, figure out your gross federal estate tax. Remember to subtract state death taxes, gift tax, tax on prior transfers, foreign death taxes, and the unified credit. Now you should have all the numbers you need.

The amount that can be paid in installments must bear the same ratio to the gross federal estate tax (reduced as just described) as the value of your business interests (only those included in the gross estate) bears to the value of the adjusted gross estate.

A formula is about the only way to translate all that tax language into English:

$$\frac{\text{Interest in closely held business}}{\text{Adjusted gross estate}} = \frac{\text{X (Tax to be paid in installments)}}{\text{Estimated federal estate tax}}$$

---

[2]Administration expenses may be claimed as either income-tax deductions or estate-tax deductions. Most practitioners feel that eligibility for installment treatment hinges on amounts *allowable* as estate-tax deductions, so that an executor's election to take these administration expenses as income tax deductions does not affect the availability of installment treatment.

[3]Code 2054 losses are defined as losses caused by casualties or theft during the administration period.

Let's assume your adjusted gross estate is $2,225,000; interest in a closely held business is $875,000, and your estimated federal estate taxes are $591,250. You could pay $232.514 in installments.

$$\frac{875,000}{2,225,000} = \frac{X}{\$591,250}$$

$$X = \$232,514$$

Your executor would have to pay the difference between $591,250 (your full tax due) and $232,514 (the amount that can be deferred), plus the first installment in the deferred amount, on or before the due date of the federal estate tax.

If you don't qualify for installment treatment, is your estate substantial enough to justify the work required to bring it into qualification? If so, the basics are simple: decrease your personal estate and increase the value of your business.

Decreasing Personal Estate/Increasing Value of the Business

Some ways of decreasing personal estate and increasing the value of your business are to:

1. Give away nonbusiness assets to family and/or charity during your lifetime.
2. Sell or borrow against nonbusiness assets and invest the proceeds in your business.
3. Hold as much accumulated earnings as you can in your business without risking the accumlated-earnings penalty.
4. Be sure your beneficiary designations on corporate retirement plans, IRAs, Keoghs, and insurance are such that these proceeds do not go into your estate.
5. Consider ways of "thinning" your estate. Some techniques will be discussed later.

One last point: in tax planning of any kind, don't let the tail wag the dog. Don't go against your preferences or your family's preferences because taxes will be decreased. Nobody enjoys paying tax—but don't get so caught up in minimizing your taxes that you lose your perspective on good financial planning for yourself and your family.

TECHNIQUES TO ELIMINATE ESTATE TAX LIABILITY

If you've investigated the methods listed previously (marital deduction, charitable bequest, and the unified credit) and your inventory reflects the advantages of current-use valuation rather than fair market values and the installment sale provisions are either not available or inadequate, then you should move on to three other techniques available to eliminate your estate tax liability:

1. Techniques that "freeze" the value of your estate and put growth and appreciation in the estate of younger family members;
2. Techniques that create estate-tax-exempt wealth;
3. Techniques that dispose of wealth already accumulated.

Let's look at each in detail.

Techniques That "Freeze the Value of Your Estate"

Capitalization

One of the best of the estate-freezing techniques is a recapitalization of your business. The federal tax code refers to this as a form of reorganization but doesn't really define the term. A recapitalization is basically a "rearrangement" of the capital structure.

Before we consider the mechanics and objectives of recapitalization, however, let's consider some fundamental decisions you should make. The first item for you to consider is what would happen to the business in the event of your death. Would the business continue to operate, or does it depend so heavily on you that without you there is no business?

If you feel the business could and should continue, what about successor management? Is there a family member to take over? Is the family member already in the business? Be honest with yourself—if your son has been a dentist for five years, don't try to convince yourself that in the event of your death, he would take over your hardware operation.

If there is no family member to take over, how about a key employee, or even an outsider experienced in your kind of business? You could arrange for that individual to buy out your family in the event of your death, through a buy/sell agreement.

Suppose you have both participating and nonparticipating family members. How do you prefer to distribute stock and control to each? How do you feel about bringing someone along to take over ultimately? How much control do you want to have? While some of these considerations are on your mind, let's look at an example of a typical recapitalization.

Assume Mr. Senior, president and 100% owner of Success, Inc. has a son George, who is an attorney and not active in the business, and a daughter, Patricia, who is active in the business. The business has a fair market value of $1,500,000. Mr. Senior's basis is only $15,000.

In a recapitalization, Mr. Senior exchanges all of his common stock for 14,000 shares of $100 par value preferred, plus 12,000 shares of nonvoting common and 150 shares of voting common.

As you can see, most of the value of the company is in preferred stock. This has effectively frozen the value of the company in the preferred, which will pay a dividend of 12%. Mr. Senior reserved an option to require liquidation if dividends are passed for a set period of time.

Now Mr. Senior can begin to make gifts of common stock, gifting nonvoting stock to George who does not participate in the business and voting stock to Patricia, who does. He may also give some nonvoting stock to Patricia to keep the gifts equitable, since he wants to retain enough voting common to control the corporation.

As he begins to remove himself more and more from the business, the preferred stock dividend will provide him with income. The continuing appreciation in the business will be reflected in the common stock Mr. Senior is gradually gifting out of his estate and into his children's estate. There will be no gift tax on these transfers if he transfers $10,000 a year or less to each of his children. (The maximum rises to $20,000 if Mrs. Senior shares in the gifting.)

Let's summarize what he has accomplished with the recapitalization:

1. He has frozen the major portion of the value of the business in preferred stock.
2. He has provided himself with a continuing source of income that will be available at retirement or to Mrs. Senior in the event of his death.
3. He has retained control of the business but has also created a way to gradually give over control.
4. He has given his children an interest in the appreciation of the business with little or no gift tax.
5. He has lowered the cost of common stock so that employees can afford to buy if Mr. Senior elects to offer them some stock.

We've seen that recapitalization can be an extremely valuable estate-tax tool and gift taxes can be easily controlled. But how about income tax? What are the income-tax consequences of recapitalization? As a general rule, no gain or loss is recognized if stock or securities in a corporation are exchanged under a plan of "reorganization" solely for stock or securities in the same corporation.[4]

That sounds pretty straightforward doesn't it? Actually, it is, but you have to be careful on two points. The principal amount of "securities" received must not exceed the principal amount of "securities" surrendered. Moreover, you cannot receive securities if no securities are surrendered. So you must in fact reorganize within the framework of your existing corporation.

The second point to be careful of involves a judicially imposed requirement. The recapitalization must have a bona fide business purpose.

The body of cases takes the predominate position that the business purpose must relate to the business itself. The estate-planning purposes of the stockholders are probably not adequate as a bona fide business purpose. Although there are dissenting cases, the IRS adheres to the view that the mere saving of taxes is not a business purpose.

Enabling family members *who participate* in the business to become shareholders or enabling employees to purchase shares is considered a bona fide business purpose. This is, of course, accomplished by putting a fairly small portion of the value of the business in the common stock and thereby lowering the purchase price. The fact that the senior stockholder(s) retain control does not violate the spirit of the requirement.

If the requirements of a tax-free reorganization are met, the basis of the preferred is the same as the basis for the common exchanged. In general, in a tax-free exchange, the basis of the property acquired is the same as the basis of the property transferred.

Intrafamily Installment Sales

Another device that "freezes" value for estate-tax purposes is an installment sale. The basics are simple: you sell an asset with appreciation potential to a junior family member who is likely to inherit the asset in any event. The appreciation is now in that person's estate—the unpaid notes (and any unspent payments you have already received) are in your estate. If you, as seller, have capital gain on the asset, you minimize your capital-gains tax by spreading the taxes over several years.

Prior to 1980, the intrafamily installment sale had enormous potential for estate planning. The Installment Sales Revision Act, however, made some very significant changes in the rules involving intrafamily installment sales. Some of the changes that simplify installment sales are:

1. The elimination of the requirement that no more than 30% of the sales price be received in the year of sale.

---

[4]Code Section 354 (a)(i).

2. The elimination of the requirement that there be two or more installments.

3. The institution of an automatic installment unless the seller elects otherwise.

While nonfamily installment sales were simplified, the act came down hard on intrafamily installment sales.

At this point you may be thinking, "Why not exchange the common stock for debt, a bond, or a note receivable? That way, the interest will be deductible to the corporation, whereas with preferred stock, the dividend is paid with postcorporate tax dollars." Well, the IRS is one step ahead of you on this one. If stock is exchanged for debt, this is not a tax-free exchange. In the case of our example, if Mr. Senior accepted debt security for his common stock he would have to recognize gain of $1,485,000.

$$\begin{array}{rl} \$1,500,000 & \text{value received} \\ -\quad 15,000 & \text{cost basis} \\ \hline \$1,485,000 & \text{taxable gain} \end{array}$$

Now comes the real zinger: Unless the transaction qualifies as a complete redemption of the shareholder's interest, the gain is considered *ordinary* gain, not long-term capital gain.

If corporate tax savings are quite large and your taxable gain is reasonable, it might still be a good way to go. Again, there's no right or wrong way—the numbers dictate the best approach.

Remember one more point, however. In the event of your death, the cost basis of your stock for your family is "stepped-up" to fair market value. Your age and health are factors in this decision as well as "the numbers."

Let me describe a scenario that was possible before passage of the Installment Sales Revision Act of 1980. Mr. Senior owns a piece of real estate having a fair market value of $250,000 for which he paid $50,000. He sells it to his son on an installment sale under the following conditions:

1. Son gives him notes for 20 equal payments of $12,500 plus 6% simple interest on the unpaid balance. (6% was the requirement under federal code section 483.)

2. Son immediately sells the property to a third party (these transactions were frequently arranged in response to a third party offer to buy) for $250,000.

3. Son may or may not give Mr. Senior "up-front" cost.

4. Son takes the $250,000 received from the sale and invests it to yield cash adequate to make the note to Mr. Senior.

The results are:

1. Mr. Senior has removed an appreciating asset from his estate and has frozen the principal amount at the value of the notes receivable from his son.
2. He has spread the recognition of gain over 20 years, which is like an interest-free loan from the government.
3. Son can invest in an appreciating asset so that his net worth position is improved.
4. Mr. Senior can "forgive" the note up to the gift-tax exemption each year or more, if he is willing to pay gift tax on the excess.

A good system—but the IRS didn't like it. The Installment Sales Revision Act of 1980 made two major changes in this scenario:

1. Recognition of gain is triggered for Mr. Senior if son sells the property within two years of the initial installment sale. Under the new law, if the sale is of marketable securities, there is no resale time limit. Any resale made at any time prior to completion of the installment payments triggers recognition of gain by the seller.
2. If Mr. Senior "forgives" an installment obligation he recognizes gain of the difference between the face value of the obligation and the basis of the obligation.

The intrafamily installment sale still has merit if the senior member sells property to a junior member that can be safely held two years or more (good real estate, for example) or that has low yield but big appreciation potential, which is inappropriate for the senior member's purposes but excellent for the junior family member.

Even if Mr. Senior wanted to transfer marketable securities, the installment sale method would still be good if these were low yield, high appreciation potential. The junior family member could hold them until the potential was realized and the senior family member would enjoy deferral for the length of that period.

Remember, the point is to freeze value for estate-tax purposes and get appreciation in the estates of younger family members. That objective can still be realized with intrafamily installment sales, although the income tax savings possibilities are limited by the new law.

The act also provides an exception to the recognition of gain at resale rule, if the second disposition occurs after the death of the senior member.

Related Persons

The rules for intrafamily transactions pertain only to transactions between "related persons." It's interesting to note who are considered "related persons." A spouse, child, grandchild, or parent is a related person, and so transactions between yourself and any one of these family members will cause your transaction to fall under the more stringent rules. But think of whom that leaves out: brothers and sisters, nieces and nephews, daughters-in-law and sons-in-law, and any other in-law.

You must approach these transactions with great care, for the IRS will be looking for "the sham." If your transaction looks like one between "related persons" disguised as a sale between unrelated persons, it will be challenged on that basis. Do get good professional help if you plan an installment sale.

Techniques That Create Tax-Exempt Wealth

It may be that freezing your estate where it is, using the marital deductions and unified credit eliminates your estate-tax liability. But does it pass on enough to your family? If not, you will want to consider some ways of creating wealth that are exempt from estate tax.

Life Insurance

Life insurance and estate tax are simple: The proceeds are exempt from estate tax if the insured names a beneficiary other than his estate or executor *and* transfers all incidents of ownership to the beneficiary or a trust more than three years before death.

It is particularly important to arrange your insurance in a way to avoid inclusion of the proceeds in your estate, since the insurance is largely for the purpose of providing cash to pay the estate tax.

Your inclination will be to make the insurance payable to the executor of the estate with the intention that he or she uses as much of the proceeds as necessary to pay federal taxes—but this approach will cause the proceeds to be included in your estate, a sort of "Catch-22."

You cannot put your beneficiary under a legal obligation to pay estate taxes or other estate obligations. If you do, the insurance is considered an asset of your estate and taxable as such. This is simple—when the beneficiary is a living person. Problems occur when the beneficiary is a trust created by the insured.

Before we consider the special problem of trusts, let's look at satisfying the conditions of the beneficiary requirement when the beneficiary is a living person. Satisfying the requirement is easy. Just don't name your estate or your executor.

Incidents of Ownership

You must *also* meet the incidents of ownership test. To meet this test, you must assign the policy and relinquish all power over the policy and its benefits.

"Incidents of ownership" has been interpreted to include:

1. Power to change the beneficiary
2. Power to surrender or cancel the policy
3. Power to assign the policy or to revoke an assignment
4. Power to pledge the policy for a loan
5. Power to borrow against the cash surrender value of the policy
6. Power to select a settlement option
7. Retention of a possible reversionary interest

The IRS is really reaching with item 7. You are considered to have a reversionary interest if there is less than 1 chance in 20 that the proceeds will revert to your estate because the beneficiaries die before you do. The odds are computed by IRS rules based on actuarial tables.

The IRS has also ruled that if you have the right at the time of your death to prevent cancellation of a policy on your life owned by your employer by purchasing the policy from him or her for its cash surrender value, you have an incident of ownership. Really reaching!

Why? Consider the amount of money involved. If you have, let us say, a $100,000 insurance policy (common in 1983) that is exempt from estate tax, and your estate is in, let's say, the 37% tax bracket, that's $37,000 in estate taxes Uncle Sam loses. If the IRS can figure out a way to include it, they're $37,000 ahead. Well worth arguing about.

As a principal of a closely held corporation, you can be considered to have incidents of ownership if you are a controlling shareholder and your corporation holds a policy on your life, unless the proceeds are payable to or for the benefit of the corporation.

Life-Insurance Trusts

Life-insurance trusts are another important consideration for creating tax-exempt wealth. See a more detailed treatment in Chapter 10.

Qualified Retirement Plans

It is possible to have the first $100,000 of proceeds of your qualified retirement plans excluded from your taxable estate, but this is not automatic.

To some extent getting favorable estate-tax treatment involves giving up some income-tax advantages. Because of this possible trade off, I'd like to describe the income-tax provisions. As the recipient or beneficiary of a qualified retirement plan, you have the choice of taking an annuity distribution or a lump-sum distribution.

Annuity Distributions   An annuity is defined as a contract or other arrangement providing for substantially equal periodic payments to a recipient for life or for a period extending at least 36 months. If you take an annuity distribution, annuity payments are taxed as ordinary income as received. Distributions not received as a lump-sum distribution are excluded from your gross estate to the extent of $100,000.

Lump-Sum Distributions   The other way to take a distribution is as a lump sum. If you take this form of distribution (and have been a plan participant for five or more taxable years), you can choose between two methods of computing your tax: part capital gain, part averageable income; or all averageable income.

You may treat the portion of the distribution attributable to employer contributions prior to 1974 as capital gain. The balance is treated as ordinary income subject to ten-year-forward income averaging. If it results in a lower tax, you may treat the entire distribution as ordinary income subject to ten-year-forward income averaging. This is strictly a numbers decision, and I always have my clients get their CPA to run the numbers both ways so they will be sure they've made the best choice.

Here is where your trade-off comes in. If you choose to take advantage of ten-year averaging, the lump-sum is included in your gross estate. Again, it's a numbers decision.

Several points need to be made:

1. To escape estate-tax exposure, you should designate a beneficiary other than your estate.
2. There is virtually no way to exclude from estate taxation the portion attributable to your own contributions to the plan. Not even an irrevocable lifetime assignment will do it. The portion that can be excluded is the employer's (your corporation's) contribution.
3. If you transfer an annuity interest, that is considered a gift of future interests and is subject to gift taxes. If the donee immediately begins receiving payments, the annual gift exclusion of $10,000 is available.

If the size and complexity of your estate make it critical that the qualified plan death benefits be excluded to the full maximum, the following items should be carefully observed:

1. Consider avoiding a lump-sum distribution to any beneficiary other than your spouse. The exception would be a beneficiary with whom you want the decision to rest regarding whether proceeds are excludable or not, depending on that individual's election to forego favorable income-tax treatment.

2. Be sure to name a contingent beneficiary. If none is named and your primary beneficiary predeceases you, the benefits fall into your estate and are exposed to the possibility of estate taxation. This is particularly important if your primary beneficiary is your spouse, because his/her death eliminates the marital deduction.

3. A lump-sum distribution to your spouse increases your gross estate by that amount. The increase is moot, however, because the marital deduction is available. Your spouse does not have to choose between favorable income-tax treatment and exclusion from the estate. Use a lump-sum distribution, if feasible, because annuity rates are rarely as good as the recipient can earn on his or her own.

4. The value of Keogh and IRA plans is excludable from estate taxation, to the extent contributions are deductible for income tax purposes. The exclusion is available only for non-lump-sum distributions.

Techniques That Dispose of Wealth Already Accumulated

Gifting

The easiest possible way to dispose of wealth already accumulated is to simply give it away. The Economic Recovery Act of 1981 makes it fairly easy to do so.

I find some confusion and misunderstanding among my clients about gifts, and I'm not surprised. The rules regarding gifts have been changed quite dramatically and fairly frequently.

Prior to the 1976 Tax Reform Act, gift-tax rates were lower than estate-tax rates, and the tax was calculated separately. The effect of these rules was that making lifetime gifts saved a lot of transfer tax. The 1976 Reform Act changed that, largely eliminating the advantage that lifetime giving had on gifts made at death.

Although the 1976 Tax Reform Act made some significant changes in the transfer tax, a provision for an annual exclusion on a gift was retained and the allowance for gift-splitting by spouses was retained.

The tax advantages that were a result of making lifetime gifts after the 1976 Tax Reform Act were:

1. *Income tax.* A gift could shift taxable income from a high-bracket donor to a low-bracket donee.

2. *Gift tax.* No tax was levied against gifts of $3,000 or less per donee per year. The limit was $6,000 if spouse gift-splitting were used.

3. *Estate tax.* Gift tax (if incurred) was excluded from the donee's gross estate and was also allowed as an offset against the estate tax.

If property likely to appreciate in value was given, the appreciation would not be taxed in the donor's estate. Any such gift was subject to the three-year rule that included gifts of life insurance or interests in property.[5]

The Economic Recovery Tax Act of 1981 did not eliminate these advantages to a significant extent, but did make some changes:

1. The annual exclusion has been raised to $10,000 per year per donee ($20,000 if gift splitting is used).

2. Appreciation of property after a gift is made still bypasses the donor's estate, even if the gift was made within three years of the donor's death.

3. Income-tax savings is less dramatic when income is shifted to a lower-bracket taxpayer because the differential between the highest and lowest income-tax brackets has been narrowed.

Several considerations should be made regarding gifts:

1. As I cautioned earlier, don't let the tail wag the dog. Can you really afford to make gifts? Suppose inflation is 8%–12% per year— will your remaining assets be adequate to support yourself? Suppose some of your investments go bad? Suppose you have a serious illness? Saving estate tax is great, but be sure you don't do it at the expense of your financial well-being in your remaining years.

2. Does the unlimited marital deduction eliminate your need to make lifetime gifts? Remember, there is also an unlimited gift-tax marital deduction.

3. If you want to give most, but not all, of your estate to your spouse, will the unified credit be enough to eliminate the estate tax on such bequests? In such a case, do you need to make lifetime gifts?

4. If you're considering gifts to family members other than your spouse, they may prefer you to make gifts to their children or grandchildren rather than "stacking" their estate. This gets more untaxed dollars to the younger generations in the family.

5. Remember that the unified credit may be used against either estate or gift transfers. If you're married, you may wish to make lifetime gifts "using the unified credit" and leave everything to your spouse at your death.

6. Making lifetime gifts may help you meet the 35% test for the deferred payment of estate taxes available to business owners.

7. Bear in mind that if you make gifts of appreciated property during

---

[5]Code Sections 2036, 2037, 2038, 2041 or 2042.

your lifetime, the donee takes your cost basis plus the gift tax attributable to appreciation. If you make such gifts at death, the donee gets a stepped-up basis equal to the fair market value of the property at time of death. (The fair market value may be established at the fair market value six months from death if the executor (trix) chooses the alternate valuation date.)

8. Although gifts made within three years of your death are not includable in your estate, any gift taxes paid are. Gift taxes are incurred if your gifts exceed $10,000 per year per donee.

9. Neither the gift nor the gift tax is included in your estate if the gift was made more than three years before death.

10. Some states have gift taxes. Check local law.

Interest-Free Loan

An interesting alternative to gifting is to make an interest-free loan to your intended donee.

The scenario goes like this. You lend your daughter $100,000 interest free. She deposits the money in a certificate of deposit (CD) drawing 10%. This amount is taxable to your daughter—not to you. If at some predetermined date, you demand repayment, your daughter collects the proceeds from the CD and repays you. Sound good? I must warn you that IRS considers it so good for the taxpayer that they would love to see it stopped.

A very significant case on this point is L. Crown.[6] In this case, three brothers made bona fide and enforceable loans of about $18 million to 21 family trusts. The commissioner sought to collect gift tax on the transaction, arguing that an amount equal to interest at an annual rate of 6% on the outstanding daily balance was a gift to the trusts.

The court took the position that because the loans were in the form of demand notes, their value at the time was unknown and unascertainable. But the commissioner argued that it could "look back" at the end of each quarter, determine what amount was outstanding and value the gift accordingly. The court not only rejected this argument, but also rejected the argument that the lender, by not demanding repayment, continuously completes the gift.

The moral is simple: If you make such a transaction, use demand notes.

However, I must in all fairness warn you that in almost every case where an interest-free loan is challenged and the court finds in favor of the taxpayer, IRS announces *nonacquiescence*. The IRS hasn't been winning, but it's clear that it doesn't like interest-free loans. If an interest-free loan appeals to you, please seek out good tax counsel before you do anything. Don't be afraid to try—just be careful.

---

[6]CA 7, 78-2 USTC 13,260,585 F2d 234, aff'g 67, TC88, CCH Dec. 35,333, Nonorg.

Private Annuities

Suppose I told you there's a way to transfer appreciated property to a junior family member; incur no gift tax on the transaction; increase your cash flow and reduce your income tax simultaneously; and remove the entire value of the appreciated property from your estate. Would you be interested? A private annuity, theoretically, will do all these magic tricks.

Suppose you own stock for which you paid $100,000. Fortunately, you chose well, and today's value of the stock is $200,000. You receive $16,000 a year in dividends. You're in the 50% tax bracket (because of other income), so you net $8,000 a year. Now you want your son to have the stock.

Giving Stock Directly

You could, of course, give him the stock directly, but that approach has two drawbacks.

1. He will take, as donee, your cost basis, so if he sells the stock he incurs capital-gains tax.
2. You will owe gift taxes on the portion of the gift that exceeds $10,000.

Selling Stocks and Gifting Proceeds

You could sell the stock and give him the proceeds but this, too, has some significant drawbacks.

1. You will recognize gain of $100,000 ($200,000 − $100,000) for a tax bill of $20,000. ($100,000 × 40% × 50%)
2. You will also owe gift taxes on the portion of the gift that exceeds $10,000.

Transfer Through Private Annuity

You could make the transfer through a private annuity. Here's how it works: Property is transferred to an individual (who is not in the business of writing annuities). That individual, in exchange, makes a commitment (normally unsecured) to make periodic payments for a specified period of time to the transferor. The normal time period is the transferor's life. The person to whom the property is transferred is called an obligor; the person to be paid a life-income stream is called an annuitant.

Let's look at the overall results of this transaction from the point of view of both parties:

1. There is no gift tax if the property transferred and the value of the annuity are the same.
2. The property transferred in exchange for the annuity is excluded from the annuitant's gross estate.
3. Recognition of gain is deferred. Recognition of capital gain will be spread out over the annuitant's life expectancy. It is as if the annuitant got an interest-free loan from the government!
4. If the stock is shares of a closely held business (perhaps the family business), the private annuity creates a market and keeps the stock in the family.
5. If the stock is not stock in the business but is stock that the son wants to sell after the annuity is established, he will have little or no capital gains if the value of the stock and the annuity are about equal.
6. Because part of every annuity payment is return of principal and part is taxable income, the income tax liability to the annuitant should be less than the tax on dividends prior to establishing the annuity.

Now let's see how the numbers work. We've assumed that you plan to transfer property with a fair market value of $200,000. Let's assume you're 60 years old. Go to the "Annuity, Life Estate and Remainder Interest Values" table in Appendix E. Look under "annuity" for male, age 60. You'll see the factor 9.1753. Divide the annuity factor into the value of the property transferred.

$$\frac{\$200,000}{9.1753} = \$21,797$$

This is the amount of the annuity required to be paid annually in order to equal the value of the property transferred. That's another improvement in your situation, from a $16,000 pre-tax yield to a $21,797 pre-tax yield.

Your income-tax liability can be figured as follows. Generally, a portion of each year's payment is excluded from income and is received tax-free. The balance is taxable as either capital gains, ordinary income, or both, depending on the property transferred to establish the annuity.

In our example, appreciated property was transferred for the annuity so we're going to have return of principal, capital gain, and ordinary income. Return of capital is excluded so let's calculate that portion first. To make the arithmetic easier to follow, let me recap the facts:

Cost basis of stocks transferred: $100,000

Fair market value of stocks transferred: $200,000

Age of annuitant: 60 years

Present value of annuity: $200,000

Excess of the present value of the annuity over the cost basis of the property transferred: $100,000.

Expected return: $479,534 ($21,797 annual payment × 22.0 life expectancy. These factors are in Appendix E.)

The exclusion ratio is:

$$\frac{\text{Cost basis}}{\text{Expected return}} = \frac{\$100,000}{\$479,534} = 20\%$$

Translation of all this arithmetic—20% of each annual payment of $21,797.00 or $4359, is considered return of capital and therefore not taxable.

Capital gains is the next calculation we need. The capital-gains portion is:

$$\frac{\text{Capital gains}}{\text{Life expectancy}} = \frac{\$100,000}{22} = \$4545$$

The balance, $12,893, is ordinary income.

After capital gains have been fully reported, 20% of each payment is return of capital and therefore excluded, but the balance of the payment will be ordinary income.

A special note here: if the annuity was established by transferring property on which you took depreciation, this transfer will trigger recapture of depreciation.

Let's look now at this same transaction from a slightly different perspective. Let's assume your son can only afford to pay you as an annuity payment what he gets as income from the property transferred. Let's further assume that the stock is "family business" stock that you don't want sold and dividends can't be increased. Does a private annuity still make sense?

The facts of transaction are:

Cost basis of stock transferred: $100,000

Fair market value of stock transferred: $200,000

Age of annuitant: 60 years

Life expectancy: 22 years

Expected return: $352,000 ($16,000/yr × 22 yrs)

Present value of annuity: $146,804

This is calculated by taking the annuity payment $16,000 yr and multiplying by the factor in Appendix E. ($16,000 × 9.1753 = $146,804.)

Note: When the value of the property transferred exceeds the present value of the annuity, the excess is treated as a gift. In this case, you would have a taxable gift of $53,196 minus the $10,000 exclusion or $20,000 exclusion, if your gift were split with your spouse.

You should be careful not to tie the obligor's commitment to pay to the income stream of the asset transferred. That would give rise to a possible claim by IRS that some portion of the transaction is includable in your estate.[7]

Now let's do our income calculation again:

$$\frac{\text{Cost basis of stock transferred}}{\text{Expected return}} = \frac{\$100,000}{\$352,000} = 28\%$$

$$\$16,000 \times 28\% = \$4,480 - \text{Return of principal}$$

Capital gains are figured as follows:

Present value of the annuity	$146,804
Minus cost-basis of property transferred	$100,000
Equals	$ 46,804
Divided by life expectancy	22
Equals:	2,127—Capital gains

The balance of the payment $9,393, is ordinary income: $16,000 − $4,480 − $2,127 = $9,393

To recap, the $16,000 payment is broken down as:

$4,480 return of capital
2,127 capital gain
9,393 ordinary income

Is a private annuity a good approach? The pages that follow sum up four options that the gentleman in my example has if his goal is to transfer stock to his son in such a way that it is out of his estate. His options are to:

1. Give the stock to the son, who then sells it.
2. Sell the stock himself and give the proceeds of the sale to the son.
3. Set up a private annuity in which the value of the annuity equals the value of the property transferred.
4. Set up a private annuity in which the value of the annuity is established by the existing cash flow in the property transferred.

---

[7]Code Section 2036.

OPTION I

Give stock to son: He sells

Income	$200,000	fair market value
Tax	100,000	cost basis
Impact	$100,000	capital gain

	40%	taxable
	$40,000	
×	50	tax bracket
	$20,000	taxes due on sale

Assume your son reinvests the proceeds at 12% ($180,000 × 12% = $21,600) and agrees to give you his after-tax yield of $10,800. The $10,000 exclusion will almost eliminate gift tax. Gifts are tax free to the recipient and nondeductible to the donor, so this aspect is tax neutral.

Gift Tax Impact	You would owe gift taxes on the fair market value of the gift minus the exclusion of $10,000 or $20,000, if your spouse consented to gift splitting.
Estate Tax	The value of stock would not be includable in your estate if you made a gift with no strings.
Net Cash Flow Impact	You have $10,800 of spendable cash. Your son has the property, but no spendable cash as a result of the transaction.

OPTION II

You sell the stock and give after tax proceeds to your son.

Income Tax Impact	$20,000 tax due on sale (same calculation as option I)

If your son invests the proceeds and gives you the after-tax yield, there is very little gift-tax due. You will receive $10,800 of tax-free income per year.

Gift Tax Impact	You will owe gift taxes on the $180,000 transferred minus the exclusion.
Estate Tax	The value of the gift would be excluded from your estate if you made the gift with no strings.

Net	You have $10,800 of spendable cash.
Cash	Your son has the property—but no spendable cash.
Flow	

OPTION III

A private annuity in which the value of the annuity equals the value of the property transferred.

Income Tax Impact	No capital gains realized on transfer of property. Capital-gains taxes are not forgiven but are deferred.
Gift Tax Impact	No gift taxes are incurred if the property transferred and the value of the annuity are the same.
Estate Tax Impact	Value of the annuity is not includable in your estate, since the annuity is extinguished at death.

If the proceeds of the annuity exceed your income needs each year and you accumulate the proceeds, you may negate some or all of this advantage.

| Net Cash Flow Impact | You will receive $21,797 per year, of which $4,359 is excluded: $4,545 is treated as capital gains and $12,893 is ordinary income. In the 50% tax bracket you will have an after-tax net of about $14,400. |

Your son is receiving $16,000 taxable proceeds, from which he must make a $21,797 nondeductible payment to you. If he sells the stock and reinvests at 12% as described in options I and II, he has taxable proceeds of $21,600 to make a nondeductible payment to you of $21,797.

OPTION IV

A private annuity in which the value of the annuity is established by existing cash flow on the property transferred. The value of the property transferred exceeds the value of the annuity.

| Income Tax Impact | No capital gains realized on transfer of the property. Capital-gains taxes are not forgiven but are deferred. |
| Gift Tax Impact | The difference between the value of the property transferred and the present value of the annuity is subject to gift tax. |

Estate Tax Impact	Transaction not includable in your estate.
Net Cash Flow Impact	You will receive $16,000 a year, of which $4,480 is excluded from taxation, $2,127 is treated as capital gains, and $9,393 is ordinary income. In the 50% tax bracket, your after-tax net is about 10,880.

Your son is receiving $16,000 a year of taxable proceeds from which he must make a $16,000 nondeductible payment.

Let's assume at this point that a private annuity has some possibilities for you. We've looked at the good points of private annuities; now let's consider the disadvantages.

The first "danger zone" to address is the fact that the annuity must be unsecured if, as the annuitant, you are to avoid immediate tax on your gain and enjoy the benefits of annuity taxation.

If the income stream from the annuity is critical to your financial well being, you must take into consideration your vulnerability and the trustworthiness of the obligor. You must also consider the danger of a fixed income in an era of inflation.

In addition, you must consider the obligor's ability to pay you. The numbers may look great, but can the person with whom you are considering an annuity afford payments in excess of the cash flow of the investment, if the numbers should work out that way?

What happens if the obligor dies before you do? Theoretically the estate must meet the annuity obligation, but personally, I prefer to have an annuitant own a life-insurance policy on the obligor to address this possibility.

An accurate valuation of the property transferred is also critical. If you are considering shares of a closely held business, you may find that a professional evaluation is money well spent.

Incidentally, your corporation may redeem your stock by issuing an annuity. If you decide to do this, be sure the annuity is not more valuable than the stock, or the IRS may claim the excess value was a dividend.

Also be very careful if you own more than 80% of the stock of the corporation or you may find your redemption treated as ordinary income rather than capital gain. The code section to watch is 1239.

Remember that another alternative is to give the property to someone other than your spouse at death, using the unified credit, leaving the balance of your estate to your spouse. At your death, your heirs get a step-up in basis to fair market value and the capital-gains tax is simply forgiven.

The relationship between transfer taxes and income taxes is one you should weigh carefully.

LIQUIDITY

You've considered every technique I've suggested. You've done your home-work and you've got your estimated estate-tax bill as low as practical. But you still have some estimated estate tax. You can see that if you died, your family and/or estate would need cash. Where would the cash come from?

If your business can afford the cash outlay, your estate can redeem shares of your closely held business in amounts equal to estate taxes and funeral and administrative expenses, and treat such redemptions as capital gains.

How does this differ from redemptions prior to death or indeed re-demptions on death for other purposes?

Code Section 303 Redemptions

The general rule holds that if a corporation makes a distribution out of earnings and profits, the distribution is treated as a dividend. This rule applies even if the distribution is by way of redemption.

Code section 302(b) deals with distributions in redemption and pro-vides three exceptions to the general rule.

Code section 303, however, provides for capital-gains treatment on redemptions of amounts equal to estate taxes and funeral and administrative expenses, if your value in the business exceeds 35% of the adjusted gross estate. The percentage test is coordinated with the test for the installment payment of estate tax that we looked at earlier.

You are allowed capital-gains treatment only to the extent that your interest is reduced directly by payment of death taxes of funeral or adminis-trative expenses. If redemptions are made in excess of the amounts allowed for death taxes and deductions allowable against federal estate taxes, the excess is treated as dividends. (Provisions of section 302 are exceptions to this provision.)

In considering if a 303 redemption is workable for your estate, make careful note of the following points:

1. The corporation must redeem the stock. This may require prior planning and/or agreements.

2. A redemption must be made on a timely basis. To be given capital-gains treatment, the redemption must be made after death and within the three-year period allowed for the assessment of estate tax. An estate-tax return must normally be filed within nine months of death. The three-year period begins 90 days after the estate tax

is filed. If an appeal from an Internal Revenue Service determination of estate tax is taken to tax court, the three-year period runs from within 60 days of the tax court decision. Your executor has the option of choosing the longer period.

3. If your will provides that two or more people will become owners of stock, be sure to point out the provision of code section 303 to them when you draw up your will. Here's why: Capital-gains treatment is available to a redeeming shareholder only to the extent that interest is reduced directly (or through a binding obligation to contribute) by any payment of death taxes or funeral or administrative expenses.

Since this provision sets a limit on the total amount of allowable code section 303 redemption, the number of shareholders who redeem are obviously limited as well.

The United States Treasury takes a first-come, first-served position Planning is necessary so that redemptions that would qualify for capital-gains treatment under code section 302 are not treated as 303 redemptions and the limit used up unnecessarily. Let's look at a hypothetical scenario. Your estate, let us assume, has "303" expenses of $175,000. Your estate includes $440,000 of closely held stock, well within the percentage requirement. You leave your stock to three beneficiaries in equal portions. Beneficiary A redeems all his stock and receives $146,667. Since he redeems first, he gets a "303" redemption for capital-gains treatment. However, a total redemption normally qualifies for capital-gains treatment, so, in effect, he "wastes" $146,667 of the $175,000 allowable limit. First-come, first-served—the Treasury does not take the responsibility for doing your estate planning!

Beneficiary B redeems. Let's assume that because of the pattern of his redemption he does not qualify for capital-gains treatment *unless* he gets a "303" redemption. Because he's redeeming second, however, he only gets the remaining allowable amount of $28,333 ($175,000 allowable minus $146,667 redeemed by beneficiary A).

Beneficiary C, of course, has no "303" redemption at all.

Additional factors to consider for a 303 redemption are:

1. Code section 303 redemptions can have an impact in deferred payment of estate taxes. If the estate or your heirs divest themselves of one-half or more of the value of their interest in the business, the deferral may be lost. An exception is made if an amount equal to the redemption is paid toward estate tax still due when the next installment payment is due.

2. If you have interests in more than one corporation, the stockholdings of all corporations that have at least 20% of their value included

in your estate may be added together to meet the 35% adjusted gross-estate test.

Life Insurance

Life insurance plays two important roles in estate planning. First, it is a very good way to create estate tax-exempt wealth. Second, it provides cash to settle taxes and other expenses.

In the last few years, there has been a major revolution in the life-insurance industry as consumers have discovered and used term insurance in unprecedented numbers.

An expanded discussion of the merits of term insurance over cash value insurance is beyond the scope of my subject matter, but I recommend Venita Van Caspel's book *Money Dynamics for the 1980's*. Her discussion of life insurance is considered classic.[8] I would like to point out, however, that with the price of term insurance so inexpensive these days, there's little excuse for leaving your estate vulnerable to liquidity problems.

Buy/Sell Agreements

In my opinion, one of the most important questions a business owner must ask himself is: "What happens to my business in the event of my death, disability, or retirement?"

It's tempting to convince yourself that you will remain in good health and will continue to be a crucial contributor to your firm's success forever—to simply beg the issue. The reality is that if you are the critical element to the success of your business, your absence, for whatever reason, may toll the death knell for your business.

It makes good sense to consider the fate of the business in the event of your death, disability, or retirement, but since we're dealing here with estate planning, let's consider only the impact of your death.

One of the first problems your estate will face is determining the value of your interest in the business. Another problem may also surface, the question of how to convert that business interest to cash. We've just seen the advantages of making code section 303 redemptions, but remember when considering this option that the corporation must have access to adequate cash in order to redeem the stock. A buy/sell agreement is a good way to address these considerations.

A buy/sell agreement is a contract among shareholders or partners; between a principal owner and key employee(s); or between a principal and the corporation itself, providing that one party will sell and another party

---

[8]If you don't find the book in your area, write Reston Publishing Co., Inc., 11480 Sunset Hills Road, Reston, VA 22090.

will buy a business interest at a prescribed price at the occurrence of a stated event. The stated event is normally the death of a shareholder but may be the disability or retirement of a shareholder.

The buy/sell agreement provides a number of advantages to you:

1. It fixes the value of your stock for estate-tax purposes. Generally, the IRS accepts this value, but a basic requirement is that there be a bona fide business arrangement and that the formula for determining price must be fair and reasonable at the time of adoption.
2. It guarantees a market for your interests in the event of your death, disability, or retirement.
3. It provides funds for the payment of death taxes and administrative expenses.
4. It may help protect a Subchapter S election by preventing transfers to shareholders who may be disqualified from owning Subchapter S shares, or shareholders who might refuse to consent to the election.
5. It assures that in the event of your death, disability, or retirement an orderly transfer of stock will take place at a fair, predetermined price.

There are several basic buy/sell agreements that address transactions at death:

1. The survivor(s) of the corporation is obligated to buy and your estate is obligated to sell your business interest.
2. The survivor(s) of the corporation has an option to buy your interest; if this option is exercised, your estate is obligated to sell.
3. Your estate has the option to sell your interest; if the option is exercised the survivor(s) of the corporation is obligated to buy.
4. There is no obligation either to buy or sell; but if your estate wants to sell, the survivor(s) or the corporation must be given the right of first refusal.

There are two basic types of agreements: cross-purchase agreements and stock-redemption agreements. With a cross-purchase agreement, each owner agrees to buy the interest of the deceased owner. With a redemption agreement, the business itself is obligated to purchase the deceased owner's interest.

Now let's look at the very important question of how funds are assured for the purchase.

Life insurance is probably the most common solution to the funding problem. With a cross-purchase agreement, each shareholder owns a life-insurance policy on the life of each other shareholder. With a stock redemption agreement, the corporation owns a life insurance policy on each shareholder whose stock is to be purchased.

When a shareholder dies, the owner of the policy collects the proceeds, which are then used to purchase the deceased shareholder's stock.

A sinking fund may be used for stock-redemption agreements, but these funds are subject to accumulated-earnings tax if they exceed $150,000 for service corporations, $250,000 for other corporations. The rationale for this position by IRS is that the accumulations serve the stockholder rather than the business.

An interesting idea is to have a tax-qualified retirement plan provide funding, by using a surviving shareholder's account to buy the stock of the deceased shareholder.

The ERISA provides that profit-sharing, stock-bonus, thrift, or savings plans in an ESOP may invest in employee securities in excess of the 10% normally applicable. Note that this provision is *not available to pension plans* but only to profit, stock, or thrift-type plans. Note also that the plans should specifically authorize such purchases. The plan may purchase life insurance for such purchases if that seems appropriate. (Refer to Chapter 6 for more information.)

Group term insurance is probably not a good approach, but I want to bring it to your attention because at first blush it appears to have a great deal of merit as a funding device for buy/sell.

Clients frequently ask why we don't set up group plans with the company shareholders as each others' beneficiaries, then have them use these group insurance proceeds to fulfill the buy/sell agreement. After all, insurance is inexpensive and tax deductible by the corporation, and the premium on the first $50,000 is tax free to the insured and the balance heavily tax favored.

The problem is that there is a strong probability that IRS will challenge on the grounds of a "transfer for value." If the transaction is construed as such the proceeds will be taxable to the recipient rather than tax-free, as they are under normal conditions.

To determine which types of buy/sell agreement, stock redemption, or cross-purchase you should use, let's consider their respective advantages and disadvantages. The first thing that will occur to you is that with several stockholders, a cross-purchase agreement can get very unwieldy, if funded with life insurance.

The number of policies required is:

$$N \times [N - 1] = \text{Number of policies required.}$$

$$N = \text{Number of shareholders.}$$

Let's assume your business is owned equally by four shareholders. To have a life-insurance-funded, cross-purchase plan requires 12 policies (4 × [4−1] = 12).

In addition to its mechanical aggravations, this approach is more costly for two reasons:

1. With life insurance, you get a "volume discount"; the larger the policy, the lower the cost per thousand.
2. Each policy has a "policy fee" of $10–$25 a year. The same policy fee is applicable on a $10,000 policy or a $1,000,000 policy as a rule.

Another consideration is that if the shareholders are of different ages, and/or own unequal percentages of the business, insurance premiums also tend to be unequal.

Assume A owns 80% of the company and is 68 years old and B owns 20% and is 30 years old. Individual A's need for life insurance on B is considerably less, and moreover, considerably cheaper, because of B's age. Shareholder B, on the other hand, needs a good deal of insurance on A's life and will find the premiums pretty steep at A's age. We would also expect, though not in every case, that a 35-year-old is at the peak of his family commitments and probably much less able to take on the added premium. If he cannot afford the premiums, and the policy lapses, there certainly will be problems with the buy/sell.

Many of these problems can be relieved with a stock redemption. This system reverses discrimination against the younger stockholder and places it onto the older stockholder, since the corporation in this case picks up the tab for the insurance.

One other consideration is that corporate creditors can obtain policies owned by the corporation. Personal creditors of individual shareholders can reach their personal policies. With term insurance there is nothing to get, so this provision doesn't really matter unless you choose cash-value insurance.

Income Tax Implications

Insurance Premiums Funding Cross-Purchase

Insurance premiums paid by shareholders to fund buy/sell agreements are not deductible. Insurance proceeds are not taxable to the recipient.

The seller of corporate shares recognizes gains of the difference between the cost basis and the purchase price. If the sale takes place as a result of the death of a shareholder, there will probably be no gain since the heirs get a step-up basis to fair market value. The surviving owners' basis in the shares they acquire is equal to their purchase price. This has the effect of increasing their cost basis.

Insurance Premiums Funding Stock Redemption

Insurance premiums paid by the corporation to fund stock redemption are not deductible to the corporation. Insurance proceeds paid to the corporation by virtue of the death of a shareholder are not taxable to the corporation.

Surviving shareholders *do not* enjoy an increase in their cost basis with a stock redemption as they do with cross-purchase. This point is even more important where the stock redemption is funded with life insurance, because insurance proceeds increase the value of the corporation. In effect, the value of shares held by surviving shareholders is greater, but there is no accompanying increase in basis.

If the estate of the deceased shareholder makes a complete termination of the shareholder's interest, the gain is treated as capital gains, and the heirs are entitled to stepped-up basis. All pre-death appreciation escapes capital-gains tax and post-death appreciation is treated as capital gain.

With either type of buy/sell, you should be careful that the insured in all cases gives up all incidents of ownership in the life insurance. Only in this way can you be sure that the policy's proceeds will not be included in the estate. (See the section on life insurance trusts in this chapter for a list of factors that create ownership in life insurance.)

I'll make one last point based on experience. Our CPA pointed out to me recently that the value of Resource Management, Inc. had increased since our last buy/sell was signed and suggested we have a new one drawn up. While reading the new document, I noticed a puzzling clause and questioned our corporate counsel about its meaning. "That's to make the buy/sell compatible with your charter and by-laws" was his response.

This is a valuable point. Be sure all of your documents are compatible. Don't provide in one document for a transaction that is specifically banned by another. As businesses grow and become more complex, their documents also grow in size and number. Compatibility of documents help to avoid other potential conflicts.

10

Trusts and Estate Tax Planning

Trusts are extremely valuable as both an estate planning tool and an income tax planning tool, but the focus of this chapter will be on the use of trusts for estate planning.

There is a wide variety of trusts, each with its own characteristics and peculiarities, but two simple principles prevail when using trusts for estate planning:

1. If you are willing to give up your property to a trust and have no further enjoyment—or, indeed, connection—with the property, and do so irrevocably, that property *will not be* includable in your gross estate.
2. If you receive income from your trust, retain the right to terminate the trust, or hold any trustee authority, regardless of distribution, the property *absolutely will be* includable in your estate.

It's the gray areas that are a problem. Have you given up some, but not all, control? Have you given up enough control to justify exclusion of the property from your estate?

KEEPING PROPERTY OUT OF YOUR TAXABLE ESTATE: BASIC REQUIREMENTS

The rules you must observe in order to keep property out of your taxable estate are:

1. You must not hold general power of appointment, which allows you to control the disposition of the property either in your own favor, the favor of your creditors, or the favor of your estate. If at your death you hold general power of appointment over trust property, it is includable in your estate. There are some exceptions to the general rule of favoring yourself, if the power is limited to health, education, support, or maintenance.

2. You must not retain for yourself the power to revoke, alter, amend or terminate your trust. If you hold this power initially, it must be surrendered more than three years before your death; otherwise the trust property is includable in your estate.

3. You must not retain a life interest. If you give property away but retain for yourself: (a) possession or enjoyment of the right to income from the property; (b) the right, either alone or in conjunction with any other person, to designate persons who shall possess or enjoy the property or its income; or (c) the right to vote stock in a "controlled corporation" for any period *not ascertainable without reference to your death* or for any period which does not in fact end before your death, code section 2036 will include such property in your gross estate.

4. You must not retain a reversionary interest. This is created when the possibility exists that ownership of the property may return to you. For example, if you put property in trust but specify that in the event of the recipient's death the property "reverts" to you, you have created a reversionary interest.

A reversionary interest exists and property is included in your estate if:

1. The intended beneficiary can have possession or enjoyment of the property only by surviving you, or,

2. The reversionary interest, with property, exceeds five percent immediately before your death. Code section 2037 governs reversionary interest and makes an exception of property transferred in trust to pay your spouse for life, with remainder of the then-surviving children, even though their enjoyment is based on survivorship. Notice, however, that if the property is placed in your trust to pay

your spouse for life and reverts to you in the event of your spouse's death, and then to your children, code section 2037 applies.

3. As stated earlier, you should not designate your estate as beneficiary of your life insurance and you should not retain any "incidents of ownership."

So far we've talked about what you have to give up. Let's talk for a moment about what rights you can retain with all trusts.

1. You can retain sole management or administrative powers. Your attorney, in drafting the documents, should specify that these powers are held and exercised in a *fiduciary* capacity. The trust instrument should also specify that you are not the fiduciary for all purposes. Be especially careful about substantive or dispositive powers.

2. You may retain the power to appoint a successor corporate trustee if the trustee resigns or is removed by judicial process.

Be sure not to retain power to replace the corporate trustee *without cause*, as this is currently being litigated. The IRS takes the position that retention of said power causes trust property to be included in the taxable estate.

The fact pattern of the case leading to this ruling gave the trustee broad discretionary powers, and many practitioners feel that for this reason the ruling will not survive a challenge, but in the meantime, your attorney should be inordinately careful.

To reinforce my original statement, to be sure trust property is not included in your estate you must make an absolute and irrevocable gift of the property to the trust and relinquish enjoyment and control of the property. If you start attaching strings, you run the risk of having the property included in your estate.

FACTORS THAT DETERMINE THE NATURE OF A TRUST

Now that we've seen some of the very general rules that apply to estate taxes and trusts in general, let's take a look at the most common trusts, and discuss their tax and nontax characteristics.

Living or Testamentary Trusts

Trusts fall into two broad categories: living trusts (intervivos) and testamentary trusts. The living trust is one that takes effect during the lifetime of the settlor (defined as "one who settles property in trust or creates a trust estate"). The testamentary trust is created by the settlor's will and takes effect at his death. (Some trusts may be either living or testamentary, depending on when you want them to begin.) Most practitioners favor living trusts for these reasons:

1. With a testamentary trust, there is some delay before the proceeds become available. The will must be probated, and the trustee must qualify. With a living trust, the proceeds become available as soon as a death certificate is presented.

2. There is some exposure of the proceeds to the estate creditors in those states where proceeds must be paid to the estate and then transferred to the trust.

3. State law varies, but many states require more rigorous periodic accounting for a testamentary trust than for a living trust.

4. Living trusts are not a matter of public record. Testamentary trusts are, because probate proceedings are matters of public record.

5. The costs of living trusts should be nominal if left unfunded or with nominal funding.

Revocable Or Irrevocable

The basic, crucial difference between revocable and irrevocable trusts is that a revocable trust allows you a great deal of freedom to control the trust.

If you set up a revocable life-insurance trust, any income earned by assets transferred to the trust is taxable to you personally. There is no completed gift to the trust and, hence, no gift tax. In the event of your death, any property in the trust is includable in your estate. Even so, a revocable life-insurance trust has many virtues:

1. It avoids probate

2. On your death, it becomes irrevocable

3. It allows your trustee to use his/her discretion in management and/or distributions.

4. It protects your beneficiaries. Although any property transferred to the trust is includable in your estate, life insurance proceeds made payable to the trust are not includable if the trust is beneficiary and you relinquish all incidents of ownership.

The irrevocable trust accomplishes everything a revocable trust does and adds some tax advantages. You must, however, give up control of your policy and risk some exposure to gift-tax liability.

Income-tax savings are fairly difficult to achieve with an irrevocable life-insurance trust. If your primary trust need is for income-tax savings you will probably be better off with a trust more favorable in this respect. This is another area in which there are no right and wrong ways. You should consider both options and perhaps even establish one of each kind of trust, if your situation dictates that such an approach makes sense. In any event, you, your CFP, and your attorney should work together very closely to make the decisions, and your attorney should draw up your trust documents.

Funded And Unfunded

Trusts can also be funded or unfunded. These terms are fairly self-explanatory.

If you make transfers of property or income to the trust, it is said to be funded. If not, it is said to be unfunded. Since you don't get an income tax break, there is very little virtue in transferring property to an insurance trust. The most common approach is to make annual gifts to the trust that are used to make premium payments.

The section that follows lists types of trusts by their income, estate, and gift-tax ramifications. Table 10–1 at the end of this chapter summarizes this material.

TYPES OF TRUSTS

Now that we have considered some of the factors that will determine the nature of your trust, let's look at some of the types of trusts available to you.

The Irrevocable Living Trust

The title "irrevocable" is quite descriptive, but my clients occasionally take the word too lightly. The *VNR Investors Dictionary*[1] by David Brownstone and Irene Franck defines an irrevocable trust as "a trust which is permanent and may not be revoked by its maker; . . . constituting passage of title to trust property and removal of that property from the estate of the trust's maker."

With an irrevocable living trust, you make an irrevocable transfer of money or property to the trust and give up all rights to enjoyment and control of the property, although you may retain management rights. Transfers may be subject to gift taxes.

The irrevocable living trust has one significant virtue: it avoids probate. This is useful since probate creates:

---

[1]The *VNR Investors Dictionary* by David M. Brownstone and Irene Franck. Van Nostrand Reinhold Company, 1981.

1. *Publicity.* The publicity of probate makes your financial affairs a matter of public record. Such items as the size of your estate, who gets what, how much, and under what conditions, become public information. A trust can be challenged and end up in court where it also becomes a matter of public record, but generally speaking, all irrevocable living trusts avoid this particular problem.

2. *Delay.* The fees to attorneys, trustees, and the executor go up in direct proportion to the size of the estate.

Now let's look at the tax treatment of an irrevocable living trust.

Income-Tax Treatment

It is possible to designate the irrevocable living trust or the beneficiary rather than the settlor liable for taxes on earnings of trust property, but the trust must be designed with care to accomplish this result. The crux, once again, is not to attach strings. If you retain enjoyment and control, the income from trust property becomes taxable to you; if you give up enjoyment and control, it does not.

If the trust is indeed irrevocable, distributed income is taxable to the beneficiary; accumulated income is taxable to the trust.

Estate-Tax Treatment

The property in an irrevocable living trust is excluded from your estate if you adhere to the general rules described earlier.

Gift-Tax Treatment

Transfers of property into an irrevocable living trust are considered "completed gifts" and, as such, subject to gift taxes. The value of the property transferred determines the value on which gift taxes are calculated.

Remember from our earlier discussion that gifts and estates are taxed by the same tax schedule and that there is an unlimited marital deduction for gifts and estates. If you set up a trust for which your spouse is the beneficiary, the transfer may qualify for this deduction. To qualify, the trust must be a general power of appointment trust, a qualifying life-income trust, or an estate trust.

Assuming for a moment that your trust does not qualify for the marital deduction, what is the impact of the gift tax? The Economic Recovery Tax Act of 1981 provides an exclusion from gift tax of $10,000 per donee per year for gifts of present interests. If your spouse consents to the gifts, the exclusion is $20,000. As trust beneficiaries are considered donees, you have as many annual exclusions as you have beneficiaries. You can use the exclusion only for gifts of present interests—not for future interests, those gifts that are to be possessed and enjoyed in the future.

Let's use a highly simplistic example. Suppose you donate cash to your trust. You specify that A is to have the interest for his/her lifetime and that on the death of A, B is to be given the cash. The annual gift-tax exclusion is available for the interest income, but not for the cash.

Gift taxation of trusts is a bit confusing because the annual exclusion applies to the present value of a gift to a trust that may be excluded. The amount of property that may be donated to the trust per donee per year without gift-tax liability depends upon the terms of the trust and such factors as age and sex of the beneficiary.

Let's take an example. You want to know exactly how much property you can transfer into a trust gift-tax free if your 15-year-old daughter is to have a present life-income interest.

Go to table on "Annuity, Life Estate and Remainder Interest Values" in Appendix E. Look under life estate, female, 6%, age 15. You'll see the factor .95314. Divide $10,000 (the gift-tax exemption) by that factor. The result, $10,491, is the value of property you may transfer free of gift tax.

Suppose you want your father, age 70, to have a present life-income interest. The factor in this case is .41294, and the value of property you may transfer free of gift tax is $24,216. If your spouse consents to the gift, you can transfer twice that much free of gift tax.

If you provide that a remainder interest follows the life estate, there is a tax on the remainder interest, and the annual exclusion is not available. The tax is based on the fair market value of the property transferred, multiplied by the factor in the table for remainder interests. The factors for remainder interest and life estate always equal 1.00.

So, returning to our first example, assume you transfer property with a fair market of $50,000 into the trust, giving your daughter a present life-income interest, and transfer the remainder to your father. Your gift tax is then based on $2,343 ($50,000 × .04686). If you do it backwards, by presenting life-income interest to your father, and leaving the remainder to your daughter, your gift tax is based on $29,353.

Remember that you only have gift taxes in the case of a "completed gift" and not all transfers to a trust result in a completed gift.

The Revocable Living Trust

The revocable living trust provides many of the same nontax advantages as the irrevocable living trusts: avoids probate, allows for continuity of income and management of assets for the survivors, allows the settlor to observe the estate fiduciaries during his/her lifetime, creates a depository for assets of the estate, allows for consolidation of assets, and insulates assets from creditors (in some states).

From a tax point of view, however, there is little virtue in a revocable living trust. Any income derived is taxable to the settlor, and the property in the trust is includable in the estate of the settlor. Since there is no "completed gift" when property is placed in a revocable living trust, there are no gift tax liabilities.

Nevertheless, the trust does have merit as an estate-planning tool, since it is very difficult for disgruntled heirs to challenge the terms of a revocable trust. In fact, these trusts are frequently used to ward off potential will contests since they are traditionally difficult to challenge successfully.

One advantage these trusts have is that you, as settlor, can revoke the trust if you wish, and you may leave the trust funded or unfunded, as you prefer.

Short-Term Trust

While the short-term trust (sometimes called a Clifford Trust) is an extremely effective financial-planning tool, its advantages as an estate-planning tool are somewhat limited.

The primary virtue of a short-term trust is its potential for splitting income among family members. You could, of course, cause the income from assets to be taxed to lower-bracket family members by simply giving them the asset, but a short-term trust accomplishes the same thing without your giving up the property permanently.

Code section 673 requires that, in order to have the income taxed to the trust and not to the settlor, the settlor must not have a reversionary interest for ten years, or until the death of the life-income beneficiary. Since the period is measured from date of transfer of property into the trust, not from date of the creation of the trust, the trust document should provide that its duration be measured from the date of the last transfer.

The fact that you have a reversionary interest after ten years or at the death of the beneficiary does not alter the fact that the trust is a taxable entity for that period.

The primary reasons for using a short-term trust are to:

1. Provide educational funds for your children. In fact, these trusts are sometimes referred to as educational trusts.
2. Support or supplement the income of an older family member. To appreciate the value of this approach, remember that the property in a short-term trust reverts to you (as settlor) on the death of the beneficiary, even if that is less than ten years from the date of the last transfer.
3. Provide for retired employees.

There has been some use of a short-term trust to transfer business property where the settlor's family is the beneficiary. The business property is then leased back to the settlor.

Income-Tax Treatment

First, note that you cannot use a short-term trust to provide support and maintenance for someone whom you are legally obligated to support. The idea of transferring in a nice dividend-producing portfolio and using those tax-advantaged dollars to raise the kids is an appealing idea. Unfortunately, if you do so, trust income is taxable to you as settlor. College costs are different, since that is not a legal obligation.

Generally speaking, if your short-term trust has been properly designed, distributed income is taxable to the beneficiary, and accumulations are taxable to the trust.

Estate-Tax Treatment

Estate-tax treatment is easy. If you as settlor retain a reversionary interest and die before the end of the short-term trust, the present value of the interest is includable in your estate.

Gift-Tax Treatment

A transfer to a short-term trust is a taxable gift. The value is determined by taking the value of the property transferred and subtracting the settlor's retained reversionary interest as computed by the table in Appendix E. If gift taxes are incurred, they are includable in your estate along with the present value of your reversionary interest.

I like to remind my clients that if they have a revocable trust, they have virtually no tax advantage. They do, however, have an opportunity to observe the trust in operation and refine its provisions. Once satisfied, they can go with an irrevocable trust.

If tax advantages are so critical that you're reluctant to wait, be careful to build in enough flexibility to allow your trustee to adjust the trust as conditions change.

Pour-Over Trust

The name is very descriptive of the function. The pour-over trust is one into which assets originating from another source are poured. Assets typically "poured-over" are assets from the settlor's will, benefits from a qualified employee benefit plan, insurance proceeds, or assets from other trusts or estates.

A pour-over trust may be either revocable or irrevocable, and its characteristics, advantages, and disadvantages are determined by that decision. Tax treatment also hinges on that decision.

A pour-over trust will avoid probate, regardless of whether it is revocable or irrevocable.

Standby Trust

A standby trust is also well described by its title. It's basically a trust that "stands by" and becomes active in the event that the settlor becomes unable to manage independently. A standby trust is normally activated by disability, although other contingencies could trigger it.

A standby trust is usually revocable and, as such, fairly neutral in terms of tax. Some settlors provide that once activated, the trust becomes irrevocable. Not all states permit standby trusts, so be sure to check local laws if you see some possibility of using one.

Generation-Skipping Trust

The primary purpose of the generation-skipping trust is to avoid exposing to a transfer tax the assets that are in the process of being transferred from one generation to another. Before the Tax Reform Act of 1976 added Chapter 13 to the code it was possible to avoid these transfer taxes by placing property in trust for two or more generations.

Let's consider a possible scenario. Mr. Senior creates a trust that pays him income for life. When he dies, his wife, Mrs. Senior, is to receive income for her life. When she dies, their children are to be paid income for their lives. When they die, any assets left in the trust are to be distributed to their children, Mr. and Mrs. Senior's grandchildren.

Now let's explore the problems and regulations pertaining to such a scenario. By the provisions of the trust, Mr. Senior postponed the ultimate disposition of his trust until the death of his children. His wife and children enjoy the benefits of the trust, and later his grandchildren will receive the trust property that has not been shrunk by estate laws. This method allows two generations to benefit from the trust, but Mr. Senior's children did not pay any estate taxes on the assets.

Congress viewed the avoidance of estate taxes by the second generation as an "injustice" and corrected it with Chapter 13 of the Tax Reform Act of 1976, which provides for a generation-skipping tax, similar to but not identical to the unified transfer tax. The tax is imposed on any trust that has two or more generations of beneficiaries. In a typical trust situation, the younger-generation beneficiaries are the settlor's children and grandchildren.

The tax is payable by the trust and is imposed when the interest of an intervening generation beneficiary (Mr. Senior's children) comes to an end, or when trust principal is paid to a beneficiary a generation younger than that of another beneficiary (Mr. Senior's grandchildren).

There are two exceptions to the generation/skipping trust:

1. The tax does not apply to transfers made from irrevocable trusts that were created on or before June 11, 1976, nor to transfers under revocable trusts or wills executed on or before June 11, 1976.

2. Up to $250,000 for each child of the settlor may be transferred to the grandchildren of the settlor free of the generation-skipping tax on taxable terminations and distributions.[2] An outright gift to a grandchild is not considered a generation-skipping transfer but is simply treated as any other gift.

Testamentary Trust

A testamentary trust is a trust created by instructions in a will. Its purpose is to provide a trust's controls and services for beneficiaries.

The settlor makes no lifetime transfers and, for this reason, the trust is relatively tax neutral, as regards the *settlor's* financial situation. The trust may, however, protect the trust assets from successive estate taxes. It must be designed carefully in order to do so.

A testamentary trust is a good device for using the unified transfer-tax credit as a means of passing assets on to succeeding generations estate-tax free. (See Chapter 9 for description of transfer tax credit.)

Charitable-Remainder Trust

A charitable-remainder trust is an extremely good financial-planning and estate-planning tool. With a charitable-remainder trust, the settlor may retain an income interest or pass it on to a trust beneficiary, dictating that the remaining interest (after the income interest has terminated) pass on to a qualified charity.

The term for which the income is paid may be a set number of years, or a period of time measured in some relationship to the lives of the beneficiaries.

Estate-tax deductions are allowed for any of the following charitable remainder trusts[3]:

1. *Annuity trust*. With an annuity trust the beneficiary receives annual distributions for life of 5% or more, based on the value of the assets *at the inception of the trust*. When the beneficiary dies, the remainder passes to charity.

2. *Unitrust*. With a unitrust, the beneficiary receives annual distributions of 5% or more based on the value of the trust assets *each year*. When the beneficiary dies, the remainder passes to charity.

3. *Pooled-income fund*. A public charity sets up a fund into which contributions are pooled for the benefit of all beneficiaries. The beneficiary receives a pro-rated annual distribution based on the

---

[2]Code Section 2613 (b)(5) and (6).

[3]Section 2055 (e)(2)(A).

income of the entire fund. When the beneficiary dies, the remainder passes to the public charity.

Income-Tax Treatment

As settlor, you are entitled to an income-tax deduction equal to the value of the remainder interest that will pass to the charity.

The deduction is, of course, subject to 50% of adjusted gross-income limitations and may be subject to a 20% or 30% limitation, depending on the kind of property being transferred.

The amount of the deduction varies according to the life expectancy of the income beneficiaries, the expected rate of return on the investment, and the type of annuity selected.

Let's look at a calculation of the income tax deduction allowable with a charitable remainder trust. Assume you are a 50-year-old gentleman and you transfer $20,000 of Runaway Success, Inc. stock to an annuity trust. You specify that the trust is to pay you 5% annually.

Go again to the "Annuity, Life Estate and Remainder Interest Values" table in Appendix E. Look under remainder (male), aged 50. You'll see the factor .32003. Your income-tax deduction in the year you made the transfer is $6,400.00 ($20,000 × .32003).

Let's further assume that you paid $5,000 for the stock. The potential capital gain of $15,000 (current value minus cost) is *avoided forever*. If the trust meets code requirements of a charitable remainder trust, it is income-tax exempt.

Income taxation to the beneficiary may be ordinary-income treatment, capital-gains treatment, excludable (if the trust invests in tax-free bonds), or tax free by virtue of being considered a distribution from principal, depending on the extent of distributions.

Estate-Tax Treatment

The value of retained-income interest is includable in your estate as settlor; however, the estate is entitled to a deduction for the value of the interest being passed in to the charity. A wash, in other words.

Gift-Tax Treatment

There is no gift tax liability unless income interest is payable to a third party. In that case, the value of the interest is subject to gift tax.

Charitable-Lead Trust

A charitable-lead trust is basically the reverse of the charitable-remainder trust. With a charitable-lead trust, the charity gets a determinable amount of income for a determinable period of time. At the end of that period, individual beneficiaries receive the remainder interest.

Aside from the altruistic motivations of simply wanting to give to charity, there are some fairly compelling gift-tax and estate-tax motivations for the settlor. For openers, if the trust is funded with property having a strong likelihood of appreciating, the settlor can pass the appreciation on to the beneficiaries without incurring gift taxes on the appreciation. This also means that appreciation on the assets and potential gift taxes are excluded from the gross estate. The settlor can thus retain control of trust assets within the family.

Income-Tax Treatment

From the settlor's point of view, income tax treatment involves a trade-off.

1. If you, as settlor, claim a tax deduction in the year you create the trust, the deduction is allowed only if in the following years the income actually produced by the trust, *including the amount paid to the charity,* is included in your income.
2. If you, as settlor, claim a tax deduction, the amount of your deduction is limited to 20% of your adjusted gross income. Excess contributions cannot be carried over.

As you would suspect, the deduction for a charitable-lead trust is rarely taken.

Estate-Tax Treatment

If the trust is in conformity with the code as regards payments to the charity and the settlor or the settlor's estate is entitled to a gift or estate tax deduction, the deduction is allowed at the time the trust is created and is based on the present value of the charitable interest.

Gift-Tax Treatment

When a charitable-lead trust is established during the lifetime of the settlor, a remainder interest is created that is subject to gift tax.

A properly structured trust can be a separate taxable entity or it may be simply a conduit through which income flows to the beneficiaries. In this event, income is taxable to the beneficiaries—not the trust.

Normally, income actually distributed by the trust to the beneficiary is taxable to the beneficiary and income accumulated by the trust is taxable to the trust.

A trust can be set up so that a portion of the income is taxable to the beneficiary and a portion is taxable to the trust. This is a good approach, since it increases the number of taxable entities.

Peculiarities in the codes governing trusts may make income from the trust taxable to the settlor, unless the trust is carefully structured.

Life-Insurance Trusts

Let's look now at the special consideration of life-insurance trusts. A life-insurance trust may be either a living trust or a testamentary trust. If a life-insurance trust is a living trust, it may be revocable, funded or unfunded, or a short-term, reversionary-type trust. Let's look at some of the advantages of life-insurance trusts.

1. They allow for a great deal of flexibility in handling distributions. If you want several people to receive a settlement, perhaps on an unequal basis, this can be handled by the trustee. Concerns such as divorce, remarriage, children of more than one marriage, and so forth, can readily be addressed.

2. Death proceeds from other employee benefit plans may be added to a life-insurance trust. This will aid in coordinating the distribution of other property added to the trust and will also aid in coordinating proper trust management.

3. It eliminates the second estate tax when the life beneficiaries die.

4. You can place restrictions and limitations on the use of funds by the beneficiaries and, in this way, protect family members who might otherwise be imprudent in the use of their inheritance. Such a provision is frequently called a "spend thrift" clause.

5. You can give your trustee investment discretion as you wish.

TABLE 10–1
Types of Trusts and their Ramifications

Type of Trust:	Irrevocable Living
General Description:	Settlor makes an irrevocable transfer of cash and/or property to the trust. Trust avoids probate.
Advantages:	Allows the settlor to arrange for continuity of management before and after death. Reduces costs by avoiding probate. Minimizes likelihood of contests from dissatisfied heirs. Permits the settlor to observe the performance of the estate fiduciaries during lifetime. May properly insulate trust from creditors.
Disadvantages:	Settlor must give up all enjoyment and control of trust assets. May expose assets to gift taxes. The costs of creating and maintaining the trust may offset some of the advantages.

TABLE 10–1
Types of Trusts and their Ramifications (continued)

Type of Trust:	*Irrevocable Living*
Tax Treatment:	Income distributed is taxable to the beneficiary.
Income Tax:	Income accumulated is taxable in the trust.
Estate Tax:	Not includable in settlor's estate.
Gift Tax:	Taxable to settlor subject to annual exclusion for present gift or income interest.
Type of Trust:	*Revocable Living*
General Description:	Settlor may or may not transfer assets to the trust.
	Settlor retains the right to revoke the trust.
	Avoids probate.
Advantages:	Avoids probate.
	Allows for continuity of income and management of assets for the survivors.
	Allows the settlor to observe the estate fiduciaries and to assess their capabilities during his/her lifetime.
	Creates a depository for assets of the estate.
	Allows for consolidation of assets and insulates assets from creditors (in some states).
Disadvantages:	Provides no tax advantages.
	Costs of creation and maintenance of trust may offset the benefits.
Tax Treatment	
Income Tax:	Income taxable to settlor.
Estate Tax:	Trust property includable in settlor's estate.
Gift Tax:	None
Type of Trust:	*Short-Term*
General Description:	Settlor will normally transfer assets to the trust.
	Trust will last for ten years or for the life of the life-income beneficiary.
	At the end of the trust term, principal reverts to the settlor.
Advantages:	Normal nontax advantages.
Disadvantages:	May expose assets to gift tax.
	Ties up assets for term of trust.
Tax Treatment	
Income Tax:	Income distributed is taxable to beneficiary.
	Income accumulated is taxable to the trust.
Estate Tax:	Present value of reversionary interest is includable in the estate of the settlor.
Gift Tax:	Taxable based on the value of the income interest.
Type of Trust:	*Pour-Over*
General Description:	Trust designed as a receptacle for assets which are "poured over" from the settlor's will for benefits from a qualified employee benefit plan, insurance proceeds, or for assets from other trusts or estates.
Advantages: Disadvantages: Tax Treatment:	Will be determined by whether the trust is revocable or irrevocable.
Type of Trust	*Standby*
General Description:	Normally revocable, but may become irrevocable if activated.
Advantages:	Allows for supervision of assets and professional management in the event of the settlor's inability to perform these duties.

TABLE 10–1

Types of Trusts and their Ramifications (continued)

Type of Trust:	*Standby*
Tax Treatment	
Income Tax:	Income taxable to settlor.
Estate Tax:	Includable in settlor's estate.
Gift Tax:	None

Type of Trust:	*Generation Skipping*
General Description:	Trust is designed to pass assets and income to successive generations. May be revocable or irrevocable. May be living or testamentary.
Advantages:	Avoids successive probate.
Tax Treatment	
Estate Tax :	Avoids successive estate taxes.
Income Tax: Gift Tax:	Depends on other decisions regarding the characteristics of the trust.

Type of Trust:	*Testamentary*
General Description:	Created by provision in the settlor's will. No property is transferred during his/her lifetime.
Advantages:	Allows for full use of the unified credit. Can avoid second taxation of assets on the death of the life beneficiary.
Tax Treatment	
Estate Tax:	Assets includable in settlor's estate.
Income Tax:	Distribution taxed to beneficiary.
Gift Tax:	None

Type of Trust:	*Charitable Remainder*
General Description:	Allows a settlor to provide a lifetime benefit to a noncharitable beneficiary— self, spouse and/or child—and to give the remainder (the property transferred) to charity.
Advantages:	Allows settlor to retain some income interest in the property without giving up estate-tax advantages.
Disadvantages:	Income is fixed as either an absolute dollar income (fixed-dollar annuity) or as a percentage of a fluctuation base (unitrust). Makes planning for future needs more difficult.
Tax Treatment	
Estate Tax:	Value of retained income interest is includable in the settlor's estate. Estate is entitled to a deduction for the value of the interest being passed on to charity.
Income Tax:	Donor (settlor) is entitled to income tax deduction equal to the value of the remainder interest that will pass to charity. Deductions allowed in the year property is transferred to the trust. The trust is income-tax exempt. Beneficiary's taxation depends on extent of distribution.
Gift Tax:	No gift-tax liability unless the income interest is payable to a third party. In that case, the value of that interest is subject to gift tax.

TABLE 10–1
Types of Trusts and their Ramifications (continued)

Type of Trust:	Charitable Lead
General Description:	Provides a charity with a determinable amount of income for a determinable period of time. At the end of the period, individual beneficiaries receive the remainder interest.
Advantages:	Allows settlor to avoid gift and estate taxes on appreciation of assets while retaining control of the assets within the family.
Disadvantages:	May create exposure to gift tax when assets are transferred.
Tax Treatment	
Estate Tax:	A deduction for the present value of the charitable interest is allowed to the settlor's estate if payments to the charity are in conformity with the Code.
Income Tax:	Settlor is allowed a tax deduction in the year the trust is created if in the following years income actually produced by the trust is included in the settlor's taxable income. This includes income paid to the trust. If a deduction is claimed, the amount is limited to 20% of adjusted gross income. Excess contributions cannot be carried over.
Gift Tax:	Remainder interest is subject to gift tax if trust is established during settlor's lifetime.

11

Case Study

On the following pages are the data for "John Jackson, Consultants," an unincorporated business, and the John Jackson family. "The Jacksons" are a composite of some of my clients—the concerns and objectives are real—the solutions are ones we actually employed.

Read the data sheets at the end of this chapter to acquaint yourself with the Jacksons, then we'll look at some recommendations. Since a complete, formal, financial plan may be as long as 40 pages or so, what follows are simply summary highlights.

The Jacksons' statement of net worth looked like this:

Net Worth

Closely Held Business Interest	$750,000
Cash	70,225
Mortgage Receivable	15,000
Personal Property	35,000
Cars	40,000
Cash Value	23,045
Real Estate Equity	386,250
	1,319,520

CONCERNS TO BE ADDRESSED BY FINANCIAL PLANNING

Their first concern was taxation. The Jacksons felt, quite justly, that their tax bill was too high.

They were undecided about whether to incorporate. The financial planning process included a comprehensive liability study on this point with all the pros and cons considered.

The Jacksons wondered if they were holding too much cash. On one hand, the reasons for holding cash were valid: the possibility of a need for cash in the business, and the necessity of paying estimated income tax. On the other hand, being in the 50% tax bracket caused the earnings on the cash to really take a beating.

Moreover, Mr. and Mrs. Jackson were so heavily involved with the business that they had not been able to explore investment opportunities and were unsure how they might invest their cash even if they were convinced they were holding too much.

Mr. Jackson wanted to consider ways of building wealth for retirement income. Since his business provided more income than he and Mrs. Jackson required as current income, he felt comfortable in committing to a fairly aggressive program. He expressed a hope that a retirement plan could address this objective so that his wealth building could be with pre-tax dollars.

Almost half of Mr. Jackson's wealth is in his business. That's very typical for a business owner and not easily rectified.

The apartment building they owned was very troublesome to them, and they considered selling it and investing the proceeds for growth and for income at his retirement while Mr. Jackson continued working.

Mr. Jackson felt good about his business but had made one decision with which he was unhappy. He had created a buy/sell agreement whereby his two key consultants could buy the business in the event of his death. Both Henry Blake and Susan Keys, his daughter, were party to the buy/sell. He had originally felt that Susan would need Henry Blake. Now, however, Susan had exhibited talent and business acumen surpassing Henry's, and Mr. Jackson wanted Susan to inherit 100% of the business.

The recommendations we made were:

1. To incorporate. Space doesn't permit going into all the advantages the Jacksons enjoyed from incorporation, but the before and after schedule that follows outlines the major advantage—tax saving. You can see for yourself how dramatic the improvement was in this point.

2. We suggested the apartment building be placed on the market.

With the $75,000–$80,000 of equity the Jacksons could realize, they should invest in five or six real estate limited partnerships which would be designed to achieve their maximum growth potential and terminate in about 5 years. The financial planning process and fee will include selection of these investments. Net financial gains should be better than those realized on the building.

3. Mr. Jackson's problem of having a large percentage of his net worth in his business is not easily solved. We've established a goal of diversifying outside his business for balance. We also suggested that he consider personally owning assets that the business can use and leasing them to the corporation.

4. With the $70,000 in cash, we suggested they

   a. Put $15,000 in a rather conservative tax shelter generating an 80% write-off ($15,000 invested resulted in $12,000 of tax deduction)

   b. Put $35,000 in a money market mutual fund for eventual payment of their tax bill and as personal emergency fund and

   c. Put $20,000 in a single-premium deferred annuity. The money in the annuity will be readily available if needed for the business, but if not, it is paying a competitive interest rate, and the interest is tax deferred.

5. In terms of making Henry Blake a party to the buy/sell, Mr. Jackson decided to change that when the current buy/sell expires. At that time, he plans to bequeath Susan $325,000 worth of the stock, which will fully use his estate tax credit, and allow her to buy the remainder from her mother, who has signed an agreement to this effect.

   This will eliminate the possibility of installment payment of estate tax in the closely held interest but, in this case, that's immaterial since Mr. Jackson is leaving everything (except the $325,000 of stock) to his wife. The marital deduction will eliminate his estate-tax bill.

   Mr. Jackson suspects that Henry Blake may leave if not included in a buy/sell but feels that he is not critical to the success of the business. He is prepared to take the risk.

6. We worked with the Jacksons' attorney to get a will drawn up. He also did all the legal work relative to the incorporation.

7. We installed a pension plan that is designed to allow for the maximum contribution for Mr. Jackson. You can see from the before and after performance that we are allowing for $53,848 in corporate retirement plan contributions. In addition, Mr. Jackson plans to give both Henry and Susan $2,000 for an IRA account.

Of the $53,848 going into the pension plan, $45,830 is going to Mr. Jackson's benefit—a full 85.1%. His annual benefit at retirement is projected at $71,040.

This plan will be considered a "top-heavy" plan, a new classification created by the tax equity and fiscal responsibility act of 1982. Top-heavy plans require minimum nonintegrated benefits for all employees as well as more rapid vesting schedules. Our plan does provide sufficient benefits for all employees but will require the necessary vesting schedule. The top-heavy rules will pertain to tax years beginning after 1983.

I thought you would find it interesting to see the sample exhibits at the end of this chapter that demonstrate some of the choices available. Notice that our choices were from a low of 44% (see Exhibit II on page 264) of the contribution going to Mr. Jackson's account to a high of 85.9%. The reason we didn't select the plan giving him only 44% is self-evident. The reason we didn't select the plan giving him 85.9% is because the total contributions were only $24,084. These percentages were made possible by having contributions and benefits integrated with Social Security.

In Mr. Jackson's case we were interested in two things: getting the maximum allowable annual contribution into the plan and favoring Mr. Jackson. A combination we could have chosen is Exhibit III and IV (see pages 265 and 266), which are designed to contribute 25% of Mr. Jackson's compensation. This combination is frequently the most advantageous to a younger principal.

You'll notice from the exhibit at the end of the chapter that the defined benefit plan favors older employees. For example, the secretary who is 45 years old is receiving 5.5% of the contributions. If you'll look at the employee census, you will see that Mr. Jackson felt it was very unlikely she would stay. The plan provides graduated vesting, which means if she leaves before six years, she forfeits a portion. Forfeited funds in a defined benefit plan reduce corporate contributions. Detailed data gathering with your financial planner reveals this kind of information and results in a plan that works for you.

With the retirement plan contribution, Mr. Jackson's compensation is effectively $120,830, but only $75,000 is taxable. The retirement plan not only allows him to save pre-tax dollars but allows him to shelter the earnings on those investments until retirement. What an improvement over the after-tax savings program he used as a sole proprietor.

I hope the case study has given you some idea of how the financial planning process works, and how dramatic the improvement in your financial situation can be with good financial planning.

We've only covered the highlights—but bear in mind that the kind of backup analysis and study that you've seen with the retirement plan goes into every aspect of your financial plan: insurance, investments, estate planning, and so forth.

I hope I've motivated you to get started!

The sample exhibits follow. I'm grateful to Lloyd Miner of Automatic Data Processing[1] for providing these actuarial studies.

---

[1]Automatic Data Processing, Pension Services Division, 22481 Aspan St., Box A, El Toro, California 92630.

	Before Incorporation			After Incorporation		
	Business	Personal with tax shelter	without tax shelter	Business	Personal with tax shelter	without tax shelter
Business Income Tax						
Business Gross	750000			750000		
Business Expenses – (Does not include Mr. Jackson's salary)	600000			600000		
Mr. Jackson's Salary	N/A			75000		
Retirement Plan Contribution	N/A			53848		
Paid to Blake & Susan for IRA	N/A			4000		
Business Net	150000			17152		
Taxable Corporate Income	N/A	N/A	N/A	17152		
Corporate tax				2573		
Personal Income Tax						
Business Net/Salary		150000	150000		75000	75000
Investment Income		25000	25000		25000	25000
Personal Deductions: Depreciation, Interest, etc.		33925	33925		33925	33925
Tax Shelter deductions		12000	-0-		12000	-0-
* IRA for Mr. & Mrs. Jackson					4000	4000
Personal Taxable Income		129075	141075		50075	62075
Personal Income Tax		48540	54539		12044	16927
Combined Tax-Business and Personal		48540	54539		14617	19500
Retained Earnings	N/A			****14579		
Personal Cash Flow						
Income		175000	175000		100000	100000
Personal Income Tax		48540	54539		12044	16927
Tax Shelter		15000	-0-		15000	-0-
IRA		-0-	-0-		4000	4000
Spendable Cash		111460	120461		68956	79073
** Additions to Net Worth		15000	-0-		***64830	49830

*Mr. Jackson was eligible for an IRA before incorporation as well as after. He just hadn't set one up.

**M/M Jackson may add some of their spendable income to their net worth

***Includes Mr. Jackson's share of the retirement plan contribution

****Could be used for Deferred Compensation to Mr. Jackson

Figure 11–1. Relevant Financial Data for the Jacksons.

EXHIBIT I
Profit Sharing Illustration for
John Jackson Consultants, Inc.
Employee Census
Eligible Employees

Name	Date of Birth	Date of Hire	Compensation*
Keyman, A	8/1/20	1/1/62	75,000.00
Salesman, A	2/1/52	1/1/77	35,000.00
Daughter, Boss	11/1/54	1/1/78	32,000.00
Secretary, A	11/1/37	1/1/79	15,000.00
Clerk, A	5/1/52	1/1/81	13,500.00
Total			170,500.00

*The compensation reported has been annualized.

EXHIBIT II

Profit Sharing Illustration for
John Jackson Consultants, Inc.

Name	S E X	Age EA	Age AA	Age RA	Service P	Service F	Service T	Total Annual Compensation	Annual Contribution		Retirement Accumulation	Monthly Income
Keyman, A	M	61	62	71	21	9	30	75,000.00	11,250.00	44.0%	159,670.	1,860.
Salesman, A	M	30	31	65	6	34	40	35,000.00	5,250.00	20.5%	1,127,229.	11,440.
Daughter, Boss	F	27	28	65	5	36	41	32,000.00	4,800.00	18.8%	1,351,820.	12,564.
Secretary, A	F	44	45	65	4	19	23	15,000.00	2,250.00	8.8%	125,470.	1,166.
Clerk, A	F	30	31	65	2	34	36	13,500.00	2,025.00	7.9%	434,788.	4,041.
Totals								170,500.00	25,575.00			

Plan Provisions
Type: Profit sharing—nonintegrated
Contribution:
  15% of covered compensation
Allocation:
  15% of participant's compensation
Compensation: All compensation
Retirement requirements
  Age: 65
  Participation: 10
Vesting schedule: 4/40

Eligibility
Minimum age: 25
Minimum service: 12 months
Minimum of 1000 hours per 12-month period
Minimum waiting period: automatic entry

Calculation Assumptions
Preretirement:
  Interest: 9%
Postretirement:
  Interest: 9%
  Mortality: 71 IAM
  Normal form: life only

EXHIBIT III

Profit Sharing Illustration for
John Jackson Consultants, Inc.

Name	S E X	Age EA	Age AA	Age RA	Service P	Service F	Service T	Total Annual Compensation	Annual Contribution	%	Retirement Accumulation	Monthly Income
Keyman, A	M	61	62	71	21	9	30	75,000.00	12,475.65	48.8%	162,445.	1,892.
Salesman, A	M	30	31	65	6	34	40	35,000.00	4,889.90	19.1%	963,224	9,777.
Daughter, Boss	F	27	28	65	5	36	41	32,000.00	4,342.00	16.9%	1,025,253.	9,535.
Secretary, A	F	44	45	65	4	19	23	15,000.00	2,035.50	8.0%	93,670.	871.
Clerk, A	F	30	31	65	2	34	36	13,500.00	1,831.95	7.2%	360,861.	3,356.
Totals								170,500.00	25,575.00			

Plan Provisions

Type: Profit sharing—integrated
Contribution:
    15% of covered compensation
Allocation:
    5.4% of compensation in excess of Social Security
    integration level, balance allocated on the basis of
    participant's compensation as a ratio to total compensation
Integration: $32,400
Compensation: All compensation
Retirement requirements
    Age: 65
    Participation: 10
Vesting schedule: Six-year graded vesting

Eligibility
Minimum age: 25
Minimum service: 12 months
Minimum of 1000 hours per 12-month period
Minimum waiting period: automatic entry

Calculation Assumptions
Preretirement:
    Interest: 9%
Postretirement:
    Interest: 9%
    Mortality: 71 IAM
    Normal form: Life only

265

EXHIBIT IV
Money Purchase Illustration for
John Jackson Consultants, Inc.

Name	SEX	Age EA	AA	RA	Service P	F	T	Total Annual Compensation	Annual Contribution		Retirement Accumulation	Monthly Income
Keyman, A	M	61	62	71	21	9	30	75,000.00	6,270.00	44.0%	81,642.	951.
Salesman, A	M	30	31	65	6	34	40	35,000.00	2,926.00	20.5%	576,370	5,850.
Daughter, Boss	F	27	28	65	5	36	41	32,000.00	2,675.20	18.8%	631,680.	5,874.
Secretary, A	F	44	45	65	4	19	23	15,000.00	1,254.00	8.8%	57,707.	536.
Clerk, A	F	30	31	65	2	34	36	13,500.00	1,128.60	7.9%	222,314.	2,067.
Totals								170,500.00	14,253.80			

Plan Provisions
Type: Money purchase—nonintegrated
Contribution:
  8.36% of covered compensation
Allocation:
  8.36% of participant's compensation
Compensation: All compensation
Retirement requirements
  Age: 65
  Participation: 10
Vesting schedule: Six-year graded vesting

Eligibility
Minimum age: 25
Minimum service: 12 months
Minimum of 1000 hours per 12-month period
Minimum waiting period: automatic entry

Calculation Assumptions
Preretirement
  Interest: 9%
Postretirement:
  Interest: 9%
  Mortality: 71 IAM
  Normal form: life only

266

Name	S E X	Age EA	Age AA	Age RA	Service P	Service F	Service T	Annual Compensation	Annual Benefit	Normal Cost		Retirement Accumulation	Social Security
Keyman, A	M	41	62	71	21	9	30	75,000.	75,000.	48,385.	81.0%	637,754.	10,492.
Salesman, A	M	25	31	65	6	34	40	35,000.	35,000.	3,164.	5.3%	352,599.	9,292.
Daughter, Boss	F	23	28	65	5	36	41	32,000.	32,000.	2,636.	4.4%	358,233.	9,232.
Secretary, A	F	41	45	65	4	19	23	15,000.	15,000.	4,199.	7.0%	167,922.	6,733.
Clerk, A	F	29	31	65	2	34	36	13,500.	13,500.	1,356.	2.3%	151,129	6,153.
Totals								170,500.	170,500.	59,740.		1,667,637.	41,902.

Plan Provisions
Type: Flat benefit—nonintegrated
Formula: 100% of average monthly compensation
Service for full benefit:
  Total: 10
Retirement requirements
  Age: 65
  Participation: 10
Compensation: All compensation
Normal form: Life only
Final averaging period:
  Any consecutive 5 which produce
  highest average monthly compensation
Maximum salary: $.00
Vesting schedule: Six-year graded vesting

Eligibility
Minimum age: 25
Minimum service: 12 months
Minimum of 1000 hours per 12-month period
Minimum waiting period: automatic entry

Calculation Assumptions
Funding method: Individual level
Preretirement:
  Interest: 6%
  Mortality: None
  Turnover: None
  Salary scale: None
  Disability:
Postretirement:
  Interest: 6%
  Mortality: 71 IAM

267

EXHIBIT VI
Defined Benefit Pension Plan for John Jackson Consultants, Inc.

Name	S E X	Age EA	AA	RA	Service P	F	T	Annual Compensation	Annual Benefit	Normal Cost		Retirement Accumulation	Social Security*
Keyman, A	M	41	62	71	21	9	30	75,000.	71,040.	45,830.	85.1%	604,080.	13,200.
Salesman, A	M	25	31	65	6	34	40	35,000.	25,280.	2,285.	4.2%	254,677.	32,400.
Daughter, Boss	F	23	28	65	5	36	41	32,000.	22,400.	1,845.	3.4%	250,763.	32,400.
Secretary, A	F	41	45	65	4	19	23	15,000.	10,500.	2,939.	5.5%	117,545.	24,600.
Clerk, A	F	29	31	65	2	34	36	13,500.	9,450.	949.	1.8%	105,791.	32,400.
Totals								170,500.	138,670.	53,848.		1,332,856.	135,000

*The Social Security amount is for benefit calculation only and does not represent participant's expected income at his normal retirement date from the social security administration.

Plan Provisions
Type: Flat benefit—integrated
Formula: 70% of average monthly compensation
plus 30% in excess of Social Security integration level
Integration: Social Security Table CC82
Service for full benefit
Total: 10
Retirement requirements
Age: 65
Participation: 10
Compensation: All compensation
Normal form: Life only
Final averaging period:
Any consecutive 5 which produce
highest average monthly compensation
Maximum salary: $.00
Vesting schedule: Six-year graded vesting

Eligibility
Minimum age: 25
Minimum service: 12 months
Minimum of 1000 hours per 12-month period
Minimum waiting period: Automatic entry

Calculation Assumptions
Funding method: Individual level
Preretirement
Interest: 6%
Mortality: None
Turnover: None
Salary scale: None
Disability:
Postretirement
Interest: 6%
Mortality: 71 IAM

EXHIBIT VII
Defined Benefit Pension Plan for
John Jackson Consultants, Inc.

Name	S E X	Age EA	Age AA	Age RA	Service P	Service F	Service T	Annual Compensation	Annual Benefit	Normal Cost		Retirement Accumulation	Social Security*
Keyman, A	M	41	62	71	21	9	30	75,000.	37,332.	24,084.	85.9%	317,448.	13,200.
Salesman, A	M	25	31	65	6	34	40	35,000.	14,832.	1,341.	4.8%	149,421.	32,400.
Daughter, Boss	F	23	28	65	5	36	41	32,000.	13,440.	1,107.	3.9%	150,458.	32,400.
Secretary, A	F	41	45	65	4	19	23	15,000.	3,600.	1,008.	3.6%	40,301.	24,600.
Clerk, A	F	29	31	65	2	34	36	13,500.	4,860.	488	1.7%	54,407.	32,400.
Totals								170,500.	74,064.	28,028.		712,035.	135,000.

*The Social Security amount is for benefit calculation only and does not represent participant's expected income at his normal retirement date from the social security administration.

Plan Provisions
Type: Unit benefit—integrated
Formula: 1% of average monthly compensation for each
year of total service plus .8% in excess of Social Security
integration level for each year of total service
Integration: Social Security Table CC82
Service for full benefit
Total: 10
Retirement requirements
Age: 65
Participation: 10
Compensation: All compensation
Normal form: Life only
Final averaging period:
Any consecutive 5 which produce
highest average monthly compensation
Maximum salary: $.00
Vesting schedule: Six-year graded vesting

Eligibility
Minimum age: 25
Minimum service: 12 months
Minimum of 1000 hours per 12-month period
Minimum waiting period: Automatic entry

Calculation Assumptions
Funding method: Individual level
Preretirement:
  Interest: 6%
  Mortality: None
  Turnover: None
  Salary scale: None
  Disability:
Postretirement:
  Interest: 6%
  Mortality: 71 IAM

269

CONFIDENTIAL INFORMATION
CONCERNING
THE
FINANCIAL PLANNING OBJECTIVES
OF

John Jackson Consultants

COMPANY

CLOSELY HELD BUSINESS INTERESTS

Name of Business ___ *John Jackson Consultants* ___

Address ___ *(Anywhere, U.S.A.* ___

Phone ___ *(123) 456-7890* ___

Nature of Business ___ *Consultants* ___

Net Fair Market Value of Entire Business $ *750,000* ___

Determined by _____ Client's Estimate

_____ Book Value

___✓___ Buy/Sell Agreement   *CPA suggested the value for the Buy/Sell*

___✓___ Professional Valuation

_____ Other _____

Tax Basis of Your Interest $ *220,000*   *at book value*

Form of Business

___✓___ Sole proprietorship   _____ Subchapter S corp.

_____ Partnership   _____ Professional corp.

_____ Business corporation   _____ Other _____

_____ Non-Profit organization

Accounting Basis ___✓___ Cash _____ Accrual

Date of Incorporation ___ *N/A* ___

Fiscal Year ___ *December 31* ___

Business was a ___ — ___ for ___ — ___ years before incorporation.

Type of Business (manufacturer, dealer, etc.) _____
                          Consultant

Is there a Buy-Sell Agreement?

_____✓_____ yes—Please provide copy and/or details   *Buy/Sell allows 2 key*
_____ no
employees to buy from the estate if John Jackson dies. Term insurance funds the buy/sell. Employees pay the insurance personally and are the beneficiaries.

At death, business is to be:

_____ Continued by heirs   _____ Inherited but not run by heirs

_____ Sold to surviving partners

_____✓_____ Sold to key employees—Is there a written agreement?

                                     _____✓_____ yes   _____ no

_____ Liquidated

_____ Other _____

_____

Please provide financial statements, balance sheets, profit and loss statements, and tax returns for the past three years and a copy of all agreements between owners and key employees or the business and key employees.

	Gross Sales	Taxable Income (to Mr. Jackson personally)	Corporate Tax	Net Profit
19 80	440, 700	84, 300	N/A	
19 81	518, 500	99, 700	N/A	
19 82	610, 000	118, 200	N/A	
19 83	750, 000	150, 000	N/A	

Fringe Benefits Provided

_____ Qualified pension plan

_____ Qualified profit sharing plan

_____ Split dollar

_____ Deferred compensation

_____ Deferred benefit plan

_____ ESOP

_____ TRASOP

_____

_____

_____

_____ Stock options

_____ Group life

_____ Long term disability

_____ Health insurance

_____ Medical reimburse

_____ Company car

___✓___ Other _*Company reimburses some travel, entertainment and educational expenses. No real benefits.*_

Please provide copies of the plan documents and the latest benefit statements.

Does the employer have any union(s)?_____ yes ___✓___ no

If yes, has there ever been good faith bargaining on the part of the union(s) for retirement

benefits? _____ yes _____ no

What is the approximate rate of employee turnover as a percent of the active group for the past five (5) years?

Year	Rate	
19**82**	**5**%	*Mr. Jackson says he's*
19**81**	**10**%	*learning ways of keeping*
19**80**	**20**%	*people. Looks for turnover*
19**79**	**40**%	*to become less of a problem*
19**78**	**40**%	*in the future.*

What is the approximate rate of salary increases over each of the past five (5) years?

Tried to match inflation, more or less

		19 **78**	19 **79**	19 **80**	19 **81**	19 **82**
Salaried employees		7 %	7 %	10 %	10 %	8 %
Hourly employees	N/A	___ %	___ %	___ %	___ %	___ %
Union employees	N/A	___ %	___ %	___ %	___ %	___ %
Other		___ %	___ %	___ %	___ %	___ %

Indicate any other pertinent information regarding the salary policy of the corporation.

Likes to give some portion as "inflation" increases, but prefers to give the major portion of increase as merit increases. Goes over the salary and increases individually with each employee when raises are announced.

Corporate tax returns filed   *N/A*

_____ Separated by corporation

_____ Consolidated return

Employee identifying number _*See tax return*_

Related corporations or entities (names, nature of enterprises, relationship of enterprises)

_____ *None* _____

Accountant

Name _*Ellen Epoch, CPA*_

Firm _*Epoch & Associates*_

Address _*Anywhere*_

_*U. S. A.*_

Telephone number _*(098) 765-4321*_

Attorney

    Name _____

    Firm _____

    Address _____

    _____

    Telephone number _____

Earnings projections:

Business is in a strong growth trend. Should increase revenues by 20%-25% per year for five years or so, then level off to about 10% growth per year. Profit margin may drop a total of 5% over next five years as growth takes place.

What cost commitment should be considered for a pension or profit sharing plan?

_____% of Payroll

_____% of Profit

_____% of Profit in excess of $ _____

$_____   Flat dollar amount

____✓____   Other *Mr. Jackson would like to put as much aside for himself as possible. Would like a plan that awards junior professional staff after they have proven themselves.*

Industry employers of concern (locally).

Details as to their compensation programs.

Do you need to be competitive to attract or retain employees?

The biggest competitors for good consultants are not other firms, but the consultants themselves leaving to set up their own shops. Mr. Jackson would like the fringe-benefits program to "tie" them to his firm in some way.

Rank the retirement plan benefits in order of importance:

_____*1*_ Tax savings *(for Mr. Jackson)*   __*N/A*__ Reduce union pressure

_____*2*_ Retain key employees   __*4*__ Gracefully retire older employees

_____*3*_ Estate conservation

_____ Other (please explain) _____

_____

_____

What are the most important factors in making your business successful? *Mr. Jackson retired from a large publicly traded firm and founded John Jackson Consultants. He has a large network of contacts in the industry and is well respected. He is very competent and inspires client loyalty by his calm, confident manner of problem solving.*

How do you feel about the future of your business?
Excellent, if Mr. Jackson's health permits him a few more years to firmly establish the business. He pins a good deal of hope in his junior staff. So concerned that if they leave, he doesn't have time to start over again and bring on new consultants.

Number of new full-time employees hired:

last year _____*1*_____

two years ago _____*1*_____

three years ago ____*1*_____

Number of full-time employees terminated:

last year _____*1*_____

two years ago _____*1*_____

three years ago ____*1*_____

What is the probable increase in full-time personnel in the next five years?

_____ ✓ less than 10   *Actually doesn't expect but two*
_____ 10–19   *more. Another professional and*
_____ 20 or more   *one para-professional.*

General specifications desired in plan

Effective date of plan_____

How much would you like to contribute as

$_____ of % _____ of compensation

Eligibility requirements

Months of service_____ (suggest 12 months to allow later vesting)

Minimum age _____ (up to age 25)

Maximum age _____ (only for defined benefit plans—cannot be lower than 55)

Normal retirement age

_____ all age 65

_____ 65 years old or ten years of participation, whichever is later

_____ Other _____

Type of plan and formula

Defined contribution _____ pension _____ profit sharing

nonintegrated _____% of compensation

integrated _____% of first $_____ of comp.

Annual plus _____% of excess

Defined Benefit

Nonintegrated

Flat percentage benefit _____% of all comp.

Unit benefit (years of service)

_____% of all comp. for each year of service. Maximum years of credited

service equals _____ years.

Integrated

Integration level

Maximum permitted by current Social Security Act

_____✓_____ yes   _____ no

Flat percentage benefit

_____ % of base plus _____% of excess

_____% of excess only

Unit benefit (years of service)

_____% of base for each year of service plus _____% of excess for

each year of service. Maximum years of credited service equals

_____ years.

_____% of excess only for each year of service.

Maximum years of credited service equals _____ years.

Target benefit

_____100_% of monthly compensation

BUSINESS INSURANCE

Key person life insurance

Insured	Title	Amount	Annual Premium
John Jackson	owner/mgr.	$750,000	

Mr. Jackson is hopeful that given one full year of gross income as insurance proceeds, his two junior consultants could survive and manage the business on their own.

Buy and sell agreement funded by life insurance

Entity _____   Cross purchase _____ ✓ _____

Insured	Title	Amount	Annual Premium
John Jackson	owner/mgr.	$750,000	

Split dollar agreements

Insured	Title	Amount	Annual Premium
	None		

Employee Census

Name	Key Person Y or N	Sex Male or Female	Date of Birth M/D/Y	Date Joined Firm M/D/Y	Compensation	Compensation Mode*	Position	Eligible Payroll	Probability they will stay for four years a. very likely b. likely c. unlikely d. very unlikely
1. John Jackson	Y	M	August 1920	1962	75,000	A	owner/ mgr.		a
2. Henry Blake	Y	M	Feb. 1952	1977	35,000	A	salesman		
3. Susan Jackson	Y	F	Nov. 1954	1978	32,000	A	consultant		
4. Secretary	N	F	Nov. 1937	1979	15,000	A	secretary		c
5. Clerk	N	F	May 1952	1981	13,500	A	clerk		a
6.									
7.									
8.									
9.									
10.									

*H—hourly W—weekly B—bi-weekly S—semi-monthly M—monthly A—annually

Owners of the Business

Name	Title	Date of Birth	% Owned or # of Shares	Annual Income from Business	Active in Business yes/no	Ownership*	Key Person Life Insurance yes/no Amount
1. John Jackson	owner/mgr.	Aug. 17, 1920	100%	$ 150,000	yes	a.	yes $ 750,000
2.							
3.							
4.							
5.							

*a. community property
b. joint tenancy with spouse
c. joint tenancy with _____
d. husband's separate property
e. wife's separate property
f. tenancy in common
g. tenancy by the entireties

CONFIDENTIAL INFORMATION
CONCERNING
THE
FINANCIAL PLANNING OBJECTIVES
OF

John Jackson

PERSONAL

PERSONAL AND FAMILY DATA

Client's Name _John Jackson_

Residence Address _Anywhere_

_U.S.A._

Home Phone _(147) 258-3690_

Occupation _Owner/mgr. - John Jackson Consultants_

Business Address _Anywhere_

Business Phone _(741) 852-0963_

Date of Birth _August 17, 1920_ Place of Birth _Louisiana_

Social Security # _123-45-6789_

Health _Excellent_ Smoker: _____ Nonsmoker: _✓_

Marital Status _Married_

Spouse's Name _Evelyn Jones Jackson_

Occupation _Homemaker_

Business Address _N/A_

Business Phone _N/A_

Date of Birth _July 2, 1924_ Place of Birth _Louisiana_

Social Security # _741-52-9863_

Health _Excellent_ Smoker: _____ Nonsmoker: _✓_

Children

Name	Date of Birth	Marital Status	Number of Children	Occupation
John Jackson, Jr.	1947	Married	2	Engineer
Michelle Jackson Le Blanc	1952	Married	2	Attorney
Theodore Jackson	1955	Married	1	Career Counselor
Susan Jackson	1954	Single	0	Consultant

Other dependents

_____ None _____

Do any dependents have health problems? _____ yes ___✓___ no

Any previous marriages? _____ yes ___✓___ no

Obligations under divorce judgments _____

_____

Are you a party to any trusts? _____ yes ___✓___ no

If yes, details: _____

_____

Have you made any lifetime gifts? _____ yes ___✓___ no

Do you wish to make lifetime gifts? ___✓___ yes _____ no

Do you have a will? _____ yes ___✓___ no

If yes, details _____

_____

Health Insurance

Major medical ___✓___ yes _____ no

Maximum $ 1,000,000 _____ Deductible $ 500 _____ Per year

Disability _____ yes ____✓____ no

Amount $_____ Per _____ Benefit period _____

Elimination period _____ Annual premium $ _____

Type of policy _____ guaranteed renewable _____ noncancellable

Annual (posttax) living expense $ __72,000_____

Annual living expense in the event of your death $ __65,000_____
  (today's dollars)   (posttax)

Annual living expense in the event of your disability $ __72,000_____
  (today's dollars)   (posttax)

Desired annual income at retirement $ __72,000_____
  (today's dollars)   (posttax)

Anticipated inflation rate per year_____ __10__ %

Are you covered under a pension plan? _____ yes ____✓____ no

If yes, please give full details: _When Mr. Jackson left the_
publicly traded firm to start John Jackson Consultants,
he took his retirement plan in a lump sum and put
it in his business.

Husband's gross income annually

  198 __2__ $ __150,000_____
  198 __1__ $ __118,200_____
  198 __0__ $ __99,700_____

Expectation regarding future income

Should increase by about 10% per year.

_____

_____

Wife's gross income annually

198___ $_____ None _____

198___ $_____

198___ $_____

Expectation regarding future income

_____ N|A _____

At what age do you plan to retire? _____ 70 _____

At what age does your spouse plan to retire? _____ N/A _____

Savings:

Passbook savings accounts

Institution	Rate %	Ownership*	Amount
First NBC	5¼	Community	$12,000

Certificates of deposit

Institution	Rate %	Date of Maturity	Ownership*	Amount
S + L	14.4	July 1984	C	$25,000
1st Hmstd.	13.2	Dec. 1983	C	$15,000

Credit union   None

_____ Rate % _____ Ownership* _____ Amount

Money market mutual funds

Institution	Average % Rate	Ownership*	Amount at date of data gathering
First Investors	12	C	$18,225

Comments: _Has cash because:_ ① _he was unsure of business growth pattern;_ ② _to pay income taxes;_ ③ _didn't know of good investment alternatives._

*CS—Client Separate
 SS—Spouse Separate
 C—Community (or joint)

Receivables

(Obligations: Notes, mortgages, accounts receivable, etc., owed to you or your spouse personally. Do not include such items owed to a business in which you or your spouse have an interest.)

Type of Receivable	Debtor	Total Balance	How is debt being repaid	Ownership*	How likely are you to collect a. very likely c. unlikely b. likely d. very unlikely
1. Mortgage	M/M Allen B. Lime	$ 15,000	Monthly on ten year amortization schedule: 1975-1985, 12%. They will a acct t mortgage when they sell their home.	C	a.
2.					
3.					
4.					
5.					
6.					
7.					
8.					
9.					

*CS—Client Separate   SS—Spouse Separate   C—Community (or joint)

Miscellaneous Personal Property: Other Assets
(automobiles, jewelry, household furniture, collections, etc.)

Nature of Property	Fair Market Value	Ownership	Year Acquired	Original Cost
1. Diamond	$10,000	C	1975	$8,200
2. Miscellaneous in Home	$15,000	C	Various	Various
3.				
4.				
5.				
6.				
7.				
8.				
9.				
10.				

Inheritances (only include those expected inheritances over $100,000.00)

Expected inheritance
of husband
             1. $ *150,000* _____ from ___*Father*___

                  age *86* _____ health __*very poor*__

             2. $_____ from _____

                  age _____ health _____

Expected inheritance
of wife   *None*   1. $_____ from _____

                  age _____ health _____

             2. $_____ from _____

                  age _____ health _____

Please rate the following financial objectives according to the following scale:

	1 of no importance	5 moderately important	10 extremely important	

1. Achieving faster asset growth   *10*

2. Increasing current income from investments   *0*

3. Paying lower income tax   *10*

4. Obtaining professional help in the management of my assets   *10*

5. Protecting assets against inflation   *10*

6. More suitably positioning investment assets   *10*

7. Supporting a family member   *0*

8. Providing college education for children   *0*

9. Retiring comfortably   *10*

10. Further building of personal wealth   *10*

11. Conserving my estate   *5*

12. Providing help and/or experience to inexperienced heirs to manage
assets   *5*

13. Protect spouse and/or children in the event of my death   *10*

14. Provide for family in the event of my disability   *10*

15. Reviewing my insurance program   _____ *5*

16. Making gifts to family members   _____ *5*

17. Making charitable gifts   _____ *5*

18. Buying or building a home   _____ *0*

19. Other _____

    _____   _____

20. Other _____

    _____   _____

Life Insurance

Type	Company	Policy Number	Insured	Owner	Beneficiary	When Iss'd	Med. (Y/N)	Acc. Dth. Bft. (Y/N)	(1) Face Amt.	(2) Cash Value	(3) Loans	(4) Net Ins. (1-2)	(5) Ann. Prem.	(6) Last Yrs. Refund (Dvdnd)	(7) Net Prem. (5-6)	(8) Lost Earnings @ 8% in Cash Value	(9) Total Cost (7+8)	(10) Cost Per Thousand (9÷4)
Whole Life	Mother's Apple Pie	123.4567	John	John	Evelyn	Dec. 1942	N	N	5,000	3,745	-0-	1255	169	-0-	169	300	469	373.70
Whole Life	Blamed Life	876.5438	John	John	Evelyn	Oct. 1949	N	Y	35,000	18,000	-0-	17000	1,033	731	302	1440	1742	102.47
Whole Life	ABC	976543	John	John	Evelyn	April 1964	N	N	3,300	1,300	-0-	2000	145	40	85	104	189	94.50

Total Cash Values $ 23,045

Minus Total Loans -$ -0-

Equals Net Cash Values =$ 23,045

Total Death Benefit $ 43,300

Total Annual Premium $ 1,327

Name: John Jackson

Date: Fall 1982

293

Real Estate Owned Personally

Location or Description	Year Acquired	Original Cost (includ. Improve-ments)	Total Fair Market Value	Client's % of Total Fair Market Value	Total Mortgage Balance	Remain-ing Period of Loan	Rents Received Monthly	Monthly Mortgage Payment	Rate of Mortgage	Owner-ship*	Equity
1. 5-Unit Apt. Bldg.	1979	$125,000	$175,000	100%	$93,750	17 yrs.	$1375	$1245	14%	C	$81,250
2. Commercial Lot	1955	15,000	75,000	100%	-0-	-0-	-0-	-0-	-0-	C	75,000
3. Home	1970	175,000	350,000	100%	120,000	18 yrs.	-0-	1205	9%	C	230,000
4.											
5.											
6.											
7.											
8.											
9.											
10.											

*Ownership: CS—Client Separate SS—Spouse Separate C—Community

A Letter to My
Fellow Practitioners

THE PERFECT CLIENT

Clients are always looking for the perfect investment, and financial planners are always looking for the perfect client. I still haven't found the perfect investment, but to me the closest thing to a perfect client is the principal in a closely held business.

There are a number of reasons why these clients are such a joy to work with. For openers, they speak the language of business. This makes it possible for you to explain rather complex recommendations with the assurance that they will understand.

My greatest pleasure, however, in working with such clients comes from the fact that they are well accustomed to taking a body of information and making decisions on a timely basis. Business owners are demanding in the sense that they expect creative thinking based on absolutely dependable information, but they are also fair decision makers when you provide the necessary information.

Business owners also appreciate the economics of your business. They understand that if you don't get compensated fairly for your time and talent, you won't be able to continue to serve their needs.

You shouldn't have problems finding these clients: There are currently about 15 million American companies, 14 million of which are defined as small businesses. Only 13,000 employ more than 500 workers. These so-called "small businesses" employ half of the private sector work force.

Recognize, however, that working with business owners is very demanding. First, you have to learn all the peculiarities of the tax law as it relates to businesses and, particularly, as it relates to transactions between the business and the business owner. You will have to work hard at staying current.

You also have to be creative. Business owners are frequently successful because they do things differently, or better, or smarter than their competition. They expect no less from their financial planner. They are rarely satisfied with "plain vanilla." If you feel that you would like to work with business owners, the following will be of interest.

Plan to Spend Some Money on Reference Materials

Industry-generated literature just won't do for this kind of client. If your background is in securities and/or insurance, you may be accustomed to getting the bulk of your education and literature through industry (seminars, trade magazines, company training, and so forth). I'd be the first to admit that much of this is excellent. At Resource Management we use industry-generated ongoing education opportunities as much as possible. My point is simply that you will have to go beyond that. You'll need good reference material *in addition to*, not instead of, industry-generated material.

I've included a reading list for you at the end of this chapter. This is by no means all the information our firm buys, but is a core that should be supplemented by several looseleaf services. To determine which of these you need, see a representative in your area for major suppliers. (A list of these is also provided.) Our business library has evolved and continues to evolve to suit our particular needs. You will probably want to experiment with services, newsletters, and magazines until you find the ones that work best for you. The reading list is simply a point of departure.

Resolve the Question of Fees and Commissions in Your Mind and in Your Firm

As more commission-oriented professionals move into financial planning, the question of fees and commissions grows more acute. You can be compensated by fees only, commissions only, or by a combination of fees and commissions. If you charge fees, you should be a registered investment advisor. Be very sure to check all federal, state, and local licensing laws before charging fees and/or commissions.

In my firm we charge fees for designing a financial plan. Where products are involved, the client can implement the plan with us or with any firm where there is already an existing relationship. We explain this verbally and then give clients a written disclosure statement. Our fee is based on the time the plan involves rather than a hard and fast relationship to income or net worth.

I'm certainly not suggesting our way is best for you or your firm, only that it works for us and our clients. You may need to experiment with fees and commissions. Don't be afraid to appoach the question openly with your clients. They will appreciate the fact that you are trying to strike a fair arrangement for both of you.

Be Active in Your Professional Community

For openers, if you are in the financial services industry and want to practice financial planning, you should be active in the International Association for Financial Planning (IAFP), and The College for Financial Planning, outgrowths of the original Society for Financial Counseling.

The Society for Financial Counseling was established in 1966 as a nonprofit organization to unite financial-services professionals committed to the concept of delivering fully integrated financial services to their clients.

The IAFP now has approximately 10,000 members. The college has confirmed about 3,000 Certified Financial Planners designations, and about 2,000 professionals are currently working towards that designation. After you have received your certification from The College for Financial Planning, you should join the Institute of Certified Financial Planners, an organization open only to Certified Financial Planners.

In my opinion, members of the financial-services industry who want to practice financial planning must be active members of IAFP. Membership requirements include professional licensing in at least one area of finance or counseling, active participation in financial planning, and subscription to the bylaws, Code of Ethics and Standards of Professional Conduct.

Membership in IAFP offers:

1. Association with other financial planning professionals
2. National conventions, midyear strategy conferences, and regional seminars
3. *The Financial Planner Magazine* (Many planners feel the magazine alone is worth the price of membership)
4. Discounts in many services and publications
5. Several newsletters to help you stay abreast of changes in our profession
6. Local chapter affiliations, which give you contact with members of various financial disciplines

Write: IAFP:
    5775 Peachtree Dunwoody Road, Suite 120C
    Atlanta, Georgia 30342

If there is no chapter in your area, write Paul Galanek at the IAFP who will help you get one started. The staff of IAFP in Atlanta is extremely hard working and very committed to the organization's goals.

  If you are not a certified financial planner, consider obtaining that designation from The College for Financial Planning through its five-course program. The five courses are:

    Introduction to financial planning
    Risk management
    Investments
    Tax planning and management
    Retirement and estate planning

Write: The College for Financial Planning
    9725 East Hampden Avenue
    Suite 200
    Denver, Colorado 80231

Certification will qualify you for membership in the Institute of Certified Financial Planners. Write:

    Institute of Certified Financial Planners
    P.O. Box 6097
    West Palm Beach, Florida 33405

  Once you have established your credentials and have made a commitment to ongoing education, you will be in a position to enjoy a clientele of the finest people in the world: business owners.

READING LIST

Loose-Leaf Services

  Loose-leaf services are provided by several major organizations. I suggest that you routinely invite their local representatives to your office and work with them until your library takes form.

American Bankers Association
1120 Connecticut Avenue NW
Washington, D.C. 20036
(202) 467-4123

American Institute of Certified Public Accountants
1211 Avenue of the Americas
New York, New York 10036
(212) 575-6200

Matthew Bender and Company, Inc.
235 E 45th Street
New York, New York 10017
(212) 661-5050

Bureau of National Affairs, Inc.
1231 25th Street NW
Washington, D.C. 20037
(202) 452-4200

Commerce Clearing House, Inc.
4025 W. Peterson Avenue
Chicago, Illinois 60646
(312) 583-8500

Institute for Business Planning, Inc.
IBP Plaza
Englewood Cliffs, New Jersey 07632

Panel Publishers
14 Plaza Road
Greenvale, New York 11548
(516) 484-0006

Prentice-Hall, Inc.
Englewood Cliffs, New Jersey 07632
(201) 592-2000

Research Institute of America, Inc.
589 5th Avenue
New York, New York 10017
(212) 755-8900

Warren, Gorham, and Lamont, Inc.
210 South Street
Boston, Massachusetts 02111
(617) 423-2020

John Wiley and Sons, Inc.
605 3rd Avenue
New York, New York 10158
(212) 850-6418

Periodicals and Newsletters

BEST'S REVIEW
    A. M. Best Company, Inc.
    Oldwick, New Jersey 08858
    Publication Office: Columbia Turnpike, Box 232
                              Rensselaer, New York 12144
    Annual Subscription: $14.00
    (monthly)

THE BRENNAN REPORTS
    Brennan Reports, Inc.
    Valley Forge Office Colony, Suite 245
    P.O. Box 882
    Valley Forge, Pennsylvania 19482
    Annual Subscription: $145.00

THE BUSINESS OWNER
    Thomas Publications, Inc.
    383 S. Broadway
    Hicksville, New York 11801
    Annual Subscription: $66.00
    (monthly)

FEDERAL TAX GUIDE REPORTS
    Commerce Clearing House, Inc.
    4025 W. Peterson Avenue
    Chicago, Illinois 60646
    Annual Subscription: $360.00
    (weekly)

FINANCIAL AND ESTATE PLANNING
    Commerce Clearing House, Inc.
    4025 W. Peterson Avenue
    Chicago, Illinois 60646
    Annual Subscription: $395.00

THE FINANCIAL PLANNER
    5775 Peachtree Dunwoody Road
    Suite 120-C
    Atlanta, Georgia 30342
    Annual Subscription: $30.00

FORBES
    Forbes, Inc.
    60 Fifth Avenue
    New York, New York 10011
    Annual Subscription: $33.00
    (biweekly)

INC. MAGAZINE
Inc. Publishing Company
P.O. Box 2538
Boulder, Colorado 80322
Annual Subscription: $45.00
(monthly)

LEGAL & TAX TRENDS
New England Mutual Life Insurance Company
Boston, Massachusetts

MONEY
Time, Inc.
3435 Wilshire Boulevard
Los Angeles, California 90010
Annual Subscription: $21.95
(monthly)

NASD (NATIONAL ASSOCIATION OF SECURITIES DEALERS, INC.)
4025 W. Peterson Avenue
Chicago, Illinois 60646
(monthly)

NATIONAL TAX SHELTER DIGEST
The Investor Group, Inc.
8550 Foust Lane, Suite 304
Dallas, Texas 75243
Annual Subscription: $30.00
(monthly)

PENSION PLAN GUIDE
Commerce Clearing House, Inc.
4025 W. Peterson Avenue
Chicago, Illinois 60646
Annual Subscription: $460.00
(weekly)

PERSONAL FINANCE
P.O. Box 974
Farmingdale, New York 11737
Annual Subscription: $78.00

REGISTERED REPRESENTATIVE
Plaza Publishing Company, Inc.
4300 Campus Drive
Newport Beach, California 92660
(monthly magazine)

THE STANGER REGISTER
P.O. Box 8
Fair Haven, New Jersey 07701
Price $180
(monthly)

THE STANGER REPORT
P.O. Box 8
Fair Haven, New Jersey 07701
Annual Subscription: $325.00
(monthly)

TAX ANGLES
P.O. Box 976
Farmingdale, New York 11737
Annual Subscription: $60.00
(12 issues)

TAX DESK BOOK FOR THE CLOSELY HELD CORPORATION
Institute for Business Planning
IBP Plaza
Dept 7102-81
Englewood Cliffs, New Jersey 07632

TAX SHELTER INVESTMENT REVIEW
Leland Publishing Company, Inc.
50 Staniford Street
Suite 800
Boston, Massachusetts 02114
Annual Subscription: $147.00
(monthly)

UNITED MUTUAL-FUND SELECTOR
United Business Service Company
210 Newbury Street
Boston, Massachusetts 02116
Annual Subscription: $65.00
(issued twice monthly)

THE VALUE LINE INVESTMENT SURVEY
Arnold Bernhard & Company, Inc.
711 Third Avenue
New York, New York 10017
Annual Subscription: $330.00
(weekly)

THE WALL STREET JOURNAL
    200 Burnett Road
    Chicopee, Massachusetts 01021
    Annual Subscription: $89.00
    (daily)

WIESBERGER INVESTMENT COMPANIES SERVICE
    Warren, Gorham & Lamont, Inc.
    210 South Street
    Boston, Massachusetts 02111
    Annual Subscription: $145.00
    (monthly & quarterly)

To locate the kind of specialized information you may need, I suggest you get a reference book called *Where To Find Business Information* by David Brownstone and Gorton Carruth, 1982, John Wiley & Sons, Inc. The book costs about $45.00 but is worth it.

APPENDICES

appendix A —————————————————————

Tax Guide Resource

Internal Revenue Service Publication #334, *Tax Guide for Small Business* (Rev. No. '81) describes four major forms of business organizations and explains the income, excise, and employment tax responsibilities of each. The publication is free. Call your local Internal Revenue Service office and ask for a copy.

appendix B

Tax Schematics

HOW TAXABLE INCOME IS CALCULATED FOR A PARTNERSHIP

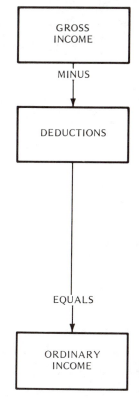

Gross receipts or sales minus cost of goods sold

Rent income (loss)
Royalty income (loss)
Net gain (or loss)
Income from other partnerships
Certain nonqualifying dividends & interest
Net farm profit (loss)

As with the sole proprietorship, these deductions are for amounts spent to make money. Such deductions would include (but not be limited to):

Salaries, bonuses, and commissions to employees
Guaranteed payments of income to partners
Rent
Interest
Taxes
Bad debts
Repairs
Depreciation
Amortization
Depletion
Retirement plans
Employee benefit programs
Other "ordinary and necessary expenses paid or incurred during the tax year related to carrying on the trade or business."

Because the partnership is not a taxable entity, the partnership's ordinary income is allocated to each partner. Each partner picks up his/her share of partnership ordinary income on his/her personal income tax return as gross income.

Unlike the sole proprietorship, however, partners will have different types of personal income from the partnership.

Partners will be allocated their pro rata share of income, interest, dividends, capital gains, etc., and may share in various types of income unequally if the partnership agreement so specifies.

Each partner is issued a Schedule K-1 of Form 1065, which specifies exactly how much of each kind of income to claim on the personal income tax return.

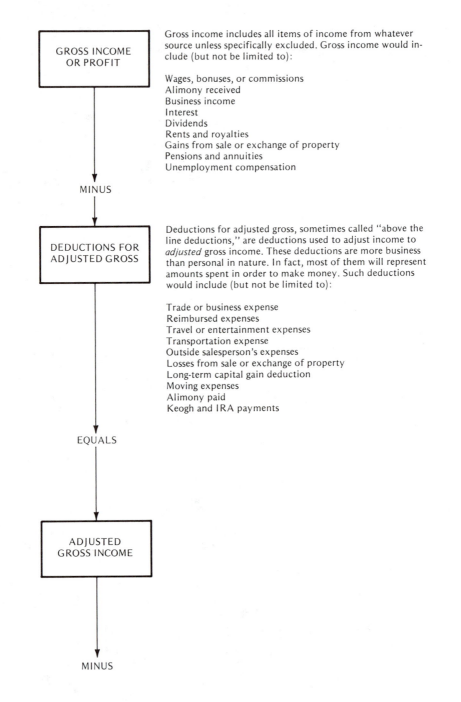

GROSS INCOME OR PROFIT

Gross income includes all items of income from whatever source unless specifically excluded. Gross income would include (but not be limited to):

Wages, bonuses, or commissions
Alimony received
Business income
Interest
Dividends
Rents and royalties
Gains from sale or exchange of property
Pensions and annuities
Unemployment compensation

MINUS

DEDUCTIONS FOR ADJUSTED GROSS

Deductions for adjusted gross, sometimes called "above the line deductions," are deductions used to adjust income to *adjusted* gross income. These deductions are more business than personal in nature. In fact, most of them will represent amounts spent in order to make money. Such deductions would include (but not be limited to):

Trade or business expense
Reimbursed expenses
Travel or entertainment expenses
Transportation expense
Outside salesperson's expenses
Losses from sale or exchange of property
Long-term capital gain deduction
Moving expenses
Alimony paid
Keogh and IRA payments

EQUALS

ADJUSTED GROSS INCOME

MINUS

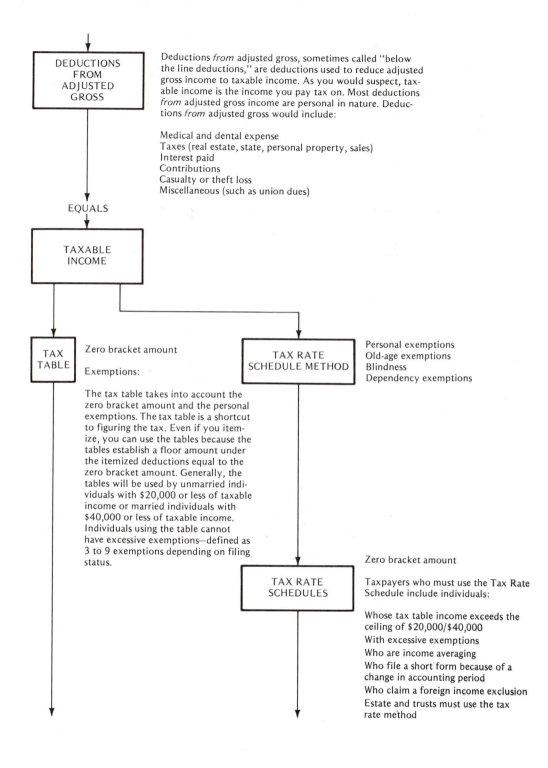

```
┌──────────────┐
│  DEDUCTIONS  │
│     FROM     │
│   ADJUSTED   │
│    GROSS     │
└──────────────┘
```

Deductions *from* adjusted gross, sometimes called "below the line deductions," are deductions used to reduce adjusted gross income to taxable income. As you would suspect, taxable income is the income you pay tax on. Most deductions *from* adjusted gross income are personal in nature. Deductions *from* adjusted gross would include:

Medical and dental expense
Taxes (real estate, state, personal property, sales)
Interest paid
Contributions
Casualty or theft loss
Miscellaneous (such as union dues)

EQUALS

```
┌──────────────┐
│   TAXABLE    │
│    INCOME    │
└──────────────┘
```

```
┌────────┐
│  TAX   │
│ TABLE  │
└────────┘
```

Zero bracket amount

Exemptions:

```
┌──────────────────────┐
│      TAX RATE        │
│  SCHEDULE METHOD     │
└──────────────────────┘
```

Personal exemptions
Old-age exemptions
Blindness
Dependency exemptions

The tax table takes into account the zero bracket amount and the personal exemptions. The tax table is a shortcut to figuring the tax. Even if you itemize, you can use the tables because the tables establish a floor amount under the itemized deductions equal to the zero bracket amount. Generally, the tables will be used by unmarried individuals with $20,000 or less of taxable income or married individuals with $40,000 or less of taxable income. Individuals using the table cannot have excessive exemptions—defined as 3 to 9 exemptions depending on filing status.

```
┌──────────────┐
│   TAX RATE   │
│  SCHEDULES   │
└──────────────┘
```

Zero bracket amount

Taxpayers who must use the Tax Rate Schedule include individuals:

Whose tax table income exceeds the ceiling of $20,000/$40,000
With excessive exemptions
Who are income averaging
Who file a short form because of a change in accounting period
Who claim a foreign income exclusion
Estate and trusts must use the tax rate method

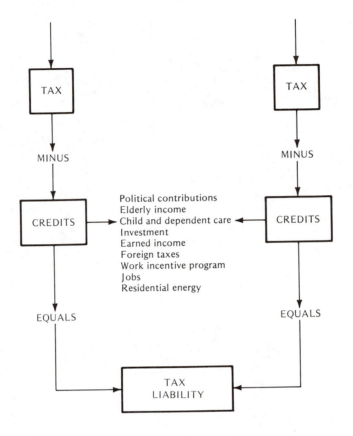

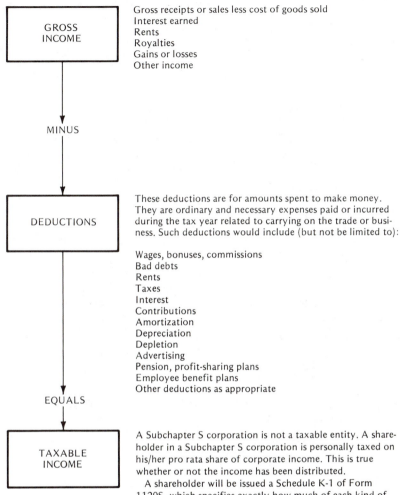

GROSS INCOME

Gross receipts or sales less cost of goods sold
Interest earned
Rents
Royalties
Gains or losses
Other income

MINUS

DEDUCTIONS

These deductions are for amounts spent to make money. They are ordinary and necessary expenses paid or incurred during the tax year related to carrying on the trade or business. Such deductions would include (but not be limited to):

Wages, bonuses, commissions
Bad debts
Rents
Taxes
Interest
Contributions
Amortization
Depreciation
Depletion
Advertising
Pension, profit-sharing plans
Employee benefit plans
Other deductions as appropriate

EQUALS

TAXABLE INCOME

A Subchapter S corporation is not a taxable entity. A shareholder in a Subchapter S corporation is personally taxed on his/her pro rata share of corporate income. This is true whether or not the income has been distributed.

A shareholder will be issued a Schedule K-1 of Form 1120S, which specifies exactly how much of each kind of income to claim on the personal income tax return.

Although a Subchapter S corporation is not a taxable entity, the capital gains tax and the minimum tax on these gains is an exception.

311

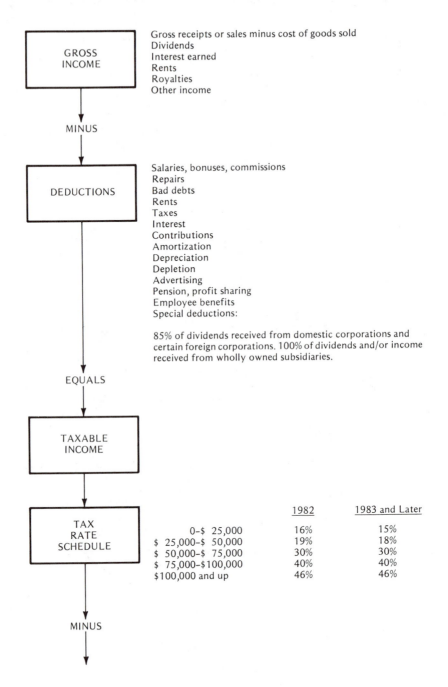

GROSS INCOME

Gross receipts or sales minus cost of goods sold
Dividends
Interest earned
Rents
Royalties
Other income

MINUS

DEDUCTIONS

Salaries, bonuses, commissions
Repairs
Bad debts
Rents
Taxes
Interest
Contributions
Amortization
Depreciation
Depletion
Advertising
Pension, profit sharing
Employee benefits
Special deductions:

85% of dividends received from domestic corporations and certain foreign corporations. 100% of dividends and/or income received from wholly owned subsidiaries.

EQUALS

TAXABLE INCOME

TAX RATE SCHEDULE

	1982	1983 and Later
0–$ 25,000	16%	15%
$ 25,000–$ 50,000	19%	18%
$ 50,000–$ 75,000	30%	30%
$ 75,000–$100,000	40%	40%
$100,000 and up	46%	46%

MINUS

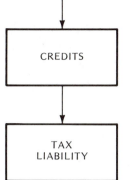

CREDITS

Foreign tax
Investment credit
Work incentive
Jobs credit
Other credits

TAX
LIABILITY

A corporation is a taxable entity and will pay taxes on its net earnings. Shareholders will pay personal taxes on any income received and on any dividends received. Dividends are paid from *after corporate tax net*—hence the complaint of double taxation on dividends.

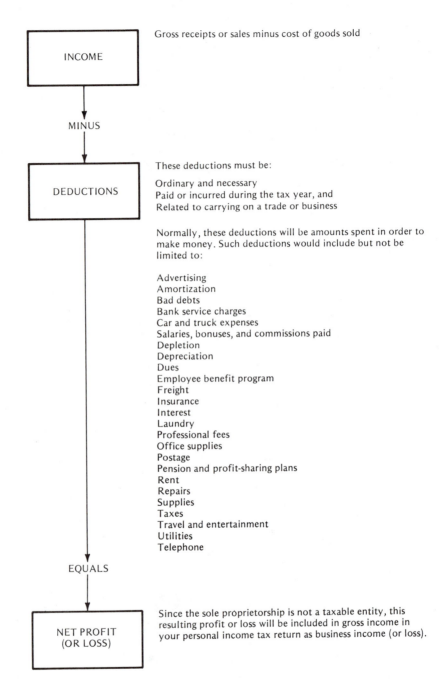

HOW TAXABLE INCOME IS CALCULATED FOR A SOLE PROPRIETOR

INCOME

Gross receipts or sales minus cost of goods sold

MINUS

DEDUCTIONS

These deductions must be:

Ordinary and necessary
Paid or incurred during the tax year, and
Related to carrying on a trade or business

Normally, these deductions will be amounts spent in order to make money. Such deductions would include but not be limited to:

Advertising
Amortization
Bad debts
Bank service charges
Car and truck expenses
Salaries, bonuses, and commissions paid
Depletion
Depreciation
Dues
Employee benefit program
Freight
Insurance
Interest
Laundry
Professional fees
Office supplies
Postage
Pension and profit-sharing plans
Rent
Repairs
Supplies
Taxes
Travel and entertainment
Utilities
Telephone

EQUALS

**NET PROFIT
(OR LOSS)**

Since the sole proprietorship is not a taxable entity, this resulting profit or loss will be included in gross income in your personal income tax return as business income (or loss).

314

HOW CAPITAL GAINS TAX IS FIGURED

A capital gain (or loss) results from the sale of a capital asset for more than (or less than) your tax basis. Basis will normally be your original purchase price *plus* costs in connection with the purchase (commissions, legal fees, and so forth) *plus* improvements *minus* depreciation.

A capital asset can be defined best by describing what *isn't* a capital asset. Capital assets are all assets except:

1. The following business-related assets:
   a. inventories
   b. accounts receivable and notes receivable
   c. depreciable property and land
2. Copyrights; literary, musical, or artistic compositions; letters or memoranda; or similar property if held by:
   a. the creator
   b. recipient of a letter or memorandum, or
   c. a person who was given the property by the creator
3. Short-term government securities
4. Government publications received free or at a reduced price

Capital assets include investments, such as securities and real estate, and personal assets, such as your home, jewelry, and automobile. The IRS has the "best worlds" on personal-use assets. Losses are not allowable but gains are taxable!

Gains and losses are characterized by the length of time you hold them as either short-term or long-term. A long-term capital gain (or loss) is the gain or loss on a sale or exchange of a capital asset that you held for more than one year. A short-term capital gain (or loss) is the gain or loss on a sale or exchange of a capital asset which you held for less than one year.

Basically, you will take the difference between short-term gains and losses; then take the difference between long-term gains and losses; then take the difference between the short-term net and the long-term net.

Assume you have a $250 short-term capital gain; a $500 capital loss; a $1,400 long-term capital gain; an $800 long-term capital gain; and a $100 long-term capital loss. You also have a $300 short-term capital loss carry-over and a $500 long-term capital loss carry-over. The calculation looks like this:

short-term capital loss	($500)
short-term capital gain	250
net short-term capital loss	($250)

short-term capital loss carry-over	($300)
net short-term loss	($550)
long-term capital loss	($100)
long-term capital gain	($2,200
net long-term capital gain	$2,100
long-term capital loss carry-over	($500)
net long-term gain	$1,600
net long-term capital gain	$1,600
net short-term capital loss	(55)
net long-term capital gain	$1,050
60% of the long-term capital gain	630
taxable long-term capital gain	$ 420

This figure is then entered on form 1040 as capital gain (or loss) in the income section.

This example is from publication 17 (Rev. Nov. 81) *Your Federal Income Tax*. To get a copy, simply call or write your local IRS office.

If your losses exceed your gains, you must figure out how much of the loss is deductible. Then you must figure how much of the loss you may deduct in the year of the loss and how much of it you carry over and use in future tax years.

Net short-term capital losses can be used to offset your income dollar-for-dollar.

Only 50% of a net long-term capital loss can be used to offset other income.

Assume you have:

short-term capital gains	$ 700
short-term capital losses	($ 800)
long-term capital gains	$ 400
long-term capital losses	($2,000)

Your deductible capital loss is figured as follows:

short-term capital losses	($800)	
minus: short-term capital gains	700	
net short-term capital loss		($100)
long-term capital losses	($2,000)	
minus: long-term capital gains	400	
net long-term capital loss	($1,600)	
minus: *half* of net long-term loss	(800)	($800)
deductible capital loss		($900)

The amount of capital loss that you can deduct in any tax year is the lesser of:

1. $3,000 or $1,500 if you are married and file a separate return.
2. Your taxable income, figured without any capital gains or losses, minus the zero-bracket amount. Do not take any deductions for personal exemptions when figuring this amount.
3. Your deductible capital loss.

If your deductible capital loss is greater than the lesser of items 1 and 2, you may carry over the unused part from year to year until fully used. When a loss is carried over, it retains its original character as long-term or short-term.

appendix C

Tax Rate Schedules

**Tax Rate Schedules for Married Individuals Filing
Joint Returns and Surviving Spouses**

	1981		1982		1983		1984	
		% on		% on		% on		% on
Taxable Income	Pay	+ Excess*	Pay	+ Excess*	Pay	+ Excess*	Pay	+ Excess*
0— $3,400	–0–	–0–	–0–	–0–	–0–	–0–	–0–	–0–
$3,400— 5,500	–0–	14	–0–	12	–0–	11	–0–	11
5,500— 7,600	$294	16	$252	14	$231	13	$231	12
7,600— 11,900	630	18	546	16	504	15	483	14
11,900— 16,000	1,404	21	1,234	19	1,149	17	1,085	16
16,000— 20,200	2,265	24	2,013	22	1,846	19	1,741	18
20,200— 24,600	3,273	28	2,937	25	2,644	23	2,497	22
24,600— 29,900	4,505	32	4,037	29	3,656	26	3,465	25
29,900— 35,200	6,201	37	5,574	33	5,034	30	4,790	28
35,200— 45,800	8,162	43	7,323	39	6,624	35	6,274	33
45,800— 60,000	12,720	49	11,457	44	10,334	40	9,772	38
60,000— 85,600	19,678	54	17,705	49	16,014	44	15,168	42
85,600—109,400	33,502	59	30,249	50	27,278	48	25,920	45
109,400—162,400	47,544	64	42,149	50	38,702	50	36,630	49
162,400—215,400	81,464	68	68,649	50	65,202	50	62,600	50
215,400—.	117,504	70	95,149	50	91,702	50	89,100	50

*The amount by which the taxpayer's taxable income exceeds the base of the bracket.

Tax Rate Schedules for Married Individuals Filing Separate Returns

Taxable Income	1981 Pay	1981 % on + Excess*	1982 Pay	1982 % on + Excess*	1983 Pay	1983 % on + Excess*	1984 Pay	1984 % on + Excess*
0— $1,700	–0–	–0–	–0–	–0–	–0–	–0–	–0–	–0–
$1,700— 2,750	–0–	14	–0–	12	–0–	11	–0–	11
2,750— 3,800	$147	16	$126	14	$115	13	$115	12
3,800— 5,950	315	18	273	16	252	15	241	14
5,950— 8,000	702	21	617	19	574	17	542	16
8,000— 10,100	1,132.50	24	1,006	22	923	19	870	18
10,100— 12,300	1,636.50	28	1,468	25	1,322	23	1,248	22
12,300— 14,950	2,252.50	32	2,018	29	1,828	26	1,732	25
14,950— 17,600	3,100.50	37	2,787	33	2,517	30	2,395	28
17,600— 22,900	4,081	43	3,661	39	3,312	35	3,137	33
22,900— 30,000	6,360	49	5,728	44	5,167	40	4,886	38
30,000— 42,800	9,839	54	8,852	49	8,007	44	7,584	42
42,800— 54,700	16,751	59	15,124	50	13,639	48	12,960	45
54,700— 81,200	23,772	64	21,074	50	19,351	50	18,315	49
81,200—107,700	40,732	68	34,324	50	32,601	50	31,300	50
107,700—.	58,752	70	47,574	50	45,851	50	44,550	50

*The amount by which the taxpayer's taxable income exceeds the base of the bracket.

Tax Rate Schedules for Head of Household

Taxable Income	1981 Pay	1981 % on + Excess*	1982 Pay	1982 % on + Excess*	1983 Pay	1983 % on + Excess*	1984 Pay	1984 % on + Excess*
0— $2,300	–0–	–0–	–0–	–0–	–0–	–0–	–0–	–0–
$2,300— 4,400	–0–	14	–0–	12	–0–	11	–0–	11
4,400— 6,500	$294	16	$252	14	$231	13	$231	12
6,500— 8,700	630	18	546	16	504	15	483	14
8,700— 11,800	1,026	22	898	20	834	18	791	17
11,800— 15,000	1,708	24	1,518	22	1,392	19	1,318	18
15,000— 18,200	2,476	26	2,222	23	2,000	21	1,894	20
18,200— 23,500	3,308	31	2,958	28	2,672	25	2,534	24
23,500— 28,800	4,951	36	4,442	32	3,997	29	3,806	28
28,800— 34,100	6,859	42	6,138	38	5,534	34	5,290	32
34,100— 44,700	9,085	46	8,152	41	7,336	37	6,986	35
44,700— 60,600	13,961	54	12,498	49	11,258	44	10,696	42
60,600— 81,800	22,547	59	20,289	50	18,254	48	17,374	45
81,800—108,300	35,055	63	30,889	50	28,430	50	26,914	48
108,300—161,300	51,750	68	44,139	50	41,680	50	39,634	50
161,300—.	87,790	70	70,639	50	68,180	50	66,134	50

*The amount by which the taxpayer's taxable income exceeds the base of the bracket.

Tax Rate Schedules for Estates and Trusts

	1981		1982		1983		1984	
		% on		% on		% on		% on
Taxable Income	Pay	+ Excess*	Pay	+ Excess*	Pay	+ Excess*	Pay	+ Excess*
0— $1,050	–0–	14	–0–	12	–0–	11	–0–	11
$1,050— 2,100	$147	16	$126	14	$115	13	$115	12
2,100— 4,250	315	18	273	16	252	15	241	14
4,250— 6,300	702	21	617	19	574	17	542	16
6,300— 8,400	1.132.50	24	1,006	22	923	19	870	18
8,400— 10,600	1,636.50	28	1,468	25	1,322	23	1,248	22
10,600— 13,250	2,252.50	32	2,018	29	1,828	26	1,732	25
13,250— 15,900	3,100.50	37	2,787	33	2,517	30	2,395	28
15,900— 21,200	4,081	43	3,661	39	3,312	35	3,137	33
21,200— 28,300	6,360	49	5,728	44	5,167	40	4,886	38
28,300— 41,100	9,839	54	8,852	49	8,007	44	7,584	42
41,100— 53,000	16,751	59	15,124	50	13,639	48	12,960	45
53,000— 79,500	23,772	64	21,074	50	19,351	50	18,315	49
79,500—106,000	40,732	68	34,324	50	32,601	50	31,300	50
106,000—.	58,752	70	47,574	50	45,851	50	44,550	50

*The amount by which the taxpayer's taxable income exceeds the base of the bracket.

Tax Rate Schedules for Single Individuals

	1981		1982		1983		1984	
		% on		% on		% on		% on
Taxable Income	Pay	+ Excess*	Pay	+ Excess*	Pay	+ Excess*	Pay	+ Excess*
0— $2,300	–0–	–0–	–0–	–0–	–0–	–0–	–0–	–0–
$2,300— 3,400	–0–	14	–0–	12	–0–	11	–0–	11
3,400— 4,400	$154	16	$132	14	$121	13	$121	12
4,400— 6,500	314	18	272	16	251	15	241	14
6,500— 8,500	692	19	608	17	566	15	535	15
8,500— 10,800	1,072	21	948	19	866	17	835	16
10,800— 12,900	1,555	24	1,385	22	1,257	19	1,203	18
12,900— 15,000	2,059	26	1,847	23	1,656	21	1,581	20
15,000— 18,200	2,605	30	2,330	27	2,097	24	2,001	23
18,200— 23,500	3,565	34	3,194	31	2,865	28	2,737	26
23,500— 28,800	5,367	39	4,837	35	4,349	32	4,115	30
28,800— 34,100	7,434	44	6,692	40	6,045	36	5,705	34
34,100— 41,500	9,766	49	8,812	44	7,953	40	7,507	38
41,500— 55,300	13,392	55	12,068	50	10,913	45	10,319	42
55,300— 81,800	20,982	63	18,968	50	17,123	50	16,115	48
81,800—108,300	37,677	68	32,218	50	30,373	50	28,835	50
108,300—.	55,697	70	45,468	50	43,623	50	42,085	50

*The amount by which the taxpayer's taxable income exceeds the base of the bracket.

Unified Transfer Tax Rate Schedules
1982

| If the amount is: | | Tentative tax is: | | | |
Over	But not over	Tax	+	%	On Excess Over
0	$ 10,000	0	18		0
$ 10,00	20,000	$ 1,800	20		$ 10,000
20,000	40,000	3,800	22		20,000
40,000	60,000	8,200	24		40,000
60,000	80,000	13,000	26		60,000
80,000	100,000	18,200	28		80,000
100,000	150,000	23,800	30		100,000
150,000	250,000	38,800	32		150,000
250,000	500,000	70,800	34		250,000
500,000	750,000	155,800	37		500,000
750,000	1,000,000	248,300	39		750,000
1,000,000	1,250,000	345,800	41		1,000,000
1,250,000	1,500,000	448,300	43		1,250,000
1,500,000	2,000,000	555,800	45		1,500,000
2,000,000	2,500,000	780,800	49		2,000,000
2,500,000	3,000,000	1,025,800	53		2,500,000
3,000,000	3,500,000	1,290,800	57		3,000,000
3,500,000	4,000,000	1,575,800	61		3,500,000
4,000,000	. . . . . .	1,880,800	65		4,000,000

1983

| If the amount is: | | Tentative tax is: | | | |
Over	But not over	Tax	+	%	On Excess Over
0	$ 10,000	0	18		0
$ 10,000	20,000	$ 1,800	20		$ 10,000
20,000	40,000	3,800	22		20,000
40,000	60,000	8,200	24		40,000
60,000	80,000	13,000	26		60,000
80,000	100,000	18,200	28		80,000
100,000	150,000	23,800	30		100,000
150,000	250,000	38,800	32		150,000
250,000	500,000	70,800	34		250,000
500,000	750,000	155,800	37		500,000
750,000	1,000,000	248,300	39		750,000
1,000,000	1,250,000	345,800	41		1,000,000
1,250,000	1,500,000	448,300	43		1,250,000
1,500,000	2,000,000	555,800	45		1,500,000
2,000,000	2,500,000	780,800	49		2,000,000
2,500,000	3,000,000	1,025,800	53		2,500,000
3,000,000	3,500,000	1,290,800	57		3,000,000
3,500,000	. . . .	1,575,800	60		3,500,000

Unified Transfer Tax Rate Schedules
1984

If the amount is:		Tentative tax is:			
Over	But not over	Tax	+	%	On Excess Over
0	$ 10,000	0	18		0
$ 10,00	20,000	$ 1,800	20		$ 10,000
20,000	40,000	3,800	22		20,000
40,000	60,000	8,200	24		40,000
60,000	80,000	13,000	26		60,000
80,000	100,000	18,200	28		80,000
100,000	150,000	23,800	30		100,000
150,000	250,000	38,800	32		150,000
250,000	500,000	70,800	34		250,000
500,000	750,000	155,800	37		500,000
750,000	1,000,000	248,300	39		750,000
1,000,000	1,250,000	345,800	41		1,000,000
1,250,000	1,500,000	448,300	43		1,250,000
1,500,000	2,000,000	555,800	45		1,500,000
2,000,000	2,500,000	780,800	49		2,000,000
2,500,000	3,000,000	1,025,800	53		2,500,000
3,000,000	. . . . . .	1,290,800	55		3,000,000

Unified Transfer Tax Rate Schedules
1985 and Thereafter

If the amount is:		Tentative tax is:			
Over	But not over	Tax	+	%	On Excess Over
0	$ 10,000	0	18		0
$ 10,00	20,000	$ 1,800	20		$ 10,000
20,000	40,000	3,800	22		20,000
40,000	60,000	8,200	24		40,000
60,000	80,000	13,000	26		60,000
80,000	100,000	18,200	28		80,000
100,000	150,000	23,800	30		100,000
150,000	250,000	38,800	32		150,000
250,000	500,000	70,800	34		250,000
500,000	750,000	155,800	37		500,000
750,000	1,000,000	248,300	39		750,000
1,000,000	1,250,000	345,800	41		1,000,000
1,250,000	1,500,000	448,300	43		1,250,000
1,500,000	2,000,000	555,800	45		1,500,000
2,000,000	2,500,000	780,800	49		2,000,000
2,500,000	. . . . .	1,025,800	50		2,500,000

Transfers Made and Decedents Dying in	Unified Credit	Amount of Transfers Not Taxed	Lowest Tax Bracket Rate
1982	$ 62,800	$225,000	32%
1983	79,300	275,000	34
1984	96,300	325,000	34
1985	121,800	400,000	34
1986	155,800	500,000	37
1987 and later	192,800	600,000	37

appendix D

Compound Tables

Future Worth of One Dollar Periodically Deposited at Compound Interest
Payable at the end of each period

Years	7% Nominal Annual Rate	8% Nominal Annual Rate	9% Nominal Annual Rate	10% Nominal Annual Rate	Years
1	1.0000 000 000	1.0000 000 000	1.0000 000 000	1.0000 000 000	1
2	2.0700 000 000	2.0800 000 000	2.0900 000 000	2.1000 000 000	2
3	3.2149 000 000	3.2464 000 000	3.2781 000 000	3.3100 000 000	3
4	4.4399 430 000	4.5061 120 000	4.5731 290 000	4.6410 000 000	4
5	5.7507 390 100	5.8666 009 600	5.9847 106 100	6.1051 000 000	5
6	7.1532 907 407	7.3359 290 368	7.5233 345 649	7.7156 100 000	6
7	8.6540 210 925	8.9228 033 597	9.2004 346 757	9.4871 710 000	7
8	10.2598 025 690	10.6366 276 285	11.0284 737 966	11.4358 881 000	8
9	11.9779 887 489	12.4875 578 388	13.0210 364 382	13.5794 769 100	9
10	13.8164 479 613	14.4865 624 659	15.1929 297 177	15.9374 246 010	10
11	15.7835 993 186	16.6454 874 632	17.5602 933 923	18.5311 670 611	11
12	17.8884 512 709	18.9771 264 602	20.1407 197 976	21.3842 837 672	12
13	20.1406 428 598	21.4952 965 771	22.9533 845 794	24.5227 121 439	13
14	22.5504 878 600	24.2149 203 032	26.0191 891 915	27.9749 833 583	14
15	25.1290 220 102	27.1521 139 275	29.3609 162 188	31.7724 816 942	15
16	27.8880 535 509	30.3242 830 417	33.0033 986 784	35.9497 298 636	16
17	30.8402 172 995	33.7502 256 850	36.9737 045 595	40.5447 028 499	17
18	33.9990 325 105	37.4502 437 398	41.3013 379 699	45.5991 731 349	18
19	37.3789 647 862	41.4462 632 390	46.0184 583 871	51.1590 904 484	19
20	40.9954 923 212	45.7619 642 981	51.1601 196 420	57.2749 994 933	20
21	44.8651 767 837	50.4229 214 420	56.7645 304 098	64.0024 994 426	21
22	49.0057 391 586	55.4567 551 573	62.8733 381 466	71.4027 493 868	22
23	53.4361 408 997	60.8932 955 699	69.5319 385 798	79.5430 243 255	23
24	58.1766 707 627	66.7647 592 155	76.7898 130 520	88.4973 267 581	24
25	63.2490 377 160	73.1059 399 527	84.7008 962 267	98.3470 594 339	25
26	68.6764 703 562	79.9544 151 490	93.3239 768 871	109.1817 653 773	26
27	74.4838 232 811	87.3507 683 609	102.7231 348 069	121.0999 419 150	27
28	80.6976 909 108	95.3388 298 297	112.9682 169 396	134.2099 361 065	28
29	87.3465 292 745	103.9659 362 161	124.1353 564 641	148.6309 297 171	29
30	94.4607 863 237	113.2832 111 134	136.3075 385 459	164.4940 226 889	30
31	102.0730 413 664	123.3458 680 025	149.5752 170 150	181.9434 249 578	31
32	110.2181 542 621	134.2135 374 427	164.0369 865 464	201.1377 674 535	32
33	118.9334 250 604	145.9506 204 381	179.8003 153 356	222.2515 441 989	33
34	128.2587 648 146	158.6266 700 732	196.9823 437 158	245.4766 986 188	34
35	138.2368 783 516	172.3168 036 790	215.7107 546 502	271.0243 684 806	35
36	148.9134 598 363	187.1021 479 733	236.1247 225 687	299.1268 053 287	36
37	160.3374 020 248	203.0703 198 112	258.3759 475 999	330.0394 858 616	37
38	172.5610 201 665	220.3159 453 961	282.6297 828 839	364.0434 344 477	38
39	185.6402 915 782	238.9412 210 278	309.0664 633 434	401.4477 778 925	39
40	199.6351 119 887	259.0565 187 100	337.8824 450 443	442.5925 556 818	40
41	214.6095 698 279	280.7810 402 068	369.2918 650 983	487.8518 112 499	41
42	230.6322 397 158	304.2435 234 233	403.5281 329 572	537.6369 923 749	42
43	247.7764 964 959	329.5830 052 972	440.8456 649 233	592.4006 916 124	43
44	266.1208 512 507	356.9496 457 210	481.5217 747 664	652.6407 607 737	44
45	285.7493 108 382	386.5056 173 787	525.8587 344 954	718.9048 368 510	45
46	306.7517 625 969	418.4260 667 690	574.1860 206 000	791.7953 205 361	46
47	329.2243 859 787	452.9001 521 105	626.8627 624 540	871.9748 525 897	47
48	353.2700 929 972	490.1321 642 793	684.2804 110 748	960.1723 378 487	48
49	378.9989 995 070	530.3427 374 217	746.8656 480 716	1057.1895 716 336	49
50	406.5289 294 724	573.7701 564 154	815.0835 563 980	1163.9085 287 970	50
51	435.9859 545 355	620.6717 689 286	889.4410 764 738	1281.2993 816 766	51
52	467.5049 713 530	671.3255 104 429	970.4907 733 565	1410.4293 198 443	52
53	501.2303 193 477	726.0315 512 783	1058.8349 429 585	1552.4722 518 287	53
54	537.3164 417 021	785.1140 753 806	1155.1300 878 248	1708.7194 770 116	54
55	575.9285 926 212	848.9232 014 111	1260.0917 957 290	1880.5914 247 128	55
56	617.2435 941 047	917.8370 575 239	1374.5000 573 447	2069.6505 671 841	56
57	661.4506 456 920	992.2640 221 259	1499.2050 625 057	2277.6156 239 025	57
58	708.7521 908 905	1072.6451 438 959	1635.1335 181 312	2506.3771 862 927	58
59	759.3648 442 528	1159.4567 554 076	1783.2955 347 630	2758.0149 049 220	59
60	813.5203 833 505	1253.2132 958 402	1944.7921 328 917	3034.8163 954 142	60

Future Worth of One Dollar Periodically Deposited at Compound Interest
Payable at the end of each period

Years	11% Nominal Annual Rate	12% Nominal Annual Rate	13% Nominal Annual Rate	14% Nominal Annual Rate	Years
1	1.0000 000 000	1.0000 000 000	1.0000 000 000	1.0000 000 000	1
2	2.1100 000 000	2.1200 000 000	2.1300 000 000	2.1400 000 000	2
3	3.3421 000 000	3.3744 000 000	3.4069 000 000	3.4396 000 000	3
4	4.7097 310 000	4.7793 280 000	4.8497 970 000	4.9211 440 000	4
5	6.2278 014 100	6.3528 473 600	6.4802 706 100	6.6101 041.600	5
6	7.9128 595 651	8.1151 890 432	8.3227 057 893	8.5355 187 424	6
7	9.7832 741173	10.0890 117 284	10.4046 575 419	10.7304 913 663	7
8	11.8594 342 702	12.2996 931 358	12.7572 630 224	13.2327 601 576	8
9	14.1639 720 399	14.7756 563 121	15.4157 072 153	16.0853 465 797	9
10	16.7220 089 643	17.5487 350 695	18.4197 491 532	19.3372 951 008	10
11	19.5614 299 503	20.6545 832 779	21.8143 165 432	23.0445 164 150	11
12	22.7131 872 449	24.1331 332 712	25.6501 776 938	27.2707 487 131	12
13	26.2116 378 418	28.0291 092 638	29.9847 007 940	32.0886 535 329	13
14	30.0949 180 044	32.3926 023 754	34.8827 118 972	37.5810 650 275	14
15	34.4053 589 849	37.2797 146 605	40.4174 644 438	43.8424 141 313	15
16	39.1899 484 732	42.7532 804 197	46.6717 348 215	50.9803 521 097	16
17	44.5008 428 053	48.8836 740 701	53.7390 603 483	59.1176 014 051	17
18	50.3959 355 139	55.7497 149 585	61.7251 381 936	68.3940 656 018	18
19	56.9394 884 204	63.4396 807 535	70.7494 061 588	78.9692 347 861	19
20	64.2028 321 466	72.0524 424 440	80.8468 289 594	91.0249 276 561	20
21	72.2651 436 828	81.6987 355 372	92.4699 167 241	104.7684 175 280	21
22	81.2143 094 879	92.5025 838 017	105.4910 058 983	120.4359 959 819	22
23	91.1478 835 315	104.6028 938 579	120.2048 366 650	138.2970 354 193	23
24	102.1741 507 200	118.1552 411 209	136.8314 654 315	158.6586 203 780	24
25	114.4133 072 992	133.3338 700 554	155.6195 559 376	181.8708 272 310	25
26	127.9987 711 021	150.3339 344 620	176.8500 982 095	208.3327 430 433	26
27	143.0786 359 233	169.3740 065 974	200.8406 109 767	238.4993 270 694	27
28	159.8172 858 749	190.6988 873 891	227.9498 904 037	272.8892 328 591	28
29	178.3971 873 211	214.5827 538 758	258.5833 761 562	312.0937 254 594	29
30	199.0208 799 265	241.3326 843 409	293.1992 150 565	356.7868 470 237	30
31	221.9131 744 984	271.2926 064 618	332.3151 130 138	407.7370 056 070	31
32	247.3236 236 932	304.8477 192 373	376.5160 777 056	465.8201 863 920	32
33	275.5292 222 995	342.4294 455 457	426.4631 678 073	532.0350 124 868	33
34	306.8374 367 524	384.5209 790 112	482.9033 796 223	607.5199 142 350	34
35	341.5895 547 952	431.6634 964 926	546.6808 189 732	693.5727 022 279	35
36	380.1644 058 226	484.4631 160 717	618.7493 254 397	791.6728 805 398	36
37	422.9824 904 631	543.5986 900 003	700.1867 377 469	903.5070 838 154	37
38	470.5105 644 141	609.8305 328 003	792.2110 136 540	1030.9980 755 495	38
39	523.2667 264 996	684.0101 967 363	896.1984 454 290	1176.3378 061 264	39
40	581.8260 664 146	767.0914 203 447	1013 7042 433 348	1342.0250 989 841	40
41	646.8269 337 202	860.1423 907 861	1146.4857 949 683	1530.9086 128 419	41
42	718.9778 964 294	964.3594 776 804	1296.5289 483 141	1746.2358 186 398	42
43	799.0654 650 366	1081.0826 150 020	1466.0777 115 950	1991.7088 332 494	43
44	887.9626 661 906	1211.8125 288 023	1657.6678 141 023	2271.5480 699 043	44
45	986.6385 594 716	1358.2300 322 586	1874.1646 299 356	2590.5647 996 909	45
46	1096.1688 010 135	1522.2176 361 296	2118.8060 318 273	2954.2438 716 476	46
47	1217.7473 691 250	1705.8837 524 651	2395.2508 159 548	3368.8380 136 783	47
48	1352.6995 797 287	1911.5898 027 609	2707.6334 220 402	3841.4753 355 932	48
49	1502.4965 334 989	2141.9805 790 923	3060.6257 669 055	4380.2818 825 763	49
50	1668.7711 521 837	2400.0182 485 833	3459.5071 166 032	4994.5213 461 370	50
51	1853.3359 789 239	2689.0204 384 133	3910.2430 417 616	5694.7543 345 961	51
52	2058.2029 366 056	3012.7028 910 229	4419.5746 371 906	6493.0199 414 396	52
53	2285.6052 596 322	3375 2272 379 457	4995.1193 400 254	7403.0427 332 411	53
54	2538.0218 381 917	3781.2545 064 992	5645.4848 542 287	8440.4687 158 949	54
55	2818.2042 403 928	4236.0050 472 791	6380.3978 852 784	9623.1343 361 202	55
56	3129.2067 068 360	4745.3256 529 525	7210.8496 103 646	10971.3731 431 770	56
57	3474.4194 445 880	5315.7647 313 069	8149.2600 597 120	12508.3653 832 218	57
58	3857.6055 834 927	5954.6564 990 637	9209.6638 674 745	14260.5365 368 728	58
59	4282.9421 976 769	6670.2152 789 513	10407.9201 702 462	16258.0116 520 350	59
60	4755.0658 394 213	7471.6411 124 255	11761.9497 923 782	18535.1332 833 199	60

Future Worth of One Dollar at Compound Interest
Payable at the end of each period

Years	7% Nominal Annual Rate	8% Nominal Annual Rate	9% Nominal Annual Rate	10% Nominal Annual Rate	Years
1	1.070 000 000	1.0800 000 000	1.090 000 000	1.1000 000 000	1
2	1.1449 000 000	1.1664 000 000	1.1881 000 000	1.210 000 000	2
3	1.2250 430 000	1.2597 120 000	1.2950 290 000	1.3310 000 000	3
4	1.3107 960 100	1.3604 889 600	1.4115 816 100	1.4641 000 000	4
5	1.4025 517 307	1.4693 280 768	1.5386 239 549	1.6105 100 000	5
6	1.5007 303 518	1.5868 743 229	1.6771 001 108	1.7715 610 000	6
7	1.6057 814 765	1.7138 242 688	1.8280 391 208	1.9487 171 000	7
8	1.7181 861 798	1.8509 302 103	1.9925 626 417	2.1435 888 100	8
9	1.8384 592 124	1.9990 046 271	2.1718 932 794	2.3579 476 910	9
10	1.9671 513 573	2.1589 249 973	2.3673 636 746	2.5937 424 601	10
11	2.1048 519 523	2.3316 389 971	2.5804 264 053	2.8531 167 061	11
12	2.2521 915 890	2.5181 701 168	2.8126 647 818	3.1384 283 767	12
13	2.4098 450 002	2.7196 237 262	3.0658 046 121	3.4522 712 144	13
14	2.5785 341 502	2.9371 936 243	3.3417 270 272	3.7974 983 358	14
15	2.7590 315 407	3.1721 691 142	3.6424 824 597	4.1772 481 694	15
16	2.9521 637 486	3.4259 426 433	3.9703 058 811	4.5949 729 864	16
17	3.1588 152 110	3.7000 180 548	4.3276 334 104	5.0544 702 850	17
18	3.3799 322 757	3.9960 194 992	4.7171 204 173	5.5599 173 135	18
19	3.6165 275 350	4.3157 010 591	5.1416 612 548	6.1159 090 448	19
20	3.8696 844 625	4.6609 571 438	5.6044 107 678	6.7274 999 493	20
21	4.1405 623 749	5.0338 337 154	6.1088 077 369	7.4002 499 433	21
22	4.4304 017 411	5.4365 404 126	6.6586 004 332	8.1402 749 387	22
23	4.7405 298 630	5.8714 636 456	7.2578 744 722	8.9543 024 326	23
24	5.0723 669 534	6.3411 807 372	7.9110 831 747	9.8497 326 758	24
25	5.4274 326 401	6.8484 751 962	8.6230 806 604	10.8347 059 434	25
26	5.8073 529 249	7.3963 532 119	9.3991 579 198	11.9181 765 377	26
27	6.2138 676 297	7.9880 614 689	10.2450 821 326	13.1099 941 915	27
28	6.6488 383 638	8.6271 063 864	11.1671 395 246	14.4209 936 106	28
29	7.1142 570 492	9.3172 748 973	12.1721 820 818	15.8630 929 717	29
30	7.6122 550 427	10.0626 568 891	13.2676 784 691	17.4494 022 689	30
31	8.1451 128 956	10.8676 694 402	14.4617 695 314	19.1943 424 958	31
32	8.7152 707 983	11.7370 829 954	15.7633 287 892	21.1137 767 454	32
33	9.3253 397 542	12.6760 496 350	17.1820 283 802	23.2251 544 199	33
34	9.9781 135 370	13.6901 336 059	18.7284 109 344	25.5476 698 619	34
35	10.6765 814 846	14.7853 442 943	20.4139 679 185	28.1024 368 481	35
36	11.4239 421 885	15.9681 718 379	22.2512 250 312	30.9126 805 329	36
37	12.2236 181 417	17.2456 255 849	24.2538 352 840	34.0039 485 862	37
38	13.0792 714 117	18.6252 756 317	26.4366 804 595	37.4043 434 595	38
39	13.9948 204 105	20.1152 976 822	28.8159 817 009	41.1447 777 893	39
40	14.9744 578 392	21.7245 214 968	31.4094 200 540	45.2592 555 682	40
41	16.0226 698 880	23.4624 832 165	34.2362 678 588	49.7851 811 250	41
42	17.1442 567 801	25.3394 818 739	37.3175 319 661	54.7636 992 375	42
43	18.3443 547 547	27.3666 404 238	40.6761 098 431	60.2400 691 612	43
44	19.6284 595 875	29.5559 716 577	44.3369 597 290	66.2640 760 774	44
45	21.0024 517 587	31.9204 493 903	48.3272 861 046	72.8904 836 851	45
46	22.4726 233 818	34.4740 853 415	52.6767 418 540	80.1795 320 536	46
47	24.0457 070 185	37.2320 121 688	57.4176 586 209	88.1974 852 590	47
48	25.7289 065 098	40.2105 731 423	62.5852 369 967	97.0172 337 849	48
49	27.5299 299 655	43.4274 189 937	68.2179 083 264	106.7189 571 534	49
50	29.4570 250 631	46.9016 125 132	74.3575 200 758	117.3908 528 797	50
51	31.5190 168 175	50.6537 415 143	81.0496 968 826	129.1299 381 677	51
52	33.7253 479 947	54.7060 408 354	88.3441 696 021	142.0429 319 844	52
53	36.0861 223 543	59.0825 241 023	96.2951 448 663	156.2472 251 829	53
54	38.6121 509 191	63.8091 260 304	104.9617 079 042	171.8719 477 012	54
55	41.3150 014 835	68.9138 561 129	114.4082 616 156	189.0591 424 713	55
56	44.2070 515 873	74.4269 646 019	124.7050 051 610	207.9650 567 184	56
57	47.3015 451 984	80.3811 217 701	135.9284 556 255	228.7615 623 902	57
58	50.6126 533 623	86.8116 115 117	148.1620 166 318	251.6377 186 293	58
59	54.1555 390 977	93.7565 404 326	161.4965 981 287	276.8014 904 922	59
60	57.9464 268 345	101.2570 636 672	176.0312 919 602	304.4816 395 414	60

Future Worth of One Dollar at Compound Interest
Payable at the end of each period

Years	*11%* Nominal Annual Rate	*12%* Nominal Annual Rate	*13%* Nominal Annual Rate	*14%* Nominal Annual Rate	Years
1	1.1100 000 000	1.1200 000 000	1.1300 000 000	1.1400 000 000	1
2	1.2321 000 000	1.2544 000 000	1.2769 000 000	1.2996 000 000	2
3	1.3676 310 000	1.4049 280 000	1.4428 970 000	1.4815 440 000	3
4	1.5180 704 100	1.5735 193 600	1.6304 736 100	1.6889 601 600	4
5	1.6850 581 551	1.7623 416 832	1.8424 351 793	1.9254 145 824	5
6	1.8704 145 522	1.9738 226 852	2.0819 517 526	2.1949 726 239	6
7	2.0761 601 529	2.2106 814 074	2.3526 054 804	2.5022 687 913	7
8	2.3045 377 697	2.4759 631 763	2.6584 441 929	2.8525 864 221	8
9	2.5580 369 244	2.7730 787 575	3.0040 419 380	3.2519 485 212	9
10	2.8394 209 861	3.1058 482 083	3.3945 673 899	3.7072 213 141	10
11	3.1517 572 945	3.4785 499 933	3.8358 611 506	4.2262 322 981	11
12	3.4984 505 969	3.8959 759 925	4.3345 231 002	4.8179 048 198	12
13	3.8832 801 626	4.3634 931 117	4.8980 111 032	5.4924 114 946	13
14	4.3104 409 805	4.8871 122 851	5.5347 525 466	6.2613 491 038	14
15	4.7845 894 883	5.4735 657 593	6.2542 703 777	7.1379 379 784	15
16	5.3108 943 321	6.1303 936 504	7.0673 255 268	8.1372 492 954	16
17	5.8950 927 086	6.8660 408 884	7.9860 778 453	9.2764 641 967	17
18	6.5435 529 065	7.6899 657 950	9.0242 679 652	10.5751 691 843	18
19	7.2633 437 262	8.6127 616 904	10.1974 228 006	12.0556 928 700	19
20	8.0623 115 361	9.6462 930 933	11.5230 877 647	13.7434 898 719	20
21	8.9491 658 051	10.8038 482 645	13.0210 891 741	15.6675 784 539	21
22	9.9335 740 437	12.1003 100 562	14.7138 307 668	17.8610 394 375	22
23	11.0262 671 885	13.5523 472 629	16.6266 287 665	20.3615 849 587	23
24	12.2391 565 792	15.1786 289 345	18.7880 905 061	23.2122 068 529	24
25	13.5854 638 029	17.0000 644 066	21.2305 422 719	26.4619 158 123	25
26	15.0798 648 212	19.0400 721 354	23.9905 127 672	30.1665 840 261	26
27	16.7386 499 516	21.3248 807 917	27.1092 794 270	34.3899 057 897	27
28	18.5799 014 462	23.8838 664 867	30.6334 857 525	39.2044 926 003	28
29	20.6236 906 053	26.7499 304 651	34.6158 389 003	44.6931 215 643	29
30	22.8922 965 719	29.9599 221 209	39.1158 979 573	50.9501 585 833	30
31	25.4104 491 948	33.5551 127 754	44.2009 646 918	58.0831 807 850	31
32	28.2055 986 063	37.5817 263 085	49.9470 901 107	66.2148 260 949	32
33	31.3082 144 529	42.0915 334 655	56.4402 118 150	75.4849 017 482	33
34	34.7521 180 428	47.1425 174 813	63.7774 393 509	86.0527 879 929	34
35	38.5748 510 275	52.7996 195 791	72.0685 064 665	98.1001 783 119	35
36	42.8180 846 405	59.1355 739 286	81.4374 123 072	111.8342 032 756	36
37	47.5280 739 509	66.2318 428 000	92.0242 759 071	127.4909 917 342	37
38	52.7561 620 855	74.1796 639 360	103.9874 317 750	145.3397 305 769	38
39	58.5593 399 150	83.0812 236 084	117.5057 979 058	165.6872 928 577	39
40	65.0008 673 056	93.0509 704 414	132.7815 516 335	188.8835 138 578	40
41	72.1509 627 092	104.2170 868 943	150.0431 533 459	215.3272 057 979	41
42	80.0875 686 072	116.7231 373 216	169.5487 632 808	245.4730 146 096	42
43	88.8972 011 540	130.7299 138 002	191.5901 025 073	279.8392 366 549	43
44	98.6758 932 810	146.4175 034 563	216.4968 158 333	319.0167 297 866	44
45	109.5302 415 419	163.9876 038 710	244.6414 018 916	363.6790 719 567	45
46	121.5785 681 115	183.6661 163 355	276.4447 841 375	414.5941 420 307	46
47	134.9522 106 037	205.7060 502 958	312.3826 060 754	472.6373 219 150	47
48	149.7969 537 702	230.3907 763 313	352.9923 448 652	538.8065 469 831	48
49	166.2746 186 849	258.0376 694 911	398.8813 496 977	614.2394 635 607	49
50	184.5648 267 402	289.0021 898 300	450.7359 251 584	700.2329 884 592	50
51	204.8669 576 816	323.6824 526 096	509.3315 954 290	798.2656 068 435	51
52	227.4023 230 266	362.5243 469 228	575.5447 028 348	910.0227 918 015	52
53	252.4165 785 595	406.0272 685 535	650.3655 142 033	1037.4259 826 538	53
54	280.1824 022 011	454.7505 407 799	734.9130 310 497	1182.6656 202 253	54
55	311.0024 664 432	509.3206 056 735	830.4517 250 862	1348.2388 070 568	55
56	345.2127 377 520	570.4390 783 543	938.4104 493 474	1536.9922 400 448	56
57	383.1861 389 047	638.8917 677 568	1060.4038 077 626	1752.1711 536 510	57
58	424.3366 141 842	715.5587 798 876	1198.2563 027 717	1997.4751 151 622	58
59	472.1236 417 445	801.4258 334 742	1354.0296 221 320	2277.1216 312 849	59
60	524.0572 423 363	897.5969 334 911	1530.0534 730 092	2595.9186 596 648	60

Annual Savings Per One Dollar Needed at Various Interest Rates to Obtain a Predetermined Amount of Capital (Sinking Fund Factors)
Payable at the end of each period

YEARLY
Compounding

Years	7% Nominal Annual Rate	8% Nominal Annual Rate	9% Nominal Annual Rate	10% Nominal Annual Rate	Years
1	1.0000 000 000	1.0000 000 000	1.0000 000 000	1.0000 000 000	1
2	0.4830 917 874	0.4807 692 308	0.4784 688 995	0.4761 904 762	2
3	0.3110 516 657	0.3080 335 140	0.3050 547 573	0.3021 148 036	3
4	0.2252 281 167	0.2219 208 045	0.2186 686 621	0.2154 708 037	4
5	0.1738 906 944	0.1704 564 546	0.1670 924 570	0.1637 974 808	5
6	0.1397 957 998	0.1363 153 862	0.1329 197 833	0.1296 073 804	6
7	0.1155 532 196	0.1120 724 014	0.1086 905 168	0.1054 054 997	7
8	0.0974 677 625	0.0940 147 606	0.0906 743 778	0.0874 440 176	8
9	0.0834 864 701	0.0800 797 092	0.0767 988 021	0.0736 405 391	9
10	0.0723 775 027	0.0690 294 887	0.0658 200 899	0.0627 453 949	10
11	0.0633 569 048	0.0600 763 421	0.0569 466 457	0.0539 631 420	11
12	0.0559 019 887	0.0526 950 169	0.0496 506 585	0.0467 633 151	12
13	0.0496 508 481	0.0465 218 052	0.0435 665 597	0.0407 785 238	13
14	0.0443 449 386	0.0412 968 528	0.0384 331 730	0.0357 461 232	14
15	0.0397 946 247	0.0368 295 449	0.0340 588 827	0.0314 737 769	15
16	0.0358 576 477	0.0329 768 720	0.0302 999 097	0.0278 166 207	16
17	0.0324 251 931	0.0296 294 315	0.0270 462 485	0.0246 641 344	17
18	0.0294 126 017	0.0267 020 959	0.0242 122 907	0.0219 302 222	18
19	0.0267 530 148	0.0241 276 275	0.0217 304 107	0.0195 468 682	19
20	0.0243 929 257	0.0218 522 088	0.0195 464 750	0.0174 596 248	20
21	0.0222 890 017	0.0198 322 503	0.0176 166 348	0.0156 243 898	21
22	0.0204 057 732	0.0180 320 684	0.0159 049 930	0.0140 050 630	22
23	0.0187 139 263	0.0164 221 692	0.0143 818 800	0.0125 718 127	23
24	0.0171 890 207	0.0149 779 616	0.0130 255 607	0.0112 997 764	24
25	0.0158 105 172	0.0136 787 791	0.0118 062 505	0.0101 680 722	25
26	0.0145 610 279	0.0125 071 267	0.0107 153 599	0.0091 590 386	26
27	0.0134 257 340	0.0114 480 962	0.0097 349 054	0.0082 576 423	27
28	0.0123 919 283	0.0104 889 057	0.0088 520 473	0.0074 510 132	28
29	0.0114 486 518	0.0096 185 350	0.0080 557 226	0.0067 280 747	29
30	0.0105 864 035	0.0088 274 334	0.0073 363 514	0.0060 792 483	30
31	0.0097 969 061	0.0081 072 841	0.0066 855 955	0.0054 962 140	31
32	0.0090 729 155	0.0074 508 132	0.0060 961 861	0.0049 717 167	32
33	0.0084 080 653	0.0068 516 324	0.0055 617 255	0.0044 994 063	33
34	0.0077 967 381	0.0063 041 101	0.0050 765 911	0.0040 737 064	34
35	0.0072 339 596	0.0058 032 646	0.0046 358 375	0.0036 897 051	35
36	0.0067 153 097	0.0053 446 741	0.0042 350 500	0.0033 430 638	36
37	0.0062 368 480	0.0049 244 025	0.0038 703 293	0.0030 299 405	37
38	0.0057 950 515	0.0045 389 361	0.0035 381 975	0.0027 469 250	38
39	0.0053 867 616	0.0041 851 297	0.0032 355 500	0.0024 909 840	39
40	0.0050 091 389	0.0038 601 615	0.0029 596 092	0.0022 594 144	40
41	0.0046 596 245	0.0035 614 940	0.0027 078 853	0.0020 498 028	41
42	0.0043 359 072	0.0032 868 407	0.0024 781 420	0.0018 599 911	42
43	0.0040 358 953	0.0030 341 370	0.0022 683 675	0.0016 880 446	43
44	0.0037 576 913	0.0028 015 156	0.0020 767 493	0.0015 322 365	44
45	0.0034 995 710	0.0025 872 845	0.0019 016 514	0.0013 910 047	45
46	0.0032 599 650	0.0023 899 085	0.0017 415 959	0.0012 629 527	46
47	0.0030 374 421	0.0022 079 922	0.0015 952 455	0.0011 468 221	47
48	0.0028 306 953	0.0020 402 660	0.0014 613 892	0.0010 414 797	48
49	0.0026 385 294	0.0018 855 731	0.0013 389 289	0.0009 459 041	49
50	0.0024 598 495	0.0017 428 582	0.0012 268 681	0.0008 591 740	50
51	0.0022 936 519	0.0016 111 575	0.0011 243 016	0.0007 804 577	51
52	0.0021 390 147	0.0014 895 903	0.0010 304 065	0.0007 090 040	52
53	0.0019 950 908	0.0013 773 506	0.0009 444 343	0.0006 441 339	53
54	0.0018 611 007	0.0012 737 003	0.0008 657 034	0.0005 852 336	54
55	0.0017 363 264	0.0011 779 629	0.0007 935 930	0.0005 317 476	55
56	0.0016 201 059	0.0010 895 180	0.0007 275 373	0.0004 831 734	56
57	0.0015 118 286	0.0010 077 963	0.0006 670 202	0.0004 390 556	57
58	0.0014 109 304	0.0009 322 748	0.0006 115 709	0.0003 989 822	58
59	0.0013 168 900	0.0008 624 729	0.0005 607 595	0.0003 625 796	59
60	0.0012 292 255	0.0007 979 488	0.0005 141 938	0.0003 295 092	60

Annual Savings Per One Dollar Needed at Various Interest Rates to Obtain a Predetermined Amount of Capital (Sinking Fund Factors)

Payable at the end of each period

Years	11% Nominal Annual Rate	12% Nominal Annual Rate	13% Nominal Annual Rate	14% Nominal Annual Rate	Years
1	1.0000 000 000	1.0000 000 000	1.0000 000 000	1.0000 000 000	1
2	0.4739 336 493	0.4716 981 132	0.4694 835 681	0.4672 897 196	2
3	0.2992 130 696	0.2963 489 806	0.2935 219 701	0.2907 314 804	3
4	0.2123 263 515	0.2092 344 363	0.2061 941 974	0.2032 047 833	4
5	0.1605 703 095	0.1574 097 319	0.1543 145 434	0.1512 835 465	5
6	0.1263 765 636	0.1232 257 184	0.1201 532 321	0.1171 574 957	6
7	0.1022 152 695	0.0991 177 359	0.0961 108 038	0.0931 923 773	7
8	0.0843 210 542	0.0813 028 414	0.0783 867 196	0.0755 700 238	8
9	0.0706 016 644	0.0676 788 888	0.0648 689 020	0.0621 683 838	9
10	0.0598 014 271	0.0569 841 642	0.0542 895 558	0.0517 135 408	10
11	0.0511 210 071	0.0484 154 043	0.0458 414 545	0.0433 942 714	11
12	0.0440 272 864	0.0414 368 076	0.0389 860 847	0.0366 693 269	12
13	0.0381 509 925	0.0356 771 951	0.0333 503 411	0.0311 636 635	13
14	0.0332 282 015	0.0308 712 461	0.0286 674 959	0.0266 091 448	14
15	0.0290 652 395	0.0268 242 396	0.0247 417 797	0.0228 089 630	15
16	0.0255 167 470	0.0233 900 180	0.0214 262 445	0.0196 154 000	16
17	0.0224 714 845	0.0204 567 275	0.0186 084 385	0.0169 154 359	17
18	0.0198 428 701	0.0179 373 114	0.0162 008 548	0.0146 211 516	18
19	0.0175 625 041	0.0157 630 049	0.0141 343 943	0.0126 631 593	19
20	0.0155 756 369	0.0138 787 800	0.0123 537 884	0.0109 860 016	20
21	0.0138 379 300	0.0122 400 915	0.0108 143 279	0.0095 448 612	21
22	0.0123 131 011	0.0108 105 088	0.0094 794 811	0.0083 031 654	22
23	0.0109 711 818	0.0095 599 650	0.0083 191 328	0.0072 308 130	23
24	0.0097 872 113	0.0084 634 417	0.0073 082 605	0.0063 028 406	24
25	0.0087 402 421	0.0074 999 698	0.0064 259 276	0.0054 984 079	25
26	0.0078 125 750	0.0066 518 581	0.0056 545 063	0.0048 000 136	26
27	0.0069 891 636	0.0059 040 937	0.0049 790 727	0.0041 928 839	27
28	0.0062 571 454	0.0052 438 691	0.0043 869 291	0.0036 644 905	28
29	0.0056 054 695	0.0046 602 068	0.0038 672 246	0.0032 041 657	29
30	0.0050 245 985	0.0041 436 576	0.0034 106 503	0.0028 027 939	30
31	0.0045 062 669	0.0036 860 570	0.0030 091 921	0.0024 525 613	31
32	0.0040 432 854	0.0032 803 263	0.0026 559 291	0.0021 467 511	32
33	0.0036 293 791	0.0029 203 096	0.0023 448 684	0.0018 795 755	33
34	0.0032 590 547	0.0026 006 383	0.0020 708 076	0.0016 460 366	34
35	0.0029 274 900	0.0023 166 193	0.0018 292 209	0.0014 418 099	35
36	0.0026 304 409	0.0020 641 406	0.0016 161 634	0.0012 631 480	36
37	0.0023 641 641	0.0018 395 924	0.0014 281 904	0.0011 067 982	37
38	0.0021 253 508	0.0016 397 998	0.0012 622 899	0.0009 699 339	38
39	0.0019 110 713	0.0014 619 665	0.0011 158 243	0.0008 500 959	39
40	0.0017 187 267	0.0013 036 256	0.0009 864 810	0.0007 451 425	40
41	0.0015 460 086	0.0011 625 982	0.0008 722 306	0.0006 532 069	41
42	0.0013 908 633	0.0010 369 577	0.0007 712 901	0.0005 726 603	42
43	0.0012 514 619	0.0009 249 987	0.0006 820 921	0.0005 020 814	43
44	0.0011 261 735	0.0008 252 102	0.0006 032 572	0.0004 402 284	44
45	0.0010 135 424	0.0007 362 523	0.0005 335 711	0.0003 860 162	45
46	0.0009 122 683	0.0006 569 363	0.0004 719 639	0.0003 384 961	46
47	0.0008 211 884	0.0005 862 064	0.0004 174 928	0.0002 968 383	47
48	0.0007 392 624	0.0005 231 248	0.0003 693 262	0.0002 603 167	48
49	0.0006 655 589	0.0004 668 576	0.0003 267 306	0.0002 282 958	49
50	0.0005 992 433	0.0004 166 635	0.0002 890 585	0.0002 002 194	50
51	0.0005 395 676	0.0003 718 826	0.0002 557 386	0.0001 756 002	51
52	0.0004 858 607	0.0003 319 279	0.0002 262 661	0.0001 540 115	52
53	0.0004 375 209	0.0002 962 763	0.0002 001 954	0.0001 350 796	53
54	0.0003 940 076	0.0002 644 625	0.0001 711 327	0.0001 184 768	54
55	0.0003 548 359	0.0002 360 715	0.0001 567 300	0.0001 039 162	55
56	0.0003 195 698	0.0002 107 337	0.0001 386 799	0.0000 911 463	56
57	0.0002 878 179	0.0001 881 197	0.0001 227 105	0.0000 799 465	57
58	0.0002 592 282	0.0001 679 358	0.0001 085 816	0.0000 701 236	58
59	0.0002 334 844	0.0001 499 202	0.0000 960 807	0.0000 615 081	59
60	0.0002 103 020	0.0001 338 394	0.0000 850 199	0.0000 539 516	60

Annual Payment Required to Amortize $1,000

Interest Years	5.00%	6.00%	7.00%	8.00%	9.00%	10.00%	11.00%	12.00%	13.00%	14.00%	15.00%	16.00%	17.00%	18.00%	19.00%	20.00%
1.0	1050.00	1060.00	1070.00	1080.00	1090.00	1100.00	1110.00	1120.00	1130.00	1140.00	1150.00	1160.00	1170.00	1180.00	1190.00	1200.00
2.0	537.81	545.44	553.10	560.77	568.47	576.20	583.94	591.70	599.49	607.29	615.12	622.97	630.83	638.72	646.63	654.55
3.0	367.21	374.11	381.06	388.04	395.06	402.12	409.22	416.35	423.53	430.74	437.98	445.26	452.58	459.93	467.31	474.73
4.0	282.02	288.60	295.23	301.93	308.67	315.48	322.33	329.24	336.20	343.21	350.27	357.38	364.54	371.74	379.00	386.29
5.0	230.98	237.40	243.90	250.46	257.10	263.80	270.58	277.41	284.32	291.29	298.32	305.41	312.57	319.78	327.06	334.38
6.0	197.02	203.37	209.80	216.32	222.92	229.61	236.38	243.23	250.16	257.16	264.24	271.39	278.62	285.92	293.28	300.71
7.0	172.82	179.14	185.56	192.08	198.70	205.41	212.22	219.12	226.12	233.20	240.37	247.62	254.95	262.37	269.86	277.43
8.0	154.73	161.04	167.47	174.01	180.68	187.45	194.33	201.31	208.39	215.58	222.86	230.23	237.69	245.25	252.89	260.61
9.0	140.70	147.03	153.49	160.08	166.80	173.65	180.61	187.68	194.87	202.17	209.58	217.09	224.70	232.40	240.20	248.08
10.0	129.51	135.87	142.38	149.03	155.83	162.75	169.81	176.99	184.29	191.72	199.26	206.91	214.66	222.52	230.48	238.53
11.0	120.39	126.80	133.36	140.08	146.95	153.97	161.13	168.42	175.85	183.40	191.07	198.87	206.77	214.78	222.90	231.11
12.0	112.83	119.28	125.91	132.70	139.66	146.77	154.03	161.44	168.99	176.67	184.49	192.42	200.47	208.63	216.90	225.27
13.0	106.46	112.97	119.66	126.53	133.57	140.78	148.16	155.68	163.36	171.17	179.12	187.19	195.38	203.69	212.11	220.63
14.0	101.03	107.59	114.35	121.30	128.44	135.75	143.23	150.88	158.67	166.61	174.69	182.90	191.24	199.68	208.24	216.90
15.0	96.35	102.97	109.80	116.83	124.06	131.48	139.07	146.83	154.75	162.81	171.02	179.36	187.83	196.41	205.10	213.89
16.0	92.27	98.96	105.86	112.98	120.30	127.82	135.52	143.40	151.43	159.62	167.95	176.42	185.01	193.72	202.53	211.44
17.0	88.70	95.45	102.43	109.63	117.05	124.67	132.48	140.46	148.61	156.92	165.37	173.96	182.67	191.49	200.42	209.45
18.0	85.55	92.36	99.42	106.71	114.22	121.94	129.85	137.94	146.21	154.63	163.19	171.89	180.71	189.64	198.68	207.81
19.0	82.75	89.63	96.76	104.13	111.74	119.55	127.57	135.77	144.14	152.67	161.34	170.15	179.07	188.11	197.24	206.47
20.0	80.25	87.19	94.40	101.86	109.55	117.46	125.58	133.88	142.36	150.99	159.77	168.67	177.70	186.82	196.05	205.36
21.0	78.00	85.01	92.29	99.84	107.62	115.63	123.84	132.25	140.82	149.55	158.42	167.42	176.54	185.75	195.06	204.45
22.0	75.98	83.05	90.41	98.04	105.91	114.01	122.32	130.82	139.48	148.31	157.27	166.36	175.56	184.85	194.23	203.69
23.0	74.14	81.28	88.72	96.43	104.39	112.58	120.98	129.56	138.32	147.24	156.28	165.45	174.73	184.10	193.55	203.07
24.0	72.48	79.68	87.19	94.98	103.03	111.30	119.79	128.47	137.31	146.31	155.43	164.68	174.02	183.46	192.97	202.55
25.0	70.96	78.23	85.82	93.68	101.81	110.17	118.75	127.50	136.43	145.50	154.70	164.02	173.43	182.92	192.49	202.12
26.0	69.57	76.91	84.57	92.51	100.72	109.16	117.82	126.66	135.66	144.81	154.07	163.45	172.92	182.47	192.09	201.77
27.0	68.30	75.70	83.43	91.45	99.74	108.26	116.99	125.91	134.98	144.20	153.53	162.97	172.49	182.09	191.75	201.47
28.0	67.13	74.60	82.40	90.49	98.86	107.46	116.26	125.25	134.39	143.67	153.06	162.55	172.13	181.77	191.47	201.23
29.0	66.05	73.58	81.45	89.62	98.06	106.73	115.61	124.67	133.87	143.21	152.66	162.20	171.81	181.50	191.24	201.02
30.0	65.06	72.65	80.59	88.83	97.34	106.08	115.03	124.15	133.42	142.81	152.31	161.89	171.55	181.27	191.04	200.85
31.0	64.14	71.80	79.80	88.11	96.69	105.50	114.51	123.69	133.01	142.46	152.00	161.63	171.32	181.08	190.87	200.71
32.0	63.29	71.01	79.08	87.46	96.10	104.98	114.05	123.29	132.66	142.15	151.74	161.40	171.13	180.91	190.73	200.59
33.0	62.50	70.28	78.41	86.86	95.57	104.50	113.63	122.93	132.35	141.88	151.51	161.21	170.97	180.77	190.62	200.49
34.0	61.76	69.60	77.80	86.31	95.08	104.08	113.26	122.61	132.08	141.65	151.31	161.04	170.83	180.65	190.52	200.41
35.0	61.08	68.98	77.24	85.81	94.64	103.69	112.93	122.32	131.83	141.45	151.14	160.90	170.71	180.56	190.44	200.34
36.0	60.44	68.40	76.72	85.35	94.24	103.35	112.64	122.07	131.62	141.27	150.99	160.77	170.60	180.47	190.37	200.29
37.0	59.84	67.86	76.24	84.93	93.88	103.03	112.37	121.84	131.43	141.11	150.86	160.67	170.52	180.40	190.31	200.24
38.0	59.29	67.36	75.80	84.54	93.54	102.75	112.13	121.64	131.27	140.97	150.75	160.58	170.44	180.34	190.26	200.20
39.0	58.77	66.90	75.39	84.19	93.24	102.50	111.92	121.47	131.12	140.86	150.65	160.50	170.38	180.29	190.22	200.17
40.0	58.28	66.47	75.01	83.87	92.96	102.26	111.72	121.31	130.99	140.75	150.57	160.43	170.32	180.25	190.19	200.14
41.0	57.83	66.06	74.66	83.57	92.71	102.05	111.55	121.17	130.88	140.66	150.49	160.37	170.28	180.21	190.16	200.12
42.0	57.40	65.69	74.34	83.29	92.48	101.86	111.40	121.04	130.78	140.58	150.43	160.32	170.24	180.18	190.13	200.10
43.0	57.00	65.34	74.04	83.04	92.27	101.69	111.26	120.93	130.69	140.51	150.37	160.28	170.20	180.15	190.11	200.08
44.0	56.62	65.01	73.76	82.81	92.08	101.54	111.13	120.83	130.61	140.45	150.33	160.24	170.18	180.13	190.10	200.07
45.0	56.27	64.71	73.50	82.59	91.91	101.40	111.02	120.74	130.54	140.39	150.28	160.21	170.15	180.11	190.08	200.06
46.0	55.93	64.42	73.26	82.39	91.75	101.27	110.92	120.66	130.48	140.34	150.25	160.18	170.13	180.09	190.07	200.05
47.0	55.62	64.15	73.04	82.21	91.60	101.15	110.83	120.59	130.42	140.30	150.22	160.15	170.11	180.08	190.06	200.04
48.0	55.32	63.90	72.84	82.05	91.47	101.05	110.74	120.53	130.37	140.27	150.19	160.13	170.10	180.07	190.05	200.04
49.0	55.04	63.67	72.64	81.89	91.34	100.95	110.67	120.47	130.33	140.23	150.16	160.12	170.08	180.06	190.04	200.03
50.0	54.78	63.45	72.46	81.75	91.23	100.86	110.60	120.42	130.29	140.21	150.14	160.10	170.07	180.05	190.04	200.03

Life Expectancy and Private Annuity Tables

Life Expectancy Table

| | Expectation of Life in Years | | | | | Mortality Rate Per 1,000 Living at Specified Age | | | | |
| | White | | Other | | | | White | | Other | |
Age in 1976 (years)	Total	Male	Female	Male	Female	Total	Male	Female	Male	Female
Under 1	72.8	69.7	77.3	64.1	72.6	15.36	14.91	11.79	25.86	21.74
1	72.9	69.8	77.2	64.9	73.3	.94	.99	.74	1.33	1.09
2	72.0	68.9	76.3	63.9	72.3	.74	.75	.59	1.11	.91
3	71.0	67.9	75.3	63.0	71.4	.60	.60	.48	.94	.75
4	70.1	67.0	74.4	62.1	70.5	.50	.50	.40	.81	.61
5	69.1	66.0	73.4	61.1	69.5	.43	.45	.34	.70	.50
6	68.1	65.0	72.4	60.2	68.5	.38	.42	.30	.62	.40
7	67.2	64.0	71.5	59.2	67.6	.35	.39	.26	.54	.34
8	66.2	63.1	70.5	58.2	66.6	.31	.35	.24	.47	.29
9	65.2	62.1	69.5	57.3	65.6	.27	.31	.21	.41	.26
10	64.2	61.1	68.5	56.3	64.6	.25	.27	.19	.37	.25
11	63.2	60.1	67.5	55.3	63.6	.25	.27	.19	.37	.26
12	62.3	59.1	66.5	54.3	62.6	.29	.35	.22	.43	.28
13	61.3	58.2	65.5	53.3	61.7	.40	.51	.27	.57	.31
14	60.3	57.2	64.6	52.4	60.7	.55	.74	.34	.77	.36
15	59.3	56.2	63.6	51.4	59.7	.72	1.00	.42	.98	.41
16	58.4	55.3	62.6	50.5	58.7	.87	1.24	.50	1.22	.48
17	57.5	54.5	61.6	49.5	57.8	1.01	1.44	.55	1.48	.56
18	56.5	53.4	60.7	48.6	56.8	1.11	1.58	.58	1.78	.65
19	55.5	52.5	59.7	47.7	55.8	1.17	1.68	.58	2.11	.76
20	54.6	51.6	58.7	46.8	54.9	1.24	1.76	.57	2.45	.88
21	53.7	50.7	57.8	45.9	53.9	1.30	1.84	.57	2.79	1.00
22	52.7	49.8	56.8	45.0	53.0	1.34	1.88	.57	3.08	1.10
23	51.8	48.9	55.8	44.2	52.0	1.35	1.85	.57	3.30	1.17
24	50.9	48.0	54.9	43.3	51.1	1.33	1.79	.58	3.47	1.23
25	50.0	47.1	53.9	42.5	50.2	1.31	1.70	.59	3.64	1.28
26	49.0	46.1	52.9	41.6	49.2	1.29	1.62	.59	3.81	1.33
27	48.1	45.2	52.0	40.8	48.3	1.28	1.56	.61	3.94	1.40
28	47.1	44.3	51.0	39.9	47.3	1.29	1.54	.63	4.02	1.46
29	46.2	43.3	50.0	39.1	46.4	1.31	1.54	.67	4.07	1.53
30	45.3	42.4	49.1	38.2	45.4	1.34	1.56	.71	4.11	1.61
31	44.3	41.5	48.1	37.4	44.6	1.38	1.58	.75	4.17	1.70
32	43.4	40.5	47.1	36.6	43.6	1.44	1.62	.81	4.29	1.80
33	42.4	39.6	46.2	35.7	42.7	1.50	1.68	.86	4.49	1.91
34	41.5	38.7	45.2	34.9	41.8	1.59	1.76	.92	4.77	2.04
35	40.6	37.7	44.2	34.0	40.9	1.69	1.86	.99	5.08	2.18
36	39.6	36.8	43.3	33.2	40.0	1.81	1.99	1.07	5.41	2.34
37	38.7	35.9	42.3	32.4	39.1	1.95	2.15	1.17	5.76	2.56
38	37.8	35.0	41.4	31.6	38.2	2.13	2.35	1.28	6.15	2.83
39	36.9	34.0	40.4	30.8	37.3	2.33	2.57	1.42	6.57	3.16

Life Expectancy Table (continued)

Age in 1976 (years)	Expectation of Life in Years					Mortality Rate Per 1,000 Living at Specified Age				
		White		Other			White		Other	
	Total	Male	Female	Male	Female	Total	Male	Female	Male	Female
40	35.9	33.1	39.5	30.0	36.4	2.56	2.83	1.56	7.04	3.52
41	35.0	32.2	38.6	29.2	35.5	2.82	3.13	1.72	7.54	3.90
42	34.1	31.3	37.6	28.4	34.6	3.10	3.46	1.90	8.07	4.27
43	33.2	30.4	36.7	27.6	33.8	3.41	3.85	2.12	8.61	4.62
44	32.4	29.5	35.8	26.8	32.9	3.74	4.27	2.35	9.18	4.97
45	31.5	28.7	34.9	26.1	32.1	4.12	4.75	2.61	9.77	5.33
46	30.6	27.8	33.9	25.3	31.3	4.52	5.27	2.89	10.42	5.73
47	29.7	26.9	33.0	24.6	30.5	4.95	5.82	3.18	11.20	6.19
48	28.9	26.1	32.1	23.9	29.6	5.40	6.41	3.47	12.14	6.72
49	28.0	25.3	31.3	23.2	28.8	5.89	7.04	3.77	13.20	7.30
50	27.2	24.4	30.4	22.5	28.0	6.42	7.74	4.09	14.36	7.94
51	26.4	23.6	29.5	21.8	27.3	7.00	8.50	4.45	15.57	8.60
52	25.6	22.8	28.6	21.2	16.5	7.63	9.32	4.84	16.77	9.27
53	24.7	22.0	27.8	20.5	25.7	8.30	10.23	5.27	17.94	9.94
54	24.0	21.3	26.9	19.8	25.0	9.02	11.21	5.74	19.11	10.61
55	23.2	20.5	26.1	19.2	24.3	9.78	12.24	6.24	20.26	11.26
56	22.4	19.7	25.2	18.6	23.5	10.60	13.37	6.78	21.49	11.96
57	21.6	19.0	24.4	18.0	22.8	11.56	14.69	7.40	23.00	12.86
58	20.9	18.3	23.6	17.4	22.1	12.70	16.25	8.11	24.88	14.01
59	20.1	17.6	22.8	16.9	21.4	13.99	18.01	8.91	27.04	15.35
60	19.4	16.9	22.0	16.3	20.7	15.42	19.94	9.80	29.56	16.99
61	18.7	16.2	21.2	15.8	20.1	16.90	21.94	10.74	32.07	18.62
62	18.0	15.6	20.4	15.3	19.5	18.29	23.96	11.62	34.06	19.74
63	17.3	14.9	19.6	14.8	18.8	19.51	25.93	12.40	35.17	20.06
64	16.7	14.3	18.9	14.3	18.2	20.65	27.91	13.15	35.63	19.88
65	16.0	13.7	18.1	13.8	17.6	21.79	29.97	13.94	35.59	19.26
70	12.9	10.9	14.4	11.3	14.3	32.38	44.20	21.62	51.87	34.29
75	10.1	8.5	11.2	9.7	12.3	50.87	67.45	37.58	74.73	54.66
80	7.9	6.6	8.5	8.6	10.9	76.55	100.28	62.16	92.85	68.28
85 and over	6.1	5.1	6.4	7.2	9.1	1,000.00	1,000.00	1,000.00	1,000.00	1,000.00

Source: U.S. National Center for Health Statistics, *Vital Statistics of the United States* (1978), annual.

Annuity, Life Estate & Remainder Interest Values (Male, 6%)

1 Age	2 Annuity	3 Life Estate	4 Remainder	1 Age	2 Annuity	3 Life Estate	4 Remainder
0	15.6175	.93705	.06295	55	10.2960	.61776	.38224
1	16.0382	.96217	.03783	56	10.0777	.60466	.39534
2	16.0283	.96170	.03830	57	9.8552	.59131	.40869
3	16.0089	.96053	.03947	58	9.6297	.57778	.42222
4	15.9841	.95905	.04095	59	9.4028	.56417	.43583
5	15.9553	.95732	.04268	60	9.1753	.55052	44948
6	15.9233	.05540	.04460	61	8.9478	.53687	.46313
7	15.8885	.95331	.04669	62	8.7272	.52321	.47679
8	15.8508	.95105	.04895	63	8.4924	.50954	.49046
9	15.8101	.94861	.05139	64	8.2642	.49585	.50415
10	15.7663	0.4593	.05402	65	8.0353	.48212	.51788
11	15.7194	.94316	.05684	66	7.8060	.46836	.53164
12	15.6698	.94019	.05981	67	7.5763	.45458	.54542
13	15.6180	.93708	.06292	68	7.3562	.44077	.55923
14	15.5651	.93391	.06609	69	7.1149	.42689	.57311
15	15.5115	.93069	.06931	70	6.8823	.41294	.58706
16	15.4576	.92746	.07254	71	6.6481	.39889	.60111
17	15.4031	.92419	.07581	72	6.4123	.38474	.61526
18	15.3481	.92089	.07911	73	6.1752	.37051	.62949
19	15.2918	.91751	.08249	74	5.9373	.35624	.64376
20	15.2339	.91403	.08597	75	5.6990	.34194	.65806
21	15.1744	.91046	.08954	76	5.4602	.32761	.67239
22	15.1130	.90678	.09322	77	5.2211	.31327	.68673
23	15.0487	.90292	.09708	78	4.9825	.29895	.70105
24	14.9807	.89884	.10116	79	4.7469	.28481	.71519
25	14.9075	.89445	.10555	80	4.5164	.27098	.72902
26	14.8287	.88972	.11028	81	4.2955	.25773	.74227
27	14.7442	.88465	.11535	82	4.0879	.24527	.75473
28	14.6542	.87925	.12075	83	3.8924	.23354	.76646
29	14.5588	,87353	.12647	84	3.7029	.22217	.77783
30	14.4584	.86750	.13250	85	3.5117	.21070	.78930
31	14.3528	.86117	.13883	86	3.3259	.19955	.80045
32	14.2418	.85451	.14549	87	3.1450	.18870	.81130
33	14.1254	.84752	.15248	88	2.9703	.17822	.82178
34	14.0034	.84020	.15980	89	2.8052	.16831	.83169
35	13.8758	.83255	.16745	90	2.6536	.15922	.84078
36	13.7425	.82455	.17545	91	2.5162	.15097	.84903
37	13.6036	.81622	.18378	92	2.3917	.14350	.85650
38	13.4591	.80755	.19245	93	2.2801	.13681	.86319
39	13.3090	.79854	.20145	94	2.1802	.13081	.86919
40	13.1538	.78923	.21077	95	2.0891	.12535	.87465
41	12.9934	.77960	.22040	96	1.9997	.11998	.88002
42	12.8279	.76967	.23033	98	1.9145	.11487	.88513
43	12.6574	.75944	.24058	98	1.8331	.10999	.89001
44	12.4819	.74891	.25109	99	1.7554	.10532	.89468
45	12.3013	.73808	.26192	100	1.6812	.10087	.89913
46	12.1158	.72695	.27305	101	1.6101	.09661	.90339
47	11.9253	.71552	.28448	102	1.5416	.09250	.90750
48	11.7308	.70885	.29615	103	1.4744	.08846	.91154
49	11.5330	.68106	.30802	104	1.4065	.08439	.91561
50	11.3329	.67997	.32003	105	1.3334	.08000	.92000
51	11.1308	.66785	.33215	106	1.2452	.07471	.92529
52	10.9267	.65560	.34440	107	1.1196	.06718	.93282
53	10.7200	.64320	.35680	108	.9043	.05426	.94574
54	10.5100	.63060	.36980	109	.4717	.02830	.97170

Annuity, Life Estate & Remainder Interest Values (Female, 6%)

1 Age	2 Annuity	3 Life Estate	4 Remainder	1 Age	2 Annuity	3 Life Estate	4 Remainder
0	15.8972	.95383	.04617	55	11.6432	.69859	.30141
1	16.2284	.97370	.02630	56	11.4353	.68612	.31388
2	16.2287	.97372	.02628	57	11.2200	.67320	.32680
3	16.2180	.97308	.02692	58	10.9980	.65988	.34012
4	16.2029	.97217	.02783	59	10.7703	.64622	.35378
5	16.1850	.97110	.02890	60	10.5376	.63226	.36774
6	16.1648	.96989	.03011	61	10.3005	.61803	.38197
7	16.1421	.96853	.03147	62	10.0567	.60352	.39648
8	16.1172	.96703	.03297	63	9.8188	.58871	.41129
9	16.0901	.96541	.03459	64	9.5592	.57355	.42645
10	16.0608	.06365	.03635	65	9.3005	.55803	.44197
11	16.0293	.96176	.03824	66	9.0352	.54211	.45789
12	15.9958	.95975	.04025	67	8.7639	.52583	.47417
13	15.9607	.95764	.04236	68	8.4874	.50924	.49076
14	15.9267	.95543	.04457	69	8.2068	.49241	.50759
15	15.8856	.95314	.04686	70	7.9234	.47540	.52469
16	15.8460	.95076	.04924	71	7.6371	.45823	.54177
17	15.8048	.94829	.05171	72	7.3480	.44088	.55912
18	17.7620	.94572	.05428	73	7.0568	.42341	.57659
19	15.7172	.94303	.05697	74	6.7645	.40587	.59413
20	15.6701	.94021	.05979	75	6.4721	.38833	.61167
21	15.6207	.93742	.06276	76	6.1788	.37073	.62926
22	15.5687	.93412	.06588	77	5.8845	.35307	.64693
23	15.5141	.93085	.06915	78	5.5910	.33546	.66454
24	15.4565	.92739	.07261	79	5.3018	.31811	.68189
25	15.3959	.92375	.07625	80	5.0195	.30117	.69883
26	15.3322	.91993	.08007	81	4.7482	.28489	.71511
27	15.2652	.91591	.08409	82	4.4892	.26935	.73065
28	15.1946	.91168	.08832	83	4.2398	.25439	.74561
29	15.1208	.90725	.09275	84	3.9927	.23956	.76044
30	15.0432	.90259	.09741	85	3.7401	.22441	.77559
31	14.9622	.89773	.10227	86	3.5016	.21010	.78990
32	14.8775	.89265	.10735	87	3.2790	.19674	.80326
33	14.7888	.88733	.11267	88	3.0719	.18431	.81569
34	14.6960	.88176	.11824	89	2.8808	.17285	.82715
35	14.5989	.87593	.12407	90	2.7068	.16241	.83759
36	14.4975	.86935	.13015	91	2.5502	.15301	.84699
37	14.3915	.86349	.13651	92	2.4116	.14470	.85530
38	14.2811	.85687	.14313	93	2.2901	.13741	.86250
39	14.1663	.84998	.15002	94	2.1839	.13103	.86897
40	14.0468	.84281	.15719	95	2.0891	.12535	.87465
41	13.9227	.83536	.16464	96	1.9997	.11998	.88002
42	13.7940	.82764	.17236	97	1.9145	.11487	.88513
43	13.6604	.81962	.18038	98	1.8331	.10999	.89001
44	13.5219	.81131	.18869	99	1.7554	.10532	.89468
45	13.3781	.80269	.19731	100	1.6812	.10087	.89913
46	13.2290	.79374	.20626	101	1.6101	.09661	.90339
47	13.0746	.78448	.21552	102	1.5416	.09250	.90750
48	12.9147	.77438	.22512	103	1.4744	.08846	.91154
49	12.7496	.76498	.23502	104	1.4065	.08439	.91561
50	12.5793	.75476	.24524	105	1.3334	.08000	.92000
51	12.4039	.74423	.25577	106	1.2452	.07471	.92529
52	12.2232	.73339	.26661	107	1.1196	.06718	.93282
53	12.0367	.72000	.27730	108	.9043	.05426	.94574
54	11.8436	.71062	.28938	109	0.4717	.02830	.97170

337

appendix F

Rule of 72 and 116

One way of looking at the return on your investments is to translate the return into the number of years required to double your money.

The rule of 72 tells you how many years it takes to double your money at a given rate of return. The formula is simply:

$$\frac{72}{\%} = \text{Years to double}$$

The rule of 72 is so simple to use, you can apply it easily and it provides good rule of thumb guidance.

To determine how long it will take to triple your money, divide the earning rate into 116. At 8%, for example, you triple your money every 14.5 years; at 12% every 9.7 years.

appendix G

What $1.00 Will Be Worth in Future Years at Various Rates of Inflation

		8%	10%	12%	15%
	5	$0.68	$0.62	$0.57	$0.50
	10	.46	.39	.32	.25
YEARS	15	.32	.24	.18	.12
FROM	20	.21	.15	.10	.06
TODAY	25	.15	.09	.06	.03
	30	.10	.06	.03	.02
	35	.07	.04	.02	.01

appendix H

Life Insurance Analysis

To determine if your insurance needs are adequately covered and at the best price, you will need to do some work.

First, get out *all* your life insurance policies and fill out the *Life Insurance Summation Sheet* that follows.

If you have any problems, ask a certified financial planner to help you and/or send the form called "Request For Policy Information" to the insurance companies with whom you have your policies. You could also call them, of course. If so, have the form handy to be sure you get all the information you need.

Completing the Life Insurance Summation Sheet will tell you exactly what you have and how much you are paying.

Next, work through the Computation of Life Insurance Needs worksheet. This will tell you how much you need.

Now, go shopping. Life-insurance rates have dropped substantially in the last few years. Remember, life insurance is priced per thousand per year. Shop around until you find your best price. Is this cheaper than what you have per thousand per year? Get the new insurance (*first!!*) then cancel the old. There's nothing sacred about a life-insurance policy. I recommend term insurance because I believe insurance and investments are two different things. I've never seen a comparison that convinced me that cash-value insurance is better than term, but you should make up your own mind.

To begin educating yourself read Chapter 13 of "Money Dynamics for the 1980's" by Venita VanCaspel, Reston Publishing Company, Inc., Reston, Virginia 22090.

340

Life Insurance Summation Sheet

Type	Company	Policy Number	Insured	Owner	Beneficiary	When Iss'd	Med. (Y/N)	Acc. Dth. Bft. (Y/N)

Total Cash Values $_____

Minus Total Loans   − $_____

Equals Net Cash Values   = $_____

Life Insurance Summation Sheet (continued)

(1) Face Amt.	(2) Cash Value	(3) Loans	(4) Net Ins. (1–2)	(5) Ann. Prem.	(6) Last Yrs. Refund (Dvdnd)	(7) Net Prem. (5–6)	(8) Lost Earnings @ ___% in Cash Value	(9) Total Cost (7 + 8)	(10) Cost Per Thousand (9 ÷ 4)

Total Death Benefit $_____

Total Annual Premium $_____

Name: _____

Date: _____

COMPUTATION OF LIFE INSURANCE NEEDS

For _____

1. Estimated burial expense . . . . $_____

2. Mortgage cancellation . . . . $_____

3. Other debt cancellation (notes, loans, etc.) . . . . $_____

4. Gifts . . . . $_____

5. Income and real estate taxes . . . . $_____

6. Estate taxes . . . . $_____

7. Estimated child care ($_____ a year for _____ years) . . . . . . $_____

8. Estimated educational costs . . . . $_____

9. Extra until family adjusts to new standard of living . . . . $_____

10. *Capital needed (see calculation below for this figure) . . . . $_____

               Total Life Insurance Needed . . . . $_____

---

*10 a. Computation of monthly income needed:

    Current monthly income . . . . $_____

    Monthly income needed by family in event of death
    (Probably 70%–80% of current monthly income) . . . . $_____

    Less: Estimated amount receivable from Social Security . . . . $_____

               Income from other sources (Spouse's job,
               investment income, etc.)

         _____ $_____

         _____ $_____

         _____ $_____ $_____

    Net income needed per month . . . . $_____

10 b. Computation of capital needed:

    Annual income needed (monthly net × 12) . . . . $_____

    Divided by expected yield on capital . . . . ÷_____%

    Equals capital needed . . . . $_____

REQUEST FOR POLICY INFORMATION

To _____

Name of Insured _____Policy Number(s) _____

By authorization of the insured, please furnish me with the information requested below:

A. Premium and Coverage Provisions:

    1. Premium due dates and amounts _____

    2. Mode of payment _____

    3. Does contract contain disability waiver or disability income feature? _____

    4. Does contract contain accidental-death-benefit provision? _____

    5. Is automatic premium loan a part of contract provision? _____

    6. If premium is other than standard, indicate reason and amount of rating

    _____

B. Dividend Information

    1. Total amount of dividend accumulations or additions _____

    2. Present cash value of dividend additions _____

    3. Amount of last dividend and how applied _____

C. Other Information:

    1. Give name and relationship of primary and secondary beneficiaries_____

    _____

    2. Indicate settlement option(s) elected _____

    3. What is the current cash-surrender value? _____

    4. Any assignment or loan against the policy?_____

    If yes

        a. Initial amount of loan _____   c. Interest rate on loan _____

        b. Present balance on loan _____   d. Terms of the loan _____

Authorization by:

_____

Date _____

Please Mail Information To:
(Write your name and address here)

appendix I ————————————

Document List*

1. Income tax returns for the last two years.

2. Wills.

3. Trust agreements.

4. Personal:

   a. life insurance policies.
   b. medical insurance policies.
   c. disability insurance policies.
   d. nonqualified annuity policies.

   Note: For a–d in item 4, please include the last policy anniversary statement furnished by the insurance company.

5. List of withholdings from your paycheck or a paycheck stub.

6. Company:

   a. life insurance plan.
   b. medical insurance plan.
   c. disability insurance plan.

*This is a list of documents we ask our clients to bring to our first meeting. If you plan to work with a Certified Financial Planner you should be prepared to provide him/her with any of these documents requested.

7. Copy of the latest statement of your retirement benefit plan. (This is a printed form sent out once a year.)

8. Fringe Benefit Statement: This is often a computer printout describing your life, health, and disability insurance together with your status in the savings and/or retirement plan.

9. Any gift tax returns filed after 12/31/76.

10. Employment contracts.

11. Pre- or post-nuptial agreements.

12. Terms of any divorce or legal separation, including alimony and child support payments.

If you are self-employed we will also need:

13. Past two years corporate income tax return and/or past two years partnership income tax return.

14. Most recent business financial statements.

15. Business buy/sell.

16. Partnership agreements.

appendix J

CONFIDENTIAL INFORMATION
CONCERNING
THE
FINANCIAL PLANNING OBJECTIVES
OF

COMPANY

CLOSELY HELD BUSINESS INTERESTS

Name of Business _____

Address _____

Phone _____

Nature of Business _____

Net Fair Market Value of Entire Business $ _____

Determined by _____ Client's Estimate

_____ Book Value

_____ Buy/Sell Agreement

_____ Professional Valuation

_____ Other _____

Tax Basis of Your Interest $_____

Form of Business

_____ Sole proprietorship   _____ Subchapter S corp.

_____ Partnership   _____ Professional corp.

_____ Business corporation   _____ Other _____

_____ Non-Profit organization

Accounting Basis   Cash _____ Accrual _____

Date of Incorporation _____

Fiscal Year _____

Business was a _____ for _____ years before
incorporation.

Type of Business (manufacturer, dealer, etc.) _____

_____

350

Is there a Buy-Sell Agreement?

_____ yes—Please provide copy and/or details

_____ no

At death, business is to be:

_____ Continued by heirs   _____ Inherited but not run by heirs

_____ Sold to surviving partners

_____ Sold to key employees—Is there a written agreement?

_____ yes   _____ no

_____ Liquidated

_____ Other _____

_____

Please provide financial statements, balance sheets, profit and loss statements, and tax returns for the past three years and a copy of all agreements between owners and key employees or the business and key employees.

	Gross Sales	Taxable Income	Corporate Tax	Net Profit
19____	_____	_____	_____	_____
19____	_____	_____	_____	_____
19____	_____	_____	_____	_____
19____	_____	_____	_____	_____

Fringe Benefits Provided

_____ Qualified pension plan

_____ Qualified profit sharing plan

_____ Split dollar

_____ Deferred compensation

_____ Deferred benefit plan

_____ ESOP

_____ TRASOP

_____

_____

_____

_____ Stock options

_____ Group life

_____ Long term disability

_____ Health insurance

_____ Medical reimburse

_____ Company car

_____ Other _____

_____

_____

Please provide copies of the plan documents and the latest benefit statements.

Does the employer have any union(s)?_____ yes _____ no

If yes, has there ever been good faith bargaining on the part of the union(s) for retirement

benefits? _____ yes _____ no

What is the approximate rate of employee turnover as a percent of the active group for the past five (5) years?

19___	_____%
19___	_____%
19___	_____%
19___	_____%
19___	_____%

What is the approximate rate of salary increases over each of the past five (5) years?

	19_____	19_____	19_____	19_____	19_____
Salaried employees	____%	____%	____%	____%	____%
Hourly employees	____%	____%	____%	____%	____%
Union employees	____%	____%	____%	____%	____%
Other	____%	____%	____%	____%	____%

Indicate any other pertinent information regarding the salary policy of the corporation.

_____

_____

_____

_____

Corporate tax returns filed

_____ Separated by corporation

_____ Consolidated return

Employee identifying number _____

Related corporations or entities (names, nature of enterprises, relationship of enterprises)

_____

_____

Accountant

Name _____

Firm _____

Address _____

_____

Telephone number _____

Attorney

Name _____

Firm _____

Address _____

_____

Telephone number _____

Earnings projections:

_____

_____

_____

_____

_____

What cost commitment should be considered for a pension or profit sharing plan?

_____% of Payroll

_____% of Profit

_____% of Profit in excess of $ _____

$_____   Flat dollar amount

_____   Other _____

_____

_____

_____

Industry employers of concern (locally).

Details as to their compensation programs.

Do you need to be competitive to attract or retain employees?

_____

_____

_____

Rank in order of importance the retirement plan benefits:

_____ Tax savings   _____ Reduce union pressure

_____ Retain key employees   _____ Gracefully retire older employees

_____ Estate conservation

_____ Other (please explain) _____

_____

What are the most important factors in making your business successful? _____

_____

_____

How do you feel about the future of your business?

_____

_____

_____

Number of new full-time employees hired:

    last year _____

    two years ago _____

    three years ago _____

Number of full-time employees terminated:

    last year _____

    two years ago _____

    three years ago _____

What is the probable increase in full-time personnel in the next five years?

    _____ less than 10

    _____ 10–19

    _____ 20 or more

General specifications desired in plan

    Effective date of plan _____

How much would you like to contribute as

    $_____ of % _____ of compensation

Eligibility requirements

    Months of service _____ (suggest 12 months to allow later vesting)

    Minimum age _____ (up to age 25)

    Maximum age _____ (only for defined benefit plans—cannot be lower than 55)

Normal retirement age

    _____ all age 65

_____ 65 years old or ten years of participation, whichever is later

_____ Other _____

Type of plan and formula

Defined contribution _____ pension _____ profit sharing

nonintegrated _____% of compensation

integrated _____% of first $_____ of comp.

Annual plus _____% of excess

Defined Benefit

Nonintegrated

Flat percentage benefit _____% of all comp.

Unit benefit (years of service)

_____% of all comp. for each year of service. Maximum years of credited

service equals _____ years.

Integrated

Integration level

Maximum permitted by current Social Security Act

_____ yes _____ no

Flat percentage benefit

_____ % of base plus _____% of excess

_____% of excess only

Unit benefit (years of service)

_____% of base for each year of service plus _____% of excess for

each year of service. Maximum years of credited service equals

_____ years.

_____% of excess only for each year of service.

Maximum years of credited service equals _____ years.

Target benefit

_____% of monthly compensation

BUSINESS INSURANCE

Key person life insurance

Insured	Title	Amount	Annual Premium

Buy and sell agreement funded by life insurance

Entity _____   Cross purchase _____

Insured	Title	Amount	Annual Premium

Split dollar agreements

Insured	Title	Amount	Annual Premium

Employee Census

Name	Key Person Y or N	Sex Male or Female	Date of Birth M/D/Y	Date Joined Firm M/D/Y	Compensation	Compensation Mode*	Position	Eligible Payroll	Probability they will stay for four years a. very likely b. likely c. unlikely d. very unlikely
1.									
2.									
3.									
4.									
5.									
6.									
7.									
8.									
9.									
10.									

*H—hourly   W—weekly   B—bi-weekly   S—semi-monthly   M—monthly   A—annually

Owners of the Business

Name	Title	Date of Birth	% Owned or # of Shares	Annual Income from Business	Active in Business yes/no	Ownership*	Key Persons Life Insurance yes/no Amount
1.							
2.							
3.							
4.							
5.							

*a. community property
b. joint tenancy with spouse
c. joint tenancy with _____
d. husband's separate property
e. wife's separate property
f. tenancy in common
g. tenancy by the entireties

Stocks and Mutual Funds Owned By Company (Common Stock Analysis)

| Name of Security | # of Shares Owned | Date of Purchase | Cost | | Market Value | | | Gain or Loss | Long Term (L.T.) Short Term (S.T.) | P/E Ratio | Earnings Per Share Latest 12 Mo. ($) | Divi- dend Yield | Five- Year Growth Rate (%) | Recom- menda- tion |
			Per Share	Total	Per Share	Total								

Emerging Liabilities

Type of Liability	Probably Will be Secured By	Likely Liability	Creditor	How Payable	Rate of Interest	Probability that liability will materialize a. very likely c. very unlikely b. likely d. unlikely
1.						
2.						
3.						
4.						
5.						
6.						
7.						
8.						
9.						

Annuities Owned by the Business

	1	2	3
Company			
Best Ratings:			
Interest Rates:			
Current			
Last Year			
Life Time			
Policy Fees			
Withdrawal Provisions			
Free Annual Withdrawal			
Surrender Penalty			
Amount of Initial Investment			
Current Value			
Death Benefits			
Lump Sum			
Annuitized			
Date Statements Issued			
Loan Provisions			

Bonds Owned by the Business (Include All Corporate, Municipal, Treasury and Government Bonds)

Name of Company, or Municipality; Type, If Government	Tax Free	Taxable	Face Value	Rate %	Maturity Date	Cost	Market Value	Recommendation

363

Limited Partnerships Owned by the Business

	1		2		3	
Name of Partnership						
General Partner Contact information (Address & Phone #)						
Annual Return—$ or %						
Expected Duration of Partnership						
Date of Initial Investment						
Amount of Investment						
19___						
19___						
19___						
19___						
19___						
	Projected	Actual	Projected	Actual	Projected	Actual
Amount of Write-Off						
19___						
19___						
19___						
19___						
19___						
General Description of Partnership						

364

Liabilities of the Business
(Outside the scope of your normal business activities)

Type of Liability	Secured By	Balance	Creditor	How Payable	Rate of Interest	Credit Line yes or no
1.						
2.						
3.						
4.						
5.						
6.						
7.						
8.						
9.						

Savings:

Passbook savings accounts

Institution	Rate %	Ownership	Amount

Certificates of deposit

Institution	Rate %	Date of Maturity	Name as it appears on the account	Amount

Credit union

	Rate %		Name as it appears on the account		Amount

Money market mutual funds

Institution	Average % Rate	Name as it appears on the account	Amount at date of data gathering

Comments: _____

_____

Receivables of the Business
(Obligations outside the scope of your normal business activities)

Type of Receivable	Debtor	Total Balance	How is debt being repaid	How likely are you to collect a. very likely c. unlikely b. likely d. very unlikely
1.				
2.				
3.				
4.				
5.				
6.				
7.				
8.				
9.				

Real Estate Owned by Business*

Location or Description	Year Acquired	Original Cost (includ. Improvements)	Total Fair Market Value	Client's % of Owner-ship	Total Mortgage Balance	Remaining Period of Loan	Total Rents Received Monthly	Total Monthly Mortgage Payment	Rate of Mortgage	Total Equity
1.										
2.										
3.										
4.										
5.										
6.										
7.										
8.										
9.										
10.										

*Note: For fractional interest, please give all figures as total for the property.

368

Life Insurance Summation Sheet

Type	Company	Policy Number	Insured	Owner	Beneficiary	When Iss'd	Med. (Y/N)	Acc. Dth. Bft. (Y/N)

Total Cash Values $_____

Minus Total Loans   − $_____

Equals Net Cash Values   = $_____

Life Insurance Summation Sheet (continued)

(1) Face Amt.	(2) Cash Value	(3) Loans	(4) Net Ins. (1–2)	(5) Ann. Prem.	(6) Last Yrs. Refund (Dvdnd)	(7) Net Prem. (5–6)	(8) Lost Earnings @ % in Cash Value	(9) Total Cost (7+8)	(10) Cost Per Thousand (9÷4)

Total Death Benefit $_____

Total Annual Premium $_____

Name: _____

Date: _____

370

appendix K ───────────────

CONFIDENTIAL INFORMATION
CONCERNING
THE
FINANCIAL PLANNING OBJECTIVES
OF

───────────────────────

PERSONAL

PERSONAL AND FAMILY DATA

Client's Name _____

Residence Address _____

_____

Home Phone _____

Occupation _____

Business Address _____

_____

Business Phone _____

Date of Birth _____ Place of Birth_____

Social Security # _____

Health _____ Smoker: _____ Nonsmoker: _____

Marital Status _____

Spouse's Name _____

Occupation _____

Business Address _____

_____

Business Phone _____

Date of Birth _____ Place of Birth_____

Social Security # _____

Health _____ Smoker: _____ Nonsmoker: _____

Children

Name	Date of Birth	Marital Status	Number of Children	Occupation

Other dependents

_____

_____

Do any dependents have health problems? _____yes _____no

Any previous marriages? _____yes _____ no

Obligations under divorce judgments_____

_____

Are you a party to any trusts? _____yes _____ no

If yes, details: _____

_____

Have you made any lifetime gifts? _____yes _____ no

Do you wish to make lifetime gifts? _____yes _____ no

Do you have a will? _____yes _____ no

If yes, details_____

_____

Health Insurance

   Major medical _____ yes _____no

   Maximum $_____ Deductible $_____ Per _____

   Disability _____ yes _____ no

   Amount $_____ Per _____ Benefit period _____

   Elimination period _____ Annual premium $_____

   Type of policy _____ guaranteed renewable _____ noncancellable

   Annual (posttax) living expense $_____

   Annual living expense in the event of your death $_____
      (today's dollars) (posttax)

   Annual living expense in the event of your disability $_____
      (today's dollars) (posttax)

Desired annual income at retirement $ _____
   (today's dollars) (posttax)

Anticipated inflation rate per year_____ %

Are you covered under a pension plan? yes _____ no

If yes, please give full details: _____

_____

_____

_____

Husband's gross income annually

    198___ $_____

    198___ $_____

    198___ $_____

Expectation regarding future income

_____

_____

_____

Wife's gross income annually

    198___ $_____

    198___ $_____

    198___ $_____

Expectation regarding future income

_____

_____

_____

At what age do you plan to retire? _____

At what age does your spouse plan to retire? _____

Savings:

Passbook savings accounts

Institution	Rate %	Ownership*	Amount

Certificates of deposit

Institution	Rate %	Date of Maturity	Ownership*	Amount

Credit union

_____ Rate % _____ Ownership* _____ Amount

Money market mutual funds

Institution	Average % Rate	Ownership*	Amount at date of data gathering

Comments: _____

_____

*CS—Client Separate
 SS—Spouse Separate
 C—Community (or joint)

Bonds and Treasury Bills, Bonds, Notes

Name of Company, or Municipality; Type, If Government	Tax Free	Taxable	Face Value	Rate %	Maturity Date	Cost	Market Value	Owner- ship*	Recommendation

*CS—Client Separate   SS—Spouse Separate   C—Community (or joint)

376

Annuities

	1	2	3
Company			
Best Ratings:			
Interest Rates:			
Current			
Last Year			
Life Time			
Policy Fees			
Withdrawal Provisions			
Free Annual Withdrawal			
Surrender Penalty			
Amount of Initial Investment			
Current Value			
Death Benefits			
Lump Sum			
Annuitized			
Date Statements Issued			
Loan Provisions			
Ownership*			

*CS—Client Separate   SS—Spouse Separate   C—Community (or joint)

Limited Partnerships

	1		2		3	
	Projected	Actual	Projected	Actual	Projected	Actual
Name of Partnership						
General Partner Contact information (Address & Phone #)						
Annual Return—$ or %						
Expected Duration of Partnership						
Date of Initial Investment						
Amount of Investment 19__ 19__ 19__ 19__ 19__						
Amount of Write-Off 19__ 19__ 19__ 19__ 19__						
Ownership*						
General Description of Partnership						

*CS—Client Separate   SS—Spouse Separate   C—Community (or joint)

Receivables

(Obligations: Notes, mortgages, accounts receivable, etc., owed to you or your spouse personally. Do not include such items owed to a business in which you or your spouse have an interest.)

Type of Receivable	Debtor	Total Balance	How is debt being repaid	Ownership*	How likely are you to collect a. very likely c. unlikely b. likely d. very unlikely
1.					
2.					
3.					
4.					
5.					
6.					
7.					
8.					
9.					

*CS—Client Separate   SS—Spouse Separate   C—Community (or joint)

379

Liabilities of Self or Spouse

(Do not include any mortgage on real estate, life insurance loans, or liabilities of a business in which you or your spouse have an interest)

Type of Liability	Secured By	Balance	Creditor	Ownership*	How Payable	Rate of Interest	Credit Line yes or no
1.							
2.							
3.							
4.							
5.							

*CS—Client Separate   SS—Spouse Separate   C—Community (or joint)

Miscellaneous Personal Property: Other Assets
(automobiles, jewelry, household furniture, collections, etc.)

Nature of Property	Fair Market Value	Ownership	Year Acquired	Original Cost
1.				
2.				
3.				
4.				
5.				
6.				
7.				
8.				
9.				
10.				

Type	Company	Policy Number	Insured	Owner	Beneficiary	When Iss'd	Med. (Y/N)	Acc. Dth. Bft. (Y/N)

Total Cash Values $_____

Minus Total Loans   − $_____

Equals Net Cash Values   = $_____

Life Insurance

(1) Face Amt.	(2) Cash Value	(3) Loans	(4) Net Ins. (1–2)	(5) Ann. Prem.	(6) Last Yrs. Refund (Dvdnd)	(7) Net Prem. (5–6)	(8) Lost Earnings @ ___ % in Cash Value	(9) Total Cost (7 + 8)	(10) Cost Per Thousand (9 ÷ 4)

Total Death Benefit $_____

Total Annual Premium $_____

Name: _____

Date: _____

Inheritances (only include those expected inheritances over $100,000.00)

Expected inheritance of husband		
1. $_____	from _____	
age _____	health _____	
2. $_____	from _____	
age _____	health _____	

Expected inheritance of wife		
1. $_____	from _____	
age _____	health _____	
2. $_____	from _____	
age _____	health _____	

Please rate the following financial objectives according to the following scale:

1 of no importance	5 moderately important	10 extremely important

1. Achieving faster asset growth   _____

2. Increasing current income from investments   _____

3. Paying lower income tax   _____

4. Obtaining professional help in the management of my assets   _____

5. Protecting assets against inflation   _____

6. More suitably positioning investment assets   _____

7. Supporting a family member   _____

8. Providing college education for children   _____

9. Retiring comfortably   _____

10. Further building of personal wealth   _____

11. Conserving my estate   _____

12. Providing help and/or experience to inexperienced heirs to manage assets   _____

13. Protect spouse and/or children in the event of my death   _____

14. Provide for family in the event of my disability   _____

15. Reviewing my insurance program   _____

16. Making gifts to family members   _____

17. Making charitable gifts   _____

18. Buying or building a home   _____

19. Other _____

_____ _____

20. Other _____

_____ _____

Stocks and Mutual Funds Owned Personally

| Name of Security | # Shares Owned | Date of Purchase | Cost | | Market Value | | Gain or Loss | Long Term (L.T.) Short Term (S.T.) | P/E Ratio | Earnings Per Share Latest 12 Mo. ($) | Dividend Yield | Five-Year Growth Rate (%) | Ownership* | Recommendation |
			Per Share	Total	Per Share	Total								

*CS—Client Separate SS—Spouse Separate C—Community

Real Estate Owned Personally

Location or Description	Year Acquired	Original Cost (includ. Improvements)	Total Fair Market Value	Client's % of Total Fair Market Value	Total Mortgage Balance	Remaining Period of Loan	Rents Received Monthly	Monthly Mortgage Payment	Rate of Mortgage	Owner-ship*	Equity
1.											
2.											
3.											
4.											
5.											
6.											
7.											
8.											
9.											
10.											

*Ownership: CS—Client Separate   SS—Spouse Separate   C—Community

appendix L————————————————

The Time Value of Money

Let's take a look at how dramatically money grows if left alone for a few years at a reasonable rate of return. Assume you use the IRA provision available to you thanks to ERTA of 1981. You faithfully deposit your $2,000 per year in a mutual fund earning 12%. Although your original motivation was the tax saving, you're delighted to discover that after ten years your $2,000 each year has grown to $35,000. (See Table L-1.) If you're quite young, let's say 20–25, so that you might work 40 more years, your $2,000 each year will grow to $1.5 million dollars. Yes, Virginia, you can become a millionaire on $2,000 per year, if you deposit it faithfully for enough years.

Suppose you have a sister who also used the IRA provision. But since she was more conservative than you, she didn't want to use a mutual fund and instead put her IRA funds in the bank and earned 8%. (Refer to Table L-1.) At the end of the fifth year you compare accounts. She has $11,733 and you have $12,705. "You took a risk for $1,000 more over five years," she points out.

You wonder if you're making a mistake, but your certified financial planner helped you select the fund you bought into and has reassured you all along that it's a good one. You decide not to change.

At the end of the tenth year, you and your sister compare accounts again. She has $28,973; you have $35,097. You feel a lot better and decide to continue the mutual-fund program.

TABLE L–1

IRA Table

$2,000 Per Year Invested at 8%, 10%, and 12%

Year	8%	10%	12%
5	11,733	12,210	12,705
10	28,973	31,874	35,097
15	54,304	63,544	74,559
20	91,523	114,549	144,104
25	146,211	196,694	266,667
30	226,566	328,988	482,665
35	344,633	542,048	863,326
40	518,113	885,185	1,534,182
45	773,011	1,437,809	2,716,460
50	1,147,540	2,327,817	4,800,036

At the twentieth year mark, you have $144,104; your sister has $91,523. Thanks to only a 4% difference each year, you now have 63% more retirement funds than your sister. Notice especially that you have deposited only $40,000 but the time value of money has grown that to $144,104.

Let's look at one more example of the time value of money. And this time let's assume you make a one time lump-sum investment at 12% and allow all earnings to be reinvested in the same account. At the end of twenty years your $10,000 has grown to $96,462 and you have ten times as much money as you started with. Suppose, however, you made a decision to deposit your money in a "guaranteed" account at 8%. At the end of twenty years you would have $46,609—half as much. (See Table L–2.)

In my years of financial counseling, I have discovered that the best way to motivate my clients to make the changes necessary to get another percentage point or so on their investments is to give them a compound interest table and encourage them to contrast their own investment alternatives at various rates over several years. I almost always get a subsequent

TABLE L–2

$10,000 Lump Sum Invested at 8%, 10%, and 12%

Year	8%	10%	12%
5	14,693	16,105	17,623
10	21,589	25,937	31,058
15	31,721	41,772	54,735
20	46,609	67,274	96,462
25	68,484	108,347	170,000
30	100,626	174,494	299,599
35	147,853	281,024	527,996
40	217,245	452,592	930,509
45	319,204	728,904	1,639,876
50	469,016	1,173,908	2,890,021

call saying, "Okay. Let's go with the changes." Financial planners call such changes "repositioning."

I've also included compound interest tables in Appendix D. Don't be intimidated by the sheer volume of numbers in the tables. They are quite simple to use, and extremely valuable. Work through the sample computation and you'll see how easy the tables are to use.

Appendix D allows you to compute how much you need to save each year at various interest rates to reach a specific goal. Accountants call this a sinking fund—and all of us need sinking funds for large financial objectives—such as retirement, second home, or children's college. There is also a table to help you determine what lump-sum commitment you need to make now to have a predetermined amount at a given point in the future.

Index